Welfare for Markets

the
LIFE
OF
IDEAS

Series Editor
Darrin McMahon, Dartmouth College

After a period of some eclipse, the study of intellectual history has enjoyed a broad re-surgence in recent years. *The Life of Ideas* contributes to this revitalization through the study of ideas as they are produced, disseminated, received, and practiced in different historical contexts. The series aims to embed ideas—those that endured, and those once persuasive but now forgotten—in rich and readable cultural histories. Books in this se-ries draw on the latest methods and theories of intellectual history while being written with elegance and élan for a broad audience of readers.

Welfare for Markets

A Global History of Basic Income

ANTON JÄGER AND
DANIEL ZAMORA VARGAS

THE UNIVERSITY OF CHICAGO PRESS   CHICAGO AND LONDON

The University of Chicago Press, Chicago 60637
The University of Chicago Press, Ltd., London
© 2023 by The University of Chicago
All rights reserved. No part of this book may be used or reproduced in any manner whatsoever without written permission, except in the case of brief quotations in critical articles and reviews. For more information, contact the University of Chicago Press, 1427 E. 60th St., Chicago, IL 60637.
Published 2023
Paperback edition 2024

33 32 31 30 29 28 27 26 25 24   1 2 3 4 5

ISBN-13: 978-0-226-82368-3 (cloth)
ISBN-13: 978-0-226-83672-0 (paper)
ISBN-13: 978-0-226-82523-6 (e-book)
DOI: https://doi.org/10.7208/chicago/9780226825236.001.0001

Library of Congress Cataloging-in-Publication Data

Names: Jäger, Anton, 1994– author. | Zamora, Daniel (Sociologist), author.
Title: Welfare for markets : a global history of basic income / Anton Jäger
    and Daniel Zamora Vargas.
Other titles: Global history of basic income | Life of ideas.
Description: Chicago ; London : The University of Chicago Press, 2023. |
    Series: The life of ideas | Includes bibliographical references and index.
Identifiers: LCCN 2022035680 | ISBN 9780226823683 (cloth) |
    ISBN 9780226825236 (ebook)
Subjects: LCSH: Basic income—History. | Basic income—Philosophy—
    History. | Economic assistance, Domestic—History. | Economic
    assistance—History.
Classification: LCC HC79.I5 J29 2023 | DDC 339.2/2—dc23/eng/20220906
LC record available at https://lccn.loc.gov/2022035680

Contents

Welfare without the Welfare State

To the liberal the task is much more difficult: how to move away from the welfare state without a decrease in welfare.... How can we have welfare without the welfare state? — Arthur Kemp, "Welfare without the Welfare State"

Money is the pimp between need and object, between life and man's means of life. — Karl Marx, *The Economic and Philosophic Manuscripts of 1844*

Twelve hundred dollars. That was the amount of the checks American citizens found deposited in their bank accounts in late March 2020, dispatched from Washington, DC, and signed by the president himself.[1] The transfer came with no strings attached, to be spent at the recipients' discretion. Just four weeks earlier, states had begun shutting down their economies to halt the spread of COVID-19, a pandemic coronavirus first recorded in the Chinese province of Wuhan in December 2019. Millions were already unemployed and behind on their bills. Hospitals and nursing homes were overrun. In the meantime, a financial scare had overtaken the stock market, while businesses had begun sending their workforces home or dumping employees en masse. Like a slow-motion train crash, the entire world economy was grinding to a halt, flinging millions off the cars. On March 28 the White House settled on a remarkable policy response: checks of $1,200 to each American, sent straight to their bank accounts.[2]

As the dollars spewed forth, a journalist reached out to Belgian philosopher Philippe Van Parijs. Over the past forty years, Van Parijs had

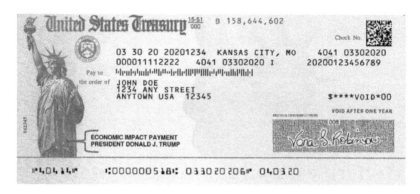

FIGURE I.I. Prototype of a March 2020 "Economic Impact Payment" issued by President Donald J. Trump.

steadily established himself as an authority on matters of distribution, social justice, and welfare. He had served as both founder and current chair of BIEN—the Basic Income Earth Network—and was a speaker of wide renown. The journalist's questions were deceptively simple. Was this the path to the permanent, unconditional basic income Van Parijs had tried to chart? And was the amount high and permanent enough?

Van Parijs, now retired after serving as Hoover Chair at the University of Louvain-la-Neuve, responded with due caution: as a short-term relief measure, President Donald Trump's "Economic Impact Payments" were a far cry from the basic income Van Parijs had been pushing since the early 1980s.[3] "In the last forty years," he claimed, "I have learned not to get excited too quickly."[4] Yet he had to admit there were *some* reasons for "opportunistic utopianism."[5] It was "true," after all, "that the idea of basic income was coming up right, left and centre," with economists pleading for "quantitative easing for the people" and politicians smuggling it into their party platforms.[6] The CARES Act was a one-off. Yet "they [did] share a most welcome virtue": they "boost . . . awareness of how much better equipped our societies and our economies would be to face challenges such as this one if *a permanent unconditional basic income were in place.*"[7]

Van Parijs indeed had reason to be optimistic. After a short coma in the 1990s, the previous decade and a half had witnessed a spectacular revival of his "basic income" proposal, from India to Alaska to Van Parijs' home turf of Belgium. After Trump's $1,200 checks to American citizens, most European countries extended and automated access to their unemployment benefits, while Jair Bolsonaro ramped up Brazil's cash-transfer machine to assist his country's poorest citizens.

Enthusiasm for the universal basic income (UBI) long preceded the COVID-19 panic. Conceived as an unconditional, continuous, and universal grant paid to every citizen, Van Parijs's proposal had galvanized spirits on both sides of the political divide in successive waves since the mid-1960s. After a nationwide debate in the United States in the early 1960s involving Michael Harrington, James Boggs, Milton Friedman, and even Martin Luther King, at the close of the decade the idea crossed the Atlantic and headed for Europe. By the early 1970s, it had been disseminated into national debates in the Netherlands, Belgium, and France and saw a renaissance in the United Kingdom after an initial interwar debate in the 1920s and 1930s. In the 1990s the proposal went global after the creation of the Basic Income Earth Network in 1986. Nearly three decades later, it proudly figures on the agendas of parties, think tanks, social movements, politicians, philosophers, community activists, and business leaders alike. Figures on the right such as Charles Murray, Jim O'Neill, Hernando de Soto, Greg Mankiw, and Christopher Pissarides applaud its capacity to eliminate outdated state bureaucracies and rigid wage regulations. Thinkers on the left such as Rutger Bregman, Paul Mason, Guy Standing, Toni Negri, and Yanis Varoufakis celebrate its ambition to move beyond the work ethic, antiquated by advances in automation and digitization. Across the spectrum, the laudation lists run long: "a practical business plan for the next step of the human journey" (Jeremy Rifkin); a "technology to make starvation and dependency relics of the past" (Desmond Tutu); and "a new social contract" (Mark Zuckerberg). All cast the UBI as "an idea whose time has come."[8]

There is noticeably little place for history in these pleas. Across the vast, sprawling literature on basic income built up in the past forty years, the origins of the idea itself have rarely been the object of sustained or separate study. Aside from honorable exceptions by Van Parijs, Yannick Vanderborght, Peter Sloman, Brian Steensland, and Walter Van Trier, the exact drivers, causes, and sources of our UBI moment remain comparatively underresearched. Most proponents of the idea trace the proposal back to early modern thinkers such as Juan Luis Vives, Desiderius Erasmus, and Thomas More, who originated a tradition continued by Condorcet, Thomas Spence, Charles Fourier, Thomas Paine, and Henry George.[9] Across this long and venerable bloodline, the idea of basic income seamlessly jumps from one epoch to another, incarnating a timeless ideal of social justice.

This Platonism also comes with casualties, however. In its tendency to "reify doctrine" and "[crave] for generality," the sharp differences that separate these previous grant proposals from our current understanding of basic income are clouded and obscured.[10] Conceived as in-kind relief measures, More's and Vives's proposals hardly come close to the cash handouts that attained prominence in the later twentieth century. And though Paine indeed hoped to pay his farmers in money, his aim was to shore up landownership, fostering a further democratization of property after the French Revolution. Most of these proposals also tied the reception of these grants to strong work requirements, far removed from a "free money" paradigm. The vast library of "invented traditions" on basic income that has been built up in the past twenty years elides these key differences between current and past versions of the grant—and tells us very little about the "political unconscious" or "plausibility structures" in which the idea was first conceived.[11]

This late arrival is easily explained. Until the mid-twentieth century, agrarian and communist precedents set strict limits on our thinking about grants. Only by the 1930s did those older languages begin to erode, both intellectually and materially. A child of this flux was the negative income tax first imagined by Milton Friedman in the early 1940s. The proposal was designed to guarantee everyone, through the fiscal system, a floor of income. Below a certain threshold, people would automatically receive money from the state rather than pay taxes. Poverty would essentially be tackled without heavy state intervention in the economy, by simply altering the distribution of income rather than by public work programs or social security systems.

As a young economist at work in the New Deal state, Friedman broke with the precepts of welfare economics dominant at the time, including the behavior control mechanisms implicit in many early welfare systems. In policy terms his proposal certainly proved too heterodox. The welfare states built on the ruins left by the two world wars had buried the prewar dedication to laissez-faire and removed parts of human life from the market altogether, including employment provisions. As Friedman's proposal proved, however, there were ways of offering minimal provision that did not impede the functioning of the market, as Friedrich Hayek also observed in his 1944 *Road to Serfdom*:

> If we strive for money, it is because it offers us the widest choice in enjoying the fruits of our efforts. . . . If all rewards, instead of being offered in money, were

offered in the form of public distinctions or privileges, positions of power over other men, or better housing or better food, opportunities for travel or education, this would merely mean that the recipient would no longer be allowed to choose and that whoever fixed the reward determined not only its size but also the particular form in which it should be enjoyed.[12]

Hayek's preference was clear: collective provision in kind would always remain potentially authoritarian. Money was "the greatest instrument of freedom ever invented," as he put it.[13] On the other side of the political spectrum, market socialists like Oskar Lange also formulated a version of the proposal. While it appealed to some economists, its overall policy uptake was marginal.

More generally, the proposal appeared deeply out of tune with the collectivist mood of the 1930s and 1940s. At the time, mass unemployment forced millions into destitution in an industrial economy, spawning workers' organizations across the world. Instead of fighting for cash, unions, workers' councils, mass parties, and policy, experts pushed for removing whole areas of our social life from the tyranny of the market, to be handed over to the state or run by workers themselves. The results were visible in public health care, public housing projects, state works programs, and free education across the Atlantic, later extended and retaken by coalitions in the Third World. In this ecosystem, unconditional cash transfers were hardly a viable idea, let alone an institutional option. Lange and Friedman would have to wait for their proposals to gather an active audience.

Their wait paid off, however. In the shifting Cold War climate of the 1950s, taken by new public management, early automation, and structural unemployment, the issue of welfare expansion became ever more fraught. Friedman's *Capitalism and Freedom* became an unexpected national best seller and his negative income tax a subject of intense debate. Tax-benefit integration and the decline of public sector provision created lasting momentum for cash-based solutions. Civil rights activists also began pushing for cash transfers, while commercial Keynesians urged US presidents John F. Kennedy and Lyndon Johnson to adopt a tax-based approach to poverty reduction. While the labor wing of the Civil Rights Movement began the 1960s with pleas for job guarantees as part of a comprehensive industrial democracy, at the close of the decade figures like Martin Luther King had warmed to cash-centered solutions.[14] By 1973 Hayek himself was again admitting that "the assurance of a certain minimum income for everyone" could form "a necessary part of the Great Society in which the individual no longer has specific claims on the members of the particular small group into which he was born."[15] Sensitive parameters had shifted since the Great Depression. Now the proposal was mentioned in think tanks, councils, and presidential memos alike.

In 1966 the American director of the Mont Pèlerin Society, Arthur Kemp, was one of the first to point out this evolving landscape. "Welfare," Kemp claimed, might be "a 'good' word . . . conjur[ing] up a condition of well-being—a sense of euphoria." Yet "anyone who was intimately acquainted with the gross inequities of . . . the public welfare system" could not "ignore . . . the immediacy of the problem."[16] Contemporary economists had already abandoned the "normative economics" propping up the New Deal order, since the former was "replete with ethical or value judgements."[17] Afterward, "a general abandonment of the previously accepted socialist principles and objectives" had led to "a heterogeneous, hodgepodge collection of programs and activities, many of which are meritorious in themselves, but some of which are incompatible with individual freedom."[18] Even if not socialist in principle, postwar welfarism would inevitably culminate in "a system that is . . . totalitarian."[19]

The New Right was hardly alone in this criticism of New Deal paternalism. On the other side of the political aisle, a New Left was also gradually turning skeptical of the old welfare order, premised on an exclusionary male model of a working breadwinner. To critics such as the socialist writer Michael Harrington or the labor activist James Boggs, the cash-centered welfare offered by basic income would sublate the New Deal order and eliminate its paternalistic vestiges.

As Kemp noted, on both left and right, "choice" was the future, in contrast to the welfare mechanisms constructed by New Deal collectivists, who did not "permit the individual to spend a decreasing proportion of his income according to his own choice and, through government, spend an increasing proportion for him on the 'good' things, thus preventing him from erring, or if you like, sinning."[20] Most agreed that "attempt[s] to alleviate poverty by an almost endless variety of governmental programs that are not only indirect and expensive but also are frequently ineffective or even produce more poverty and suffering rather than less."[21]

Cash transfers presented an elegant middle way here. They avoided utopianism and a sclerotic public sector, but they also had little time for laissez-faire minimalism, reconciling the market with a modicum of security. "The liberal task," Kemp noted, was to imagine a "welfare without the welfare state."[22] And although the guaranteed income was "not likely to bring about the millennium," it could "be used to increase somewhat individuals' abilities to use their time, energies and resources in whatever ways they wish."[23] Some recipients "might buy LSD or gin or racetrack tickets instead of bread and housing. But then the problem is not poverty but something else. . . . freedom in a most fundamental sense."[24]Written at the height of Johnson's War on Poverty, Kemp's provocation rallied welfarist critics. Economists such as Hyman Minsky saw the negative income tax as indicating "an inability to make the production process respond to social goals."[25] To them, a "resort to taxation transfers as a substitute for income from factor payments" hinted at a dangerous retreat of the planning state and the domestication of a more radical Keynesianism.[26] More dangerous in the context of the 1970s, a basic income could make voters join a deflationary bloc hostile to potentially inflationary wage demands on behalf of workers. Kemp's criticism nonetheless proved premonitory for forces across the spectrum. As the transactional politics of the New Deal era gave way to the more speculative, public relations–driven media campaigns of the 1960s and 1970s, cash transfers became an elegant way of conducting social bargaining without passing through corporatist channels. With its own public-private welfare state, the United States saw the first policy experiments in this direction.[27] Unlike the European welfare states that had instituted extensive socializations of the wage, American unions faced a triumphant ruling class that had won a relatively capital-intensive war and thereby "forced [unions] to build their own bureaucratically managed, private welfare states."[28] Coupled with the fear of "workerless factories" caused by automation, cash transfers now not only seemed thinkable but necessary.[29]

As one observer noted at the time, Friedman's "means to help poor people is now supported by almost all economists—be they of the left, the center, or the right, as well as by three of our last four presidents (though often in disguised form)."[30] Propped up by an economics profession that sought to render welfare "market-conforming" and a New Right and New Left fed up with New Deal paternalism, Friedman's negative income tax and Harrington's guaranteed income seemed to have a rosy future.[31]

This changing climate applied both at home and abroad. As Europeans began to creep into their own Fordist crisis a decade later, Kemp's criticism began to migrate—from Washington, New York, and Detroit to Paris, Turin, London, and Amsterdam. Throughout the 1970s, the crisis of an older welfare ideal allowed new social movements to embrace the perspective of a guaranteed income, moving beyond the workerist bent of the Old Left. Full employment increasingly appeared as "a strange experience in the history of capitalism"; job seeking and inflation returned to figures "unimaginable to most people twenty years earlier."[32] Yet claims for public works or centralized investment were sidelined on the political spectrum, opening up space for guaranteed income schemes.

By the mid-1980s, the window opened by the post-Fordist 1970s already seemed to be closing. Market reformers won office on disinflationary platforms, liquidating public housing stocks, imposing structural adjustment programs and privatizing state assets. A conservative counterrevolution suspicious of "money for nothing" and "the eternal dole" was in full swing.[33] In all these conservative cases, however, the basic income also witnessed a "victory in defeat." In this postindustrial landscape, the fiscal apparatus was expanded and floors of income were promoted to compensate for the deregulation of labor markets and cuts in public services.

Across national contexts, a new redistributive market liberal paradigm nurtured the idea in policy circles, claiming that a "liberal social policy designed to maintain minimum standards of comfort . . . justifies no other social services other than those which involve transfers of income" and would "alleviate poverty without the need for trade union activity, public ownership, or central planning."[34] Although the proposal never became an institutional reality in the 1980s and 1990s, it silently installed itself as the distant, asymptotic horizon of a new welfare world.

This was hardly an exclusively Western development. In a Third World reeling from structural adjustment and faltering development, the career of cash transfers seemed even more propitious. In the aftermath of the market reform programs of the 1980s and 1990s, many former developing nations found themselves without adequate state capacity to support their populations. Whether in Brazil, South Africa, or India, cash transfers became an attractively simple way of doing welfare for an age of crumbling state capacity, mounting public debt, and competitive disinflation. More than a weapon for neoliberal shock therapy, however, these measures also twinned well with the New Keynesian economics of the 1990s, including a renewed precedence on poverty alleviation over development. A distinctly new civil society, with its own types of "poverty knowledge," now began to bolster it as a program. A "transfer paradigm" imposed itself as an indispensable framework within institutions such as the International Monetary Fund, the United Nations, the World Bank, and the International Labour Organization, where policy entrepreneurs such as

Guy Standing and William Easterly rethought social justice through a market-friendly lens. The UBI offered them "a floor without a ceiling" for a world that had given up hope of reversing market dependency and deindustrialization altogether. In the United States, in turn, the rise of cash benefits ran in tandem with a new vision of public administration "[assuming] a fragmented society of individuals where each person acts as his own regulator in a grand market of risk and reward."[35]

In the 2010s, when Europe seemed to undergo its own structural adjustment process, basic income steadily found its way back to the Old World. The scheme proposed a "techno-populist explosion" in which technocrats and populists both arose on the ruins of an older party democracy. Here the basic income fused with a radically new way of thinking about redistribution: the abstract universality of the money form came to triumph over the concrete universality of a decommodified public sector with full employment provisions. Basic income became the utopia for a world that had lost faith in utopias. Rather than a stand-alone policy prescription, basic income here acts as a prism refracting a series of epochal changes in late-century political culture. Foremost among these were deindustrialization and the crisis of organized party democracy—itself resulting in a global depoliticization of needs and "market turn" that straddled left and right, running parallel to "a crisis of politics as a form of human activity."[36] This broader context also offers answers as to what could unite *all* pro-UBI forces in the same camp. Scholars have been grappling for years with the proposal's attraction across the spectrum. From its inception in the interwar period to nowadays, the idea has been promoted by socialists, Keynesians and neoliberals alike. Under different labels, it counted advocates spanning from presidential candidates and Nobel Prize economists to Silicon Valley entrepreneurs. But what exactly do David Graeber, Milton Friedman, Charles Murray, Yannis Varoufakis, and Mark Zuckerberg have in common? While authors have tried to pin this unusual trajectory on "neoliberalism," "post-Fordism," a "Californian ideology," or, more generally as the "utopia for realists," a careful study of its origins and conditions of possibility indicates that the bipartisan appeal of basic income can be traced back to deeper intellectual and material shifts.[37] What the wide array of proponents actually share is less a coherent ideology-whether it be libertarianism or postworkerism-than a specific way of thinking about needs, poverty and the state that was slowly formulated in the interwar period, only to triumph in the decades following the Second World War.

There had always been marked differences between left- and right-wing versions, of course. For the first, a duly generous basic income would facilitate tactical withdrawal from the labor market and increase bargaining power for workers. To the right, a more frugal transfer would foster market participation and weaken wage rigidities. As usual, some basic income thinkers moved from a critique of the state to a critique of labor, others from a critique of labor to a critique of the state. Across the postwar debate, left-wing proponents were also careful to emphasize their differences with right-wing versions. Yet a vocal argument about quantity also hid a silent overlap on quality: both left and right premised their arguments on a critique of publicly provided, in-kind benefits, which stipulated the collective determination of needs. As a subspecies of the same cash transfer family, the convergence between both camps appeared far less surprising: both on left and right, the hope now became to provide welfare "for" and not "outside of" markets.

A closer look at the successes of the basic income over the past thirty years also makes it clear that the cross-partisan appeal of the UBI tapped into deeper institutional dynamics beyond the purview of pure intellectual history. Indeed, the conditions under which basic income could succeed require careful study, not only the divorce of redistributive considerations from the hierarchies of need or notions of duty and citizenship that were common in the postwar welfarist conceptions. This also included the monetization of poverty, sidelining more structural definitions and the slow displacement of the postwar planning state by a more market-friendly "transfer state," using the fiscal apparatus for social policy rather than state-led full employment programs.

More than economic necessity, this "new politics of distribution" pioneered in the 1960s United States and the 2000s Global South also arose from profound structural changes affecting all global democracies.[38] In the latter sense, the shared factor between UBI advocates was less a coherent ideology than a specific relation to politics and the state: a change embodying the most significant cultural and economic transformation since the end of the Cold War.

In that sense, any history of basic income's utopia cannot be a history of basic income alone. Through the lens of the proposal, we observe changing views of economic justice, social rights, state provision, markets, and political organization, refracted through a policy unique in its disrespect for ideological boundaries. This was also an intrinsically *global* story, bringing together activists from Delhi to Brussels to Detroit. These activists were embedded in research communities, reading groups, and political parties on a planet increasingly united in its market dependency. The globalization of basic income spoke to that shared vocabulary of forms and concepts birthed by the second capitalist globalization. Most prominently, however, the basic income can tell us something prominent about the rise of neoliberalism. Although the basic income idea was in part conceptualized by thinkers foundational for the neoliberal tradition, its appeal was never exclusive. Rather than tracking a homogeneous "left" or "right" for the proposal, the story of basic incomes points to a deeper shift of policy paradigms: fiscal Keynesians, New Leftists, and neoclassicists all came to support cash transfers for their own distinct reasons. Yet behind a seemingly technical proposal there always stood a set of specific assumptions—on labor, needs, the state, social citizenship. Although never distinctly neoliberal, its tenor was always decidedly *market friendly*: it supposed that money would remain the basic means of rationing access to goods, and that it would continue to mediate between "life and our means of life." From the 1940s to the 2010s, the guaranteed income dreamed up by Van Parijs and other activists also never turned into a policy reality. Rival proposals, from expanded public services to property-owning democracy, also found their place in many party platforms. In practice, however, it was clear that basic income was winning *a* battle of ideas, pushing welfare discussions and policy closer and closer to its regulatory ideal.

In this history basic income also functioned as much more than an "idea." Instead, the story told here forces us to look at the material forces that lent the idea its plausibility and attraction, which then allowed the idea to steer material forces in turn. Tying together economics, culture, and policy, the history told here can *only* be a "social history of ideas": a "social-contextual" story resting on the claim that the "questions confronting political thinkers are framed not only at the level of philosophy, political economy, or high politics but also by the social interactions outside the political arena and beyond the world of texts."[39] None of this implies collapsing writings on basic income into a nebulous "material base," but it does blur the borders between specialists and laymen, pamphleteers and philosophers, radically expanding the range of contexts in which the thinkers on basic income wrote.[40]

This also has consequences for how we think out the traditions that fed into the current basic income moment. Neoliberals, Keynesians, and antiwork leftists did not invent the markets, states, and welfare institutions that figured in their basic income visions. Their ideas were never the exclusive *engines* of economic, social, and political change that drove the past fifty years of basic income thinking. Yet they did provide orientation to the pilots at the wheel, a compass for policy makers, activists, and politicians. Like any compass, these ideals of basic income both reflected an established global field of forces *and* indicated a specific direction of travel, charging intellectual historians with an agenda of their own (as Christopher Hill once remarked, while "steam is essential to driving a railway engine," "neither a locomotive nor a permanent way can be built out of steam").[41] Or as Angus Burgin put it:

> Every story about the last fifty years will have to be a story about social practices, cultural norms, political praxis, or the transformation of the state. But it is also, crucially, a story about *ideas*: how changing circumstances led people to understand their economic lives in new ways, and how those novel understandings, in turn, affected their actions. . . . Exploring the interplay between ideas and circumstances helps us to recognize the contingency of current assumptions about political economy, and to understand how and why some beliefs persisted long after the contexts that produced them were "all but obliterated."[42]

For citizens in the 1970s worried about falling profits, the decline of the work ethic, deindustrialization, and persistent poverty amid plenty, the compass of basic income proved entrancing enough. As with any compass, however, the history of basic income also brings into view other forces that shaped our thinking on markets, states, welfare, and policy in the past fifty years. These span the rise of neoliberalism, the end of development, the birth of a new regulatory state, shifts from fiscal to monetary policy, and the secular crisis of mass politics across the globe.[43] Although always versions of older questions, these problems are very much *ours*, and they are unlikely to be best understood by time-traveling back to the fifteenth or sixteenth century. The basic income Van Parijs "opportunistically" dreamed of after Trump's 2020 checks might indeed still be a long way off. Its effects on our political culture, however, have become impossible to deny. They deserve a proper history.

CHAPTER ONE

An Anti-Mythology

"... a teleology imposed upon historic chaos" — C. L. R. James, "On the Negro in the Caribbean" (1943)

In March 1975, librarians at the French National Archives stumbled upon a strange batch of documents in their collection. Some years before, an anonymous donor had deposited in their library a file titled "Les dossiers secrets d'Henri Lobineau," including a document tracking the French aristocracy's lineage from AD 914 to about 1280, back to the first Merovingian king. About five years later Paris police confirmed that the confidence man Pierre Plantard had smuggled the documents into the collection sometime in the late 1960s. He admitted to planting the false family history in the Republic's archives as a member of the "Priory of Sion," a neochivalric society he founded in 1956, supposedly started by crusader Godfrey of Bouillon, with purported grand masters such as Leonardo da Vinci, Isaac Newton, and Mary Magdalene. Plantard's motives also came to light: proving his consanguinity with the Merovingian kings—and consequently with Jesus Christ himself—would justify his claim to the throne of France.[1]

It is hard to find a more brazen example of an "invented tradition" than the forgery Plantard performed.[2] As more than a mythic hoax, however, Plantard's "search for origins" also has an interesting counterpart in the existing histories of basic income. Like Plantard's family tree, the growing popularity of the UBI as a "five-hundred-year-old idea" has gone hand in hand with its insertion into an old and mighty family tree, encompassing thinkers from Thomas More to Thomas Paine to Milton Friedman.[3] Some authors openly trace the basic income to the late Roman republic and its attempts at popular land redistribution, placing the Roman Gracchus brothers in the same basket with Elon Musk and Jeff Bezos.[4] Rutger Bregman's *Utopia for Realists* similarly claims that "Thomas More dreamed about [basic income] in his book *Utopia* in 1516," a vision later rechanneled through figures such as Paine, Henry George, and Richard Nixon.[5] Guy Standing pushes the dawn of basic income even further back, suggesting that the Athenian reformer Ephilates—who introduced payments to citizens for jury service—was "the true originator of the basic income."[6]

Teleologies always come in imprudent and less imprudent versions, and some basic income scholars have paid very close attention to context. Walter Van Trier's book *Every One a King* (1995), for instance, provides a richly textured analysis of basic income thinking in interwar Britain and its relation to heterodox currents of economic thought, from Social Credit to early Keynesianism.[7] Peter Sloman's *Transfer State* (2018) tracks the birth of a British basic income movement to the 1920s and 1930s, when later competitors of the Beveridge plan sought more market-friendly variants of the rising welfare state, later extended into postwar "redistributive market liberalism" and an ascendant New Left.[8] This prudence remains all too rare, however. Most histories of the basic income exhibit what Hayden White termed a "teleological temptation"—a "bias in favor of order" for which "earlier events" can be understood only from the perspective of a "narrative's ending," in which blips and misfits are "subliminally edited out."[9] While the "history itself might not be teleological," the writing of the story "inescapably leaves us with the same 'teleological' feeling as fiction does, for it is difficult, if not impossible, not to read the ending point of a given narration as an implicit telos."[10] Broadly, most existing histories of basic income rest on the assumption that writers "in other periods were asking the same questions and facing the same problems as those of the historian and *his* world."[11]

What would a history of basic income look like without this telos? First, it would imply letting go of what J. G. A. Pocock and John Dunn call a tendency to "mythologise" given works by reading our own presuppositions into them "as a whole," making all history an "enterprise in the present."[12] Second, it would require specifying an object. For the basic income, this implies singling out its unique aspects: unconditional, individual, and

TABLE I.I. **Varieties of basic grants**

Timeline	A priori requirements	A posteriori expectations
(a) Continuous (b) One-off	(a) Means-tested (b) Universal (c) Conditionality	(a) Work requirements (b) Property ownership (c) Discretionary

Characteristics	Concepts	Authors
a, a, c	Negative Income Tax	Milton Friedman, George Stigler, James Tobin, Robert Lampman
a, b, a	Juliet Rhys-Williams's "New Social Contract," French personalists' "minimum vital"	Emmanuel Mounier, Alexandre Marc, Daniel Rops
a, b, c	Basic Income, Social Dividend, National Dividend, State Bonus, Minimum Abondant, Vagabond's wage, Guaranteed Income	Bertrand Russell, Oskar Lange, Joseph Charlier, Dennis & Mabel Milner, Jan Tinbergen, Robert Theobald, Philippe Van Parijs
a, c, c	Earned Income Tax Credit	
b, b, b	Land Grant	Thomas Paine, Thomas Spence
b, b, c	Basic/Capital Endowment, Citizen's Stake	François Huet, Anne Alstott & Bruce A. Ackerman

universal.[13] Most important, however, the basic income is *monetary* and not provided in kind. Rather than providing specific public goods, it leaves it to recipients to decide how they want to spend the grant.[14]

Since the early 1960s, historians in Quentin Skinner's and J. G. A. Pocock's Cambridge tradition have built a rich literature relativizing our notions of "liberalism," "socialism," and "anarchism," embedding these traditions in their contexts, unraveling their coherence, and, most important, eschewing large-scale teleological claims.[15] More than the rediscovery of lost authors or themes, terms such as "republicanism," "democracy," and "liberalism" have steadily lost their fixity in this literature. Strangely enough, these tectonic movements in intellectual history have left the field of basic income studies conspicuously intact. Many scholars seem to have no problem with pinning a transhistorical label on the idea, endowing it with an immutability rarely found in other conceptual accounts.[16] More than robbing the UBI of its history, such an account would allow for a better understanding of the processes that gave us our current basic income — or of what its conditions of possibility were.

Two devices will prove helpful as we track these discontinuities. The first distinguishes "a priori" from "a posteriori" conditions on the reception of grants (see table 1.1).[17] What conditions do recipients have to fulfill

to receive grants, and what expectations—both implicit and explicit—
are tied to them after their receipt? The second factor spans traditions
that drove grant ideology in the eighteenth and nineteenth centuries—
"agrarianism" and "producerism."[18] The first centered on how a republican regime could achieve stability. In its modern, eighteenth-century
version, this tradition hinged on what form of land distribution would be
suitable for a stable republican political order. An older Roman debate
over "agrarian law" set the coordinates for this thinking, reaching back to
classical republicanism and its sumptuary restrictions on property holding. The second was a producerist tradition that insisted on the centrality of a work ethic to this republican order.[19] In both traditions, property
ownership and republican rule were closely connected, spanning citizens'
duty to take part in productive work.[20] Both traditions formed an integral
part of a broader "politics of property" that ran across the eighteenth and
nineteenth century and sought to redistribute factors of production to citizens rather than increase income for wage-dependent workers.[21]

In the end, it was the erosion of these older political "languages," as
Skinner calls them, that opened space for new notions of cash transfers
to emerge in the 1930s and 1940s.[22] During the interwar and early postwar period, mass proletarianization, rural depopulation, state planning,
and industrial expansion displaced the grammar of the older "politics of
property." In this transitional period, thinkers such as Milton Friedman,
Lady Juliet Rhys-Williams, Abba Lerner, Oskar Lange, and Jan Tinbergen all began to reimagine welfare through a new market-friendly lens.
Their new version decoupled itself from the traditions that had structured
the grant tradition before—most prominently around "sovereign consumers" rather than "sovereign producers." They also let go of the emphasis
on property redistribution or credit creation that had characterized this
thinking on grants. Rather than inscribing the UBI into a dubious teleology, such a "radically historicist" history fixes our eyes both on shocks
that rocked twentieth-century capitalism and on how these shocks turned
basic income into an elegant tool to deconstruct and rethink social policy.

Agrarian Law in Anglo-American Republicanism

Thomas Paine opens his 1797 pamphlet *Agrarian Justice Opposed to Agrarian Law, and to Agrarian Monopoly* with a striking claim: Every citizen has
the right to an income.[23] "The plan I have to propose," Paine informs read-

ers, is to "create a National Fund, out of which there shall be paid to every person, when arrived at the age of twenty one years, the sum of fifteen pounds sterling, as a compensation in part, for the loss of his or her natural inheritance, by the introduction of the system of landed property."[24] The grant would be coupled with "the sum of ten pounds per annum, during life, to every person now living, of the age of fifty years, and to all others as they shall arrive at that age."[25]

Although Paine continued to publish until his death in 1809, *Agrarian Justice* proved to be his last contribution to the global republic of letters. Drafted during a stay at the house of American minister James Monroe, *Agrarian Justice* was printed in Paris in the rue Ménilmontant and later sold by booksellers from Paris to Westminster. "Written in the winter of 1795 and 96," as Paine recalled, the pamphlet was later consecrated as one of the first written examples of basic income.[26]

Yet matters quickly become more complicated. *Agrarian Justice* goes on to clarify that the payment would be a one-off; after calculating the costs and numbers of England's national capital, Paine hopes that his plan would "immediately relieve and take out of view three classes of wretchedness—the blind, the lame, and the aged poor"—and also would "furnish the rising generation with means to prevent their becoming poor" without ever "deranging or interfering with any national measures."[27] Most important, the plan "would multiply . . . the national resources; for property, like vegetation, increases by offsets"; and "when a young couple begin the world, the difference is exceedingly great whether they begin with nothing or with fifteen pounds a piece."[28] "With this aid," that couple "could buy a cow, and implements to cultivate a few acres of land; and instead of becoming burdens upon society, which is always the case where children are produced faster than they can be fed, would be put in the way of becoming useful and profitable citizens."[29] "National domains also would sell the better if pecuniary aids were provided to cultivate them in small lots," redistributing land by stealth without interfering with existing property arrangements.[30]

Paine's pamphlet looked both backward and forward with its alternative to the infamous "agrarian law." In 1793 the French Convention had passed a law condemning to death any person proposing the adoption of the law in question.[31] Instead, the regime began redistributing expropriated church lands to peasants who had been released from their demesnes. Some radicals sought to go beyond these measures, however. French radical Gracchus Babeuf, for instance, had died under the guillotine in 1797 after advocating land redistribution, an event that likely stimulated Paine's plan to publish. Paine had also served as one of the framers of the 1793 constitution that rendered Babeuf's law illegal, but he still harbored hopes of a breaking up of the large estates.[32] The French constitution of the year III in 1795, however, had taken a step back on suffrage expansion and introduced a censitary qualification, reducing the electorate to propertied men.[33] The redistribution provoked calls for emulation across the Channel, where the so-called Speenhamland system tied agricultural laborers to their parishes for minor cash relief. Yet Paine also initiated a radical departure from ancien régime assumptions on poor relief. As Gregory Claeys notes, by uncoupling welfare from the precepts of Christian charity—exemplified by Edmund Burke's plea for benevolence in his 1798 *Thoughts and Details on Scarcity* or Malthus's later *Essay on the Principle of Population*—Paine inaugurated a new epoch in social justice thinking.[34] Following Condorcet, he turned relief from a "favor" into a "national responsibility," properly carrying the Atlantic Revolutions into the realm of the social.[35]

Paine's pamphlet also took a position in a much older debate. To American readers the subtitle of the publication proclaiming "Agrarian Justice Opposed to Agrarian Law" "would have transported them back to the Roman history in which their republican ardour was kindled."[36] Within this republican tradition, "agrarian laws" stipulated the necessity of an equitable holding of land for a stable republic and sought to organize this division through cyclical surges of redistribution.[37] The best known of these precedents were part of the Licinian Law of 367 BC, which put an upper limit on landownership and imposed restrictions on cattle holding.[38] The measures also included a slight redrawing of public lands using the notion of the *ager publicus*.[39] Later, the Sempronian Laws of 133 BC put forward by Tiberius and Gaius Gracchus stood out as the most open attempt to transfer land from wealthy landowners to poorer Roman citizens.[40] Although the laws were passed through the Senate, aristocratic control over state finances thwarted their implementation, leading to the assassination of the Gracchus brothers and pushing the republic deeper and deeper into civil strife.[41] Their status thus remained tainted for posterity: set within the story of Roman decline, the laws appeared as a mere prelude to the dictatorship.

Unsurprisingly, Rome's agrarian laws also had a fraught history in republican thought as a whole. Before 1600, political thinkers had usually shunned the option, preferring anti-interference or abolishing private property altogether.[42] Classical Roman historiography operated as an ominous precedent here. There, the civil wars launched by the Gracchi were imputed to popular jealousy that sought to destroy Rome's careful *concordia* between plebs and patriciate. As Cicero argued in his *De legibus* and *De officiis*, for instance, the laws of the Gracchi were "ruinous" and brought about a "complete revolution in the State," robbing "one man of what belongs to him . . . to give another man what does not belong to him."[43] Renaissance thinkers usually followed Cicero on this score. Thomas More,[44] for instance, dismissed agrarian laws as "poultices continually applied to sick bodies that are past cure," while Machiavelli cast them as a "plague" and "cause of the destruction of the republic."[45] In Machiavelli's view, the Gracchi had rightly tried to close the widening gap between *grandi* and *popolo*, but they had done so through dangerously direct means: the agrarian law had "turned Rome upside down."[46]

More's hostility to the agrarian law also matters for those claiming him as a grandfather of the basic income. More's work was inspired by an England in which enclosures had accelerated rapidly in the 1400s, coupled with increasing militancy after the Black Death in the late 1300s. With the further extinguishing of England's customary rights, a growing number of farm laborers found themselves without access to land, "devoured" by sheep imported by improving landlords.[47] All this raised a question of equal landownership, yet More consistently followed Cicero in condemning the agrarian laws as dangerous. "It would be far more to the point to provide everyone with some means of livelihood, so that nobody is under the frightful necessity of becoming, first a thief, and then a corpse."[48] Philippe Van Parijs and Yannick Vanderborght claim that More proposed a guaranteed income with this statement.[49]

Contemporary translations usually render the expression "proventus vitae" as "adequate income." In later passages, however, More signals that his handout would be paid in kind rather than in money (*proventus* in medieval Latin referring to produce or growth, not to moneyed handouts).[50] "Revive agriculture and the wool industry," he added, "so that there is plenty of honest, useful work for the great army of unemployed." Later on, More's correspondent claims there are "ample provisions" for this task, "including crafts [and] labour on the fields," which would be available "if people do not choose a life as a criminal."[51] Two aspects sharply separate More's proposal from today's basic income proposals: their distribution in kind, and their connection to common landownership.

The same set of differences emerge in the nineteenth-century theorist Thomas Skidmore, "one of the first proponents of an unconditional basic endowment"[52] to proponents. In *The Rights of Man to Property* (1829), Skidmore claimed that a just constitution would stipulate the need to add up all the property of "each citizen, association, corporation, and other persons" together with "State property," from which a "dividend would be made."[53] Inheritance laws would form no obstacle to the plan, since auction was "to supersede all wills by means of which, property may daily transmit itself to the approaching generation."[54] Rather than a cash grant, Skidmore's setup would entail a constant rotation of property, maintaining citizens' access to productive resources (a scheme akin to the "asset egalitarianism" of Paine and Jefferson).[55] "Whenever nations have ceased to exist," Skidmore noted, "it has been because there has prevailed in them no system, or theory of government, whereby property should be as nearly equal among the people."[56]

The most prominent of English Speenhamland critics was English publicist Thomas Spence, a prominent member of the London radical scene. A correspondent of Paine's, Spence had read *Agrarian Justice* in the late 1790s, but he disagreed with his emphasis on land taxes. In a 1796 reply to Paine's pamphlet, Spence claimed Paine had accepted British land concentration and risked eliminating existing public provisions in hospitals. In his "The Rights of Infants," Spence advocated a redistribution of surplus rents to persons in need organized around the parish structure of Speenhamland. Unlike Paine, however, he claimed that this surplus could not be accrued by taxing landed estates. Instead, it should be levied on *all* taxable property. This "overplus" should be "divide[d] . . . fairly and equally among all the living souls in the parish, whether male or female; married or single; legitimate or illegitimate; from a day old to the extremist age; making no distinction between the families of rich farmers and merchants, and the families of poor labourers and mechanics."[57]

Spence thus countered the minimalism of the Speenhamland approach by seeking a more generous grant regime. This regime itself, however, was never to be turned into a permanent source of relief. Instead, Spence's republicanism revolved around the same producerist principles as Paine's. "May we not ask," he inquired at the end of the pamphlet, "who improved the land? Did the proprietors alone work and toil at this improvement?"[58] Spence thus hoped to break up large estates and allow them to be occupied by laborers. Rather than offering laborers relief from the world of work, Spence's plan was to put labor on the pedestal and allow workers to purchase their land.

In America this property-centered tradition persisted into nineteenth-century republican theory, undergoing its own modifications against a dynamic capitalist economy, hoping to "prevent the enormous accumulation of property in a few hands" by "confiscation without compensation," inscribed into a constitutional code.[59] This was a radical option rarely taken up by most agrarians. The Jacksonian labor Democrat Orestes Brownson, for instance, followed Jefferson in his 1830 proposal by insisting that abolishing inheritance would "elevate the labouring classes" and make "each man . . . free and independent."[60] "The young man, starting in life," he claimed, "receives his portion, which serves him for an outfit, as a capital with which to commence operations. With this he goes forth into the world and has what he can honestly acquire."[61] Although the means to acquire this property would be monetary (taking the form of a "cash endowment"), Brownson's final aim again was to re-create a class of independent landowners.[62] An emphasis on work also remained central for Brownson. If one could "strip labor of the degrading ideas now associated with it" and "render it as honorable, as much in keeping with the character of the gentleman, as fox-hunting is in England," "nobody would shun it."[63] An orderly property regime, in turn, would make it so that "labor . . . comes to be performed by the enlightened and cultivated" and "by men who own the capital on which they labor," thus making it worthy "in the estimation of all, and soon be sought as an agreeable pastime."[64] The call to labor was to be assured by a constitutional injunction to "accumulate within reasonable bounds."[65]

Later nineteenth-century thinkers found their own routes around Brownson's hurdle. Populists such as Henry George, Edward Bellamy, and Ignatius Donnelly, for instance, sidestepped redistribution by opting for a "land tax." This would rectify unjust ownership by channeling taxes on property into public funds. George, in turn, also hoped for "the salutary effect of an agrarian law without the iniquity."[66] Borrowing from Jefferson and Paine, George opened his 1879 *Progress and Poverty* with the claim that the "value [was] taken by society for social needs" when "one man can command the land upon which others must labor," thereby appropriating "the producer of their labor as the price of his permission to labor."[67] Land taxes would allow recipients to regain property ownership, redistributing funds to facilitate further landownership. A land value tax would compensate the propertyless for the loss of their divine rights. (George stopped short of following Paine on unconditionality, however, and preferred to distribute land taxes into the coffers of the state, which would use the funds to build public infrastructure.)

Even when contemporaries *did* eschew the possibility that their grant might be put to uses other than landed independence — as in Edward

Bellamy's "credit card" system in *Looking Backward* (1889)—a duty to labor remained central.[68] In Bellamy's view, "every person" was "free to spend his income as he pleases; but it is the same for all, the sole basis on which it is awarded being the fact that the person is a human being."[69] When the interlocutor in *Looking Backward* inquired into potentially perverse effects, the protagonist disregarded them. "The amount of effort alone," he noted, "is pertinent to the question of desert."[70] As Jamie Bronstein notes, Bellamy's plan thereby still "mandated participation in the economy"—anyone who decided to opt out or "not to contribute his labor to the large corporation that is the United States" would "be left with no possible way to provide for his existence. He would have excluded himself from the world, cut himself off from his kind, in a word, committed suicide."[71] In Bellamy's view, a refusal to work amounted to nothing less than an act of social secession.

From the revolutionary 1770s onward, thinkers like Paine, Spence, and Skidmore both broke with an old welfare regime and worked their way around the implications of an older agrarian law tradition. More than a "politics of income," theirs remained a "politics of property" above all. Before them, thinkers like Erasmus, More, and Vives thought of welfare programs in kind as alternatives. Although parts of these programs resembled the current basic income, their being encased in a larger vision—"the agrarian law without agrarian law"—put them at odds with the schemes celebrated by Van Parijs, Standing, and Bregman.

Grants and the Critique of Labor in European Socialism

Europe was hardly an exception to this agrarian rule. Like its American counterpart, grant thinking on the Continent in the eighteenth and nineteenth centuries began with an intimate relationship with property ownership, tracking its heritage of Paine's Jacobin engagement and the agrarian law schemes launched in the French Revolutionary years. Early socialists such as Charles Fourier and Victor Considérant justified minimum provision from within the perspective of socialized industry rather than through Paine's republic of smallholders. Some grant thinkers such as Sismondi or Mably hoped to recreate the yeomanry destroyed by land concentration.[72] Later thinkers in the century such as Karl Marx, Pierre-Joseph Proudhon, and Louis Blanqui completely broke with the agrarian frame.[73] Instead, they returned to the communal ownership advocated by

More, proposed alternative forms of credit creation, or sought an expansion of public employment. Yet, though these writers broke with the previous agrarian law traditions, this move never entailed a full endorsement of unconditional grants. Proudhon, for instance, imagined a society of small producers (mainly peasants and artisans) who could enter into a "series of equal market exchanges."[74] Freeing up currency and credit would make it possible to lease out land under eminent domain, halting the commodification of labor underway in the industrial regime.[75] Proudhon also saw this "people's bank"' (*Banque du peuple*) as an explicit alternative to agrarian laws in their older sense: "Here we have no expropriation, no bankruptcies, no agrarian law, no community, no State meddling and no trespass against inherence or family ... only the annihilation of net income by means of the competition from the National Bank which is to say, freedom, naught but freedom."[76]

The first nineteenth-century socialist singled out as a mature basic income proponent was French socialist Charles Fourier. Celebrated by Marx and Engels as the first utopian socialist, Fourier launched his political career in 1792 with the unruly *Theory of the Four Movements*, rising to prominence later in the decade. First mentions of Fourier's grant came in his 1803 "Lettre de Fourier au Grand Juge," which stipulated the need for a "decent minimum."[77] He later extended this thesis in his 1836 *La fausse industrie morcellée*. The book famously polemicized against the "civilized order" and argued for an "abundant minimum" if the "natural means of subsistence" such as hunting and farming had been monopolized by the few.[78] This minimum could then function as a wedge to force employers to provide better working conditions. Fourier never insisted on the monetary nature of his "minimum," however. Rather, he looked for "satisfaction of a minimum for the poor" with "clothes" and "food stock," public housing, and agricultural plots as chief remedies.[79] His cooperative communities, or "phalansteries," were to provide a "food guarantee" and "decent maintenance" coupled with vouchers in kind that could be traded in the communes.[80] Fourier's "minimum income" would be "paid in kind," since there was to be no money in Fourier's system.[81] Once these statelets had offered "excellent dinners" and "wines of their choosing," every participant would become a "small proprietor."[82]

Fourierists such as Victor Considérant in turn did advocate a "minimum" as "the basis of freedom and the guarantee of the emancipation of the proletarian," but this option again entailed no cash transfers.[83] ("Make revolutions, decrees, constitutions, proclaim every sort of republic," Considérant claimed in his 1845 *Exposition abrégée du système phalanstérien de Fourier*, and "you will done absolutely have DONE ABSOLUTELY NOTHING for serious liberty, the true, real liberty of the masses, if society does not guarantee to every man, woman and child a sufficient MINIMUM of existence ... clothes, housing, food and all necessary things for the maintenance of their lives and the social independence of their personality."[84]) Rather than monetary handouts, Considérant's phalansteries would produce a list of goods in kind and distribute them to their members.[85] If one could retrieve the "satisfactions of work" and "break with the mutilating aspects of contemporary employment," industrialism would attain its true and final form.[86]

There were exceptions to this rule. The writer who came closest to an unconditional understanding of the basic income was Belgian jurist and writer Joseph Charlier. Charlier—a Fourierist—shared his master's concerns with industrial minimums. In his *Solution du problème social, ou Constitution humanitaire, basée sur la loi naturelle, et précédée de l'exposé des motifs* (published in 1848 in Brussels in a nearly perfect parallel to Marx and Engels's *Manifesto*), Charlier defended a "territorial dividend" funded by property taxes à la Spence, which could compensate proletarians for the unequal distribution of land.[87]

Charlier's plan was ambitious in its generality. His dividend came with no family, gender, or age limits and was to be received from the cradle onward. "It is a very big mistake," Charlier noted in the *Solution*, "to let the spur of needs be the driving force of industrial activity."[88] Labor was of course to remain central in socialist currents. Yet since "the attraction of labour is only situated in the advantages it procures," it was therefore "obvious that the more these advantages are real, the more love for labour will develop; and the more they are sterile, the more it will burn out."[89] Charlier thereby instituted a break with the previous grant regime by uncoupling his dividend from both property ownership *and* work requirements.[90]

Charlier's dividend did retain a productivist edge, however. Through his minimum, the "overall consumption of products would no longer be allowed to degrade labor," and hence "the speed of the flow will be in proportion to the number of consumers and will inevitably enhance manufacturing activity."[91] If individuals did decide to remain idle, the forces of social stigma would ruthlessly execute their task. "All alone," Charlier continued, a recipient would "have to carry the burden of his misbehavior, since the public will no longer be so naïve as to help him by means of charity, given that everyone knows that in this case the misery has been caused by the one who suffers from it."[92]

Here then was the first official basic income—obligation-free, individual, and monetary. Charlier's marginality as a figure, however, also was testimony to the untimeliness of his proposal.[93] Despite several "sustained attempts to discover more information," Charlier "remain[ed] much of a mystery" to later scholars, while his name was "considered only in passing in many of the standard sources on the history of socialism in Belgium." "No substantial study of either his life or [his] work" appeared until a century after his death.[94] His "territorial dividend" remained an utter political orphan.[95]

The reasons for this obscurity are not surprising. When drafting his *Solution* in the Brussels of 1848, Charlier was flanked by two of socialism's most important theorists, Karl Marx and Friedrich Engels, drafting their own *Communist Manifesto*. As critics and legatees of the Fourierist school, Marx and Engels both rejected Babeuf's emphasis on agrarian law redistribution, instead returning to More's emphasis on public ownership. Here Marxian socialism still centered on the "producer" as an emancipatory subject and looked forward to the perfection of an economy in kind. This skepticism was already visible in Marx's comments on the Speenhamland system of the 1790s, which was to compensate for wage decreases.[96] It also became explicit in Marx's later criticisms of Proudhonist writers' money schemes.[97]

The tenacity of this "work centric" view can be gauged by the nineteenth-century reception history of Paul Lafargue's *The Right to Be Lazy*. When Friedrich Engels charged Eduard Bernstein with the task of translating Lafargue's book, Bernstein began by downplaying the tract's serious intent.[98] In his introduction, Bernstein decided to leave out the controversial subtitle ("refutation of the 'right to labor'")[99] and removed contentious passages elegizing idleness. "It would almost be possible," Bernstein stated in the German introduction to the edition, "to read this work as a piece of satire," since the tract's "biting sarcasm" and "relentless frankness" could assist labor in "fighting hypocrisy and moral cowardice in our own ranks."[100] Lafargue's book, in Bernstein's view, should best be read as a "series of stimulating thoughts" rather than a doctrinal commitment to the "right to be lazy."[101] Bernstein's ambivalent attitude toward Lafargue's text became a fixture of later Social Democratic Party and Soviet literature: Georges Sorel castigated Lafargue's tract as burdened with an "incorrigible lightness" and a "great pretension," rejecting its "paradoxes, gags and naivetés."[102] No Soviet edition was issued until the late 1980s.[103]

Until the 1920s, this "producerist" tradition retained a strong hold on the European socialist imagination. As Dutch socialist Ferdinand Domela

Nieuwenhuis had it, since "labor is the source of each and every piece of wealth and civilization," the "general product of labor" implied "a general universal duty to labor."[104] Communists like Rosa Luxemburg were even more vocal about the requirement. "In order that everyone in society can enjoy prosperity," she claimed in a 1918 pamphlet, "everybody must work. Only somebody who performs some useful work for the public at large, whether by hand or brain, can be entitled to receive from society the means for satisfying his needs."[105] "A general requirement to work for all who are able to do so . . . is a matter of course in a socialist economy."[106] Two years later, Vladimir Lenin reiterated the same point in a speech to a Russian Congress of Mineworkers, claiming that the "strong influence the Soviet power in Russia" made it clear "that power should be vested in those who work—he who does not work, shall not eat, but he who does work is entitled to a voice in the state . . . and can influence matters of state. That is a simple truth, and millions of working-class people have understood it."[107] Even when smallholder property had receded into the distance and agrarian laws no longer held sway on republicans' imagination, a strong suspicion of cash grants remained.

The "State Bonus" in Interwar British Thought, 1918–42

Interwar Britain offered one of the very first locations of a genuinely new mode of grant thinking. These ideas loosened connections with the producerist and agrarian traditions of the previous period and experimented with modes of unconditionality that had been absent. They also revolved around a new model of the "consumer" that displaced the older "sovereign producer" of socialist thinkers. These all decreed the centrality of the labor contract. Among these was the "state bonus" promoted by Quaker engineers Dennis and Mabel Milner in 1918. After the war, the York couple argued that "every individual, all the time, should receive from a central fund some small allowance in money which would be just sufficient to maintain life and liberty if all else failed."[108] The scheme envisioned a weekly payment of five shillings per person that would basically extend existing targeted benefits for servicemen's families to all citizens.[109]

The Milners thereby initiated a crucial departure from earlier grant thinking, which generally tied grants to an older property paradigm. In their view the bonus "must not be too much, since some are lazy, and if luxury were possible without work, they would be glad of the opportunity to rest." Yet they immediately countered this possibility by insisting that "if many were idle," "the contributions to the central fund would be reduced," with the bonus "correspondingly reduced."[110] Moreover, although "land" did not play an important role in the argument, the Milners presupposed that laborers would use their "national sum" to reacquire a modicum of property values. Much like Paine before them, they still believed that "most people are agreed that everyone ought to have access to the land."[111] As they stated in their pamphlet *The State Bonus*, "That in our existing civilisation this right is denied, so that it would seem only reasonable for Civilization to give in exchange the cash equivalent of what a man could grow with very little effort."[112] "Obviously," they stated, "giving the equivalent in cash is a great deal simpler than reorganising our whole land system"—a remnant of the earlier agrarian law problem.[113] Landed independence was not forfeited completely, however, and the Milners continued to believe that the grant would be used to acquire property above all. The bonus would also prove a capacious instrument in the fight over production rather than consumption, while labor would use it "to reinforce, not only [its] demand for a larger share in the fruits of industry, but also for a greater control of the machinery of Production itself."[114] Although the scheme was rejected by the Labour Party, it found its way to G. D. H. Cole and later market socialists, proponents of a "social dividend" such as Abba P. Lerner, Oskar Lange, and Fred Taylor. In Labour circles, however, its reception was far less enthusiastic—as a Labour Party committee concluded in the early 1920s, "we have already upon our agenda nationalisation, workers' control, the raising of all wages, the raising of unemployment insurance, to say nothing of the scores of minor measures it is more in accord with our principles to establish high wages and high unemployment benefit, than to offer merely the means to live."[115]

In the same month that the Milner couple launched their dividend scheme, British philosopher Bertrand Russell put forward his "vagabond's wage." More than his Quaker counterparts, Russell snapped the strings with the agrarian law tradition and saw little reason to rearrange property. His "wage" was modeled on a medieval ideal of artistry that would allow for a self-expression rendered impossible by employment. Russell proposed a version of basic income that was obligation-free, individual, and universal. "Under this plan," he claimed, "every man could live without work," and recipients would "bring colour and diversity into the life of the community."[116] Like Charlier's before him, however, Russell's proposal was as neglected as it was radical, inciting little or no policy interest.

A more promising avenue for basic income thinking was opened by the Social Credit movement of the 1920s and 1930s. Driven by the social reformer Major C. H. Douglas and the Canadian Social Credit lobby, these proposals focused on public control over the money supply as the main solution to industrial unrest and underconsumption. In 1922 engineer-turned-economist Major Douglas—a Cambridge graduate—proposed to pay out a monthly national dividend to simplify existing social security schemes and support private initiative across society.[117] Douglas's proposed separation between "A" and "B" payments—the one covering financial costs, the other material capital goods—led to a theorem claiming that scarce capital would come to block production.[118] Private financiers would have an incentive to hoard money and drive up asset prices. If the state were to inject liquidity into the system, however, incentives to hoard would decrease and production would retake its natural course. This inflationary method would have the effect of depreciating idle capital and make it easier for citizens to take part in economic activity, spreading available capital across society. If "financial credit was directly controlled by the consumers in the interests of the Community as a whole," the "amount of financial credit in circulation would tend more and more to become an accurate reflection of the National Real Credit," and "economic development would have been carried another step forward."[119] Douglas hoped his dividend would spur consumption, coupled with a strong incentive to work.

Douglas's scheme found a welcome audience in some Labour circles. All in all, however, the movement left little imprint on interwar socialist politics writ large. The antifinancial ambition of the scheme played a paramount role in this ambition—including its potential overlap with anti-Semitic themes. Douglas's "A + B" theorem became a guiding mantra for these credit movements in the 1930s, which saw private control over money creation as the main source of industrial depression and a driver of "wage slavery."[120] Traced back to the credit ideology of Proudhon, Edward Kellogg, and Henry Charles Carey in the 1850s and 1860s, social credit also operated in a transitional period between the property-based vision of nineteenth-century reformers and the consumer making headway in the Keynesian tradition. It thus ended as an option midway between producerism and consumerism. Russell's and Douglas's marginality became ever clearer over the decade, however. Guild socialist G. D. H. Cole, in his 1929 book *The Next Ten Years in British Social and Economic Policy*, stated that his "Dividend for All" was to be attributed according to "need rather than

labour contribution," thereby introducing the convertibility clause celebrated by later writers (Cole was familiar with the Milners' scheme and
probably encountered Douglas's proposals in a Labour reading group). In
his *Principles of Economic Planning*, for instance, he stated the necessity
"for everybody to have at least a minimum income"[121] that would allow
people to buy what they need beyond basic needs. At the same time, he
worried that a "State Bonus" based purely on "need" would rule out the
possibility of "combining an incentive to work with safeguards against destitution."[122] Cole's social dividend was dependent on one's "proven readiness" to play a part "in the common tasks and duties of the whole community."[123] The state, as Cole saw it, would remain "a great democratically
organised body of producers," firmly in charge of "the methods of production."[124] This body could use a "dividend for all" with a wider program
of civil reconstruction but stipulate strong work requirements.[125] As Ben
Jackson and Peter Sloman have noted, Cole repeatedly expressed worries
about free-riding and tied his grant to "a proven readiness to play one's
part in the common tasks and duties of the whole community."[126]

John Maynard Keynes encountered a similar basic income in a letter
sent to him by Fabian banker George Wansbrough in December 1939.
The letter proposed a "workers' income," in which "every family would
receive an income on a scale equivalent to present unemployment insurance benefits" with "wages . . . very much lower than they are at present."[127] In a reply in December 1939 Keynes said he considered the idea
"important and excellent," with a deserved place "in any Utopian political
programme," but also thought it "unthinkable that it could be introduced
in war time." "Some moves in the right direction" could be undertaken, of
course; Keynes himself had tried to introduce a similar permanent payment into the Labour platform in the 1930s.[128] Yet the proposal would
remain a "waste . . . in such conditions" and too far beyond orthodoxy.[129]
Three years later the success of the Beveridge Report—with its strong
emphasis on being service-based—worked against Keynes's hope of replacing unemployment insurance with family allowances.

American debates tended toward a similar arrangement. Louisiana
Governor Huey Long's 1931 "homestead grant"—pegged at $5,000 a
year—was premised on the "politics of property" of a previous Jeffersonian age. As Long hoped, farmers could use the handout to acquire a little
property and move up the property ladder. Long's "Share the Wealth"
program not only stipulated an upper limit on financial holding; conceived
in kind, it also included a wide public-sector program ranging free child

care for Louisiana's children to providing families with radios, automobiles, and washing machines.[130] With this would come a $6,000 homestead grant with which families could acquire rural property.[131] Long tracked these proposals all the way back to the old Hebrew agrarian laws: "Who cares what consequences may come following the mandates of the Lord, of the Pilgrims, of Jefferson, Webster and Lincoln?"[132]

The 1940s also saw more significant departures from these grant assumptions, however. One of these was the income plan devised by Lady Juliet Rhys-Williams, an English aristocrat who became a leading figure within Liberal Party circles in the 1940s. In 1943 she advocated a "new social contract" in the form of a universal benefit allocated weekly, replacing "all other forms of payment" and without a means test, to each citizen above age eighteen. An alternative to the Beveridge plan, her idea constituted an implicit normalization of casual labor (mostly for rural employers), but it also refused the emphasis on the male breadwinner at the heart of the Beveridge model. "Married women and those acting as unpaid housekeepers," Rhys-Williams argued, "would receive the benefits of the contract without being required to register for employment."[133] Although her plan was never implemented, its focus on cash transfers financed by general taxation as an alternative way to tackle poverty established, as Sloman notes, "tax-benefit integration . . . as a market liberal cause, rooted in a critique of both Fabian paternalism and the labourist assumptions of the National Insurance system."[134]

Rhys-Williams's criticisms mainly centered on the employment efforts Beveridge proposed. The Beveridge plan was "open to criticism," she noted in *Something to Look Forward To* (1943), "on the grounds that it fails to provide any security for the independent worker, who comes badly out of the Scheme."[135] As she continued, "the real objection to the Beveridge Scheme does not lie in its shortcomings in respect of the abolition of want, which could be made good, but in *its serious attack upon the will to work*."[136] "There can be little doubt," she finished, "that the Beveridge Plan, if put into full operation, will have the effect of undermining the will to work of the lower-paid workers to a probably serious and possibly dangerous degree."[137] Most visibly in *Something to Look Forward To*, however, Rhys-Williams's producerist principles stipulated that workers' "consumption" mattered only to the degree that it implied an underlying commitment to production. Rhys-Williams also retained a commitment in the form of a labor contract. Indeed, as Peter Sloman noted, to be eligible under her scheme, "each adult citizen would sign a contract with the state, promising to work to the best of their ability—full-time for men, part-time for single women and young widows without dependent children—in return for their allowance."[138] Those who refused to sign the contract would not be eligible for the payments. Moreover, unlike the Milners, she saw no need to treat her grant as a stepping-stone to land redistribution—an option that casual agricultural labor ruled out. She thus moved beyond the last remnants of the "in kind" paradigm that held sway in the nineteenth century.

$$* \quad * \quad *$$

Before a singular interwar boom, grant thinking had moved around a triple axis—landownership, socialization, and work requirements. All of these made a purely monetary and unconditional basic income difficult to theorize, let alone institute it as a policy.

The parameters of this previous grant regime were stringent. To writers as diverse as Paine, Brownson, Cole, Fourier, and Milner, "state bonuses" or "land grants" placed productive citizens at the center of their polity. Both groups did have "one preoccupation in common," as Bertrand de Jouvenel noted: both wanted to eliminate the effects of an unequal distribution of property.[139] The 1920s and 1930s would form a transitional period between the producerism of the agrarian law tradition and new ideas and visions of the figure of the consumer. Not only would this shift initiate a retreat from the sphere of production as the arena for the "battle over needs," for the first time the basic income would endow citizens with a "right to consume" beyond landownership or the compulsion to work.

The move away from capital grants also ran parallel to the rise of a new policy regime—the shift from a "politics of property" to a "politics of income." For the first, the redistribution of factors of production was essential. By the start of the twentieth century, however, the disappearance of an artisanal layer of workers and a new fiscal revolution allowed a right to income to compete with the older right to land. As de Jouvenel concluded:

> What was demanded in the name of social justice over thousands of years was land redistribution. This may be said to belong to a past phase of history when agriculture was by far the major economic activity. . . . agrarian egalitarianism may be said to embody two notions: one that natural resources are not to be engrossed, the other that fair rewards can be obtained only when the supply of capital is evenly spread out. The socialist solution [was] the destruction of private property as such.[140]

Only in the 1940s did thinkers decisively move away from these traditions. Figures such as Oskar Lange, Abba Lerner, Jan Tinbergen, William
Hutt, Fred M. Taylor, Juliet Rhys-Williams, and Milton Friedman had already offered proximate versions of this basic income. When their ideas
began to be accepted, however, the success was undeniable: first in the
United States, then in Europe and the Global South, cash transfers began
to acquire a deep and abiding attraction to generations of activists, policy
makers, and philosophers. Under this new set of circumstances, the idea of
basic income had become not only thinkable but plausible too. With these
parameters in place, Plantard's history began to make sense.

CHAPTER TWO

Milton Friedman's Negative Income Tax and the Monetization of Poverty

Almost no matter how you would define a free market, it will imply inequalities at the bottom of the scale which you, like I, would find socially intolerable. — Milton Friedman, Letter to Robert de Fremery, 1947

B efore he became one of the most famous economists of the twentieth century and a leading figure in the "Chicago school" of economics, Milton Friedman held a series of positions within the US federal government. Far from his achieving a straight track to academic tenure, Friedman's career prospects had remained rather uncertain until he was appointed associate professor at the University of Chicago in 1946. When he and his wife, Rose Director, graduated from the University of Chicago in 1933, for instance, there were few university jobs available for economists and, as both recalled in their memoirs, American academia was rife with anti-Semitism.[1] Friedman went without an academic position until 1940, when he was hired as a visiting professor at the University of Wisconsin. This was not an edifying experience, mainly because the university denied him tenure in 1941 despite protests from Friedman's students, including Walter Heller, who would later become President Kennedy's chairman of the Council of Economic Advisers.[2] For the ensuing four years Friedman would work within federal institutions. The timing was propitious. The growth of the federal agencies resulting from the New Deal and the war effort had multiplied the positions for economists in Washington, DC. In later life he joked that, "ironically," the New Deal had been a "lifesaver" for the couple, transforming Friedman into what Rose called a "knowledgeable government bureaucrat."[3] He was therefore not yet strongly politicized but was essentially a brilliant statistician who voted for Roosevelt in 1936,[4] had—according to his brother-in-law Aaron Director—"very strong New Deal leanings," and would later describe himself as a "Norman Thomas-type socialist."[5]

During his years at federal agencies, Friedman was mostly remembered as a "first-class technician" rather than the free-market crusader he would later become.[6] His intellectual rigor and technical capacity led to successive positions at the National Resources Committee (1935–37), designing and implementing the largest study of consumer income, then at the National Bureau of Economic Research (NBER) (1937–41) as a research assistant for Simon Kuznets studying national income and wealth, before he was hired at the Division of Tax Research of the Treasury Department (1941–43), ironically implementing withholding tax at the source,[7] and, finally, in the Statistical Research Group (1943–45) using his capacities as a statistician to improve war matériel and techniques. Far from a "lost" period in his career, it was precisely during these years that Friedman thought out his worldview and garnered some of his most important insights about social policy.[8]

One of his ideas would become especially popular in the following decades: the negative income tax (NIT). Friedman had first drafted a version of his proposal while he was at the US Treasury in the early years of World War II working on the general reform of the income tax. "It arose," he recalled, "as part of the thinking about an appropriate structure of the income tax which would take care of averaging fluctuating incomes over time."[9] It also revolutionized the thinking on grants prevalent until the 1920s. At that time he discussed the proposal mainly with colleagues such as his former student Walter Heller, but also with Louis Shere and William Vickrey under Henry Morgenthau's administration.[10] Although at first he restricted the idea to those who were employed, by the late 1940s Friedman would "see the virtues of it as an alternative to welfare programs"[11] and extend its application to guarantee everyone a floor of unconditional income through the tax system.[12] Considered quite marginal at first, the proposal would later be endorsed by more than a thousand economists with a wide array of political affiliations, from the Keynesian James Tobin to the openly neoliberal George Stigler.[13] By the late 1960s large-scale experiments were carried out in several American and Canadian cities while in 1969 President Richard Nixon, initially presenting himself as a firm opponent of the idea, tried to implement a version of it through his Family Assistance Plan (FAP), though it never made it past legislative brokering in the Senate.

Guaranteed income proposals would flourish in later decades, but Friedman's negative income tax constituted one of the first and most coherent versions of a noncontributory guaranteed cash transfer scheme. Of course, when he drafted his idea in the early 1940s, Friedman relied on an already rich variety of proposals aimed at guaranteeing a minimum income, and he openly admitted that the idea had "been in the air for a long time" and "was not originally [his]."[14] It was only in the interwar period that Friedman noticed a proliferation of proposals meant to reshape the distribution of income. Often obscured by the success of the Beveridge plan, these alternative ideas[15] would encompass Bertrand Russell's 1918 "vagabond wage," the "national dividend" promoted by the social credit theory of C. H. Douglas, Arthur C. Pigou's proposal of a minimum income in *The Economics of Welfare*, or the proposal Edward Bellamy put forward in *Looking Backward*, which Friedman used in his classes at the University of Wisconsin in 1940 and 1941.[16] The most influential formulation Friedman relied on to shape his own NIT as an alternative to Social Security was, he acknowledged, "the literature associated with Lady Rhys-Williams and the idea of the social dividend."[17] This proposal for a "social dividend" was first put forward by the market socialist Oskar Lange, whose work was very much discussed at the University of Chicago owing to the presence of the Cowles Commission,[18] and then by Abba P. Lerner in the mid-1930s.[19] Lerner in particular—who befriended Friedman and George Stigler in the late 1930s[20]—had argued in *The Economics of Control* for a "social dividend" distributed through the tax system.[21]

But unlike its predecessors, Friedman's NIT openly rejected any behavioral control of recipients and an emphasis on work. He also refused to stipulate any "duties" that would come with his guaranteed income. The idea's "antipaternalist" design, especially its disregard for work requirements, contrasted strongly with the very labor-centered versions of the postwar welfare state *and* with many earlier guaranteed income proposals. This was particularly true of Juliet Rhys-Williams's 1943 tax benefit reform. Her plan, which Friedman described as being "identical"[22] to his own, in fact diverged from his on a crucial dimension. As Peter Sloman has observed, the first version of Rhys-Williams's proposal was accompanied by a strong conditional clause by which workers would sign a "social contract" committing themselves to full participation in the labor market.[23] Only in later versions of her proposal did the work requirement and its contractual dimension disappear.[24] In fact, Friedman's disconnection of income from any type of *duty* strongly contrasted not only with nineteenth-century poor relief and social security schemes, but also with the modern notion of "rights." Rights were rarely thought to be independent of an understanding of citizenship and its accompanying range of duties, in particular the duty to work. In that regard the emphasis Friedman put on recipients' freedom to make "their own choices"[25] made the NIT one of the earliest and most successful proposals for a genuine guaranteed income.

Although an important literature has focused on Friedman's NIT as a policy proposal,[26] its exact sources and intellectual significance in the later development of guaranteed income proposals remain comparatively underresearched. The proposal's explicit break with the contractual constraints of the preceding grant tradition was accompanied by a desire to experiment with the features of a newly fiscal state, which seemed to offer market-friendly avenues for welfare expansion and for tempering bureaucratic elephantiasis. New interwar economic debates on welfare economics, needs, and the state as a social planner shaped innovative ways to tackle poverty and inequality. Far from dividing economists into clear political camps or "schools," these discussions were also articulated along new boundaries. They slowly elevated the price system rather than collective provision and public services as the most efficient way to allocate goods in society according to diverse individual preferences.[27] Debates opposing economists and policy makers on the *extent* of the transfers and their effects on incentives rather than on the means of redistribution were their main legacy. From this perspective, the history of Friedman's negative income tax locates the rising popularity of "cash" rather than "in kind" transfers in larger shifts and changes within the interwar and midcentury economics profession, involving not only self-identified neoliberals but self-described Keynesians as well. For a proper understanding of the inception of Friedman's NIT, three developments are of particular importance: the divorce of redistributive considerations from politically constituted needs leading Friedman to promote maximizing choice rather than in-kind welfare; the hollowing out of preexisting notions of equality in which the state played a key role by replacing it with a monetary and market-friendly conception of poverty; and, finally, with the rise of mass taxation during the war, a fiscalization of social policy.

From Collective Needs to Individual Preferences

When Friedman first drafted his proposal, the American economics profession still operated under the imposing lodestar of British welfare economics. Canonically embodied in the work of the economists Alfred Marshall and Arthur Cecil Pigou,[28] this body of work relied on one of the most famous assumptions in modern economics: that the "marginal utility of wealth" declined as wealth increased. This perspective owed much to the Benthamite argument that "the greatest happiness of the greatest number" was to be seen as "the measure of right and wrong."[29] The utilitarianism underlying welfare economics thus decreed that society should be organized to maximize total utility. This utilitarian view implied that extra funds given to a rich and well-endowed individual would always translate into less additional happiness than would funds given to a poor one.[30] Transferring a unit of income from the rich to the poor would thus decrease the happiness of the rich, but by less than the happiness gained by the poor. As David Grewal noted, the consequence was that "social welfare policies that directed benefits to the poor at the expense of the rich would have the property of increasing total social utility."[31]

This perspective naturally led to two supporting theses. First, it implied a certain homogeneity in utility functions between different individuals (assuming an equal capacity for satisfaction). And second, it implied that it would make sense to sum or subtract utilities as if utility were as measurable as weight, assuming the possibility of interpersonal comparisons. While authors operating in this tradition often remained politically neoclassical in their vision of economics (implying notably, with few exceptions, a distrust for high minimum wages and union bargaining), their utilitarian framework still committed them to a vision of utility maximization cast in Benthamite terms. Pigou, for instance, famously wrote that it was "evident that any transference of income from a relatively rich man to a relatively poor man of similar temperament, since it enables more intense wants to be satisfied at the expense of less intense wants, must increase the aggregate sum of satisfaction."[32]

However, this vision of utility and interpersonal comparison, unlike Bentham's, was strongly tied to a conception of normative needs as objective and universal, in contrast to subjective preferences.[33] What these thinkers generally denoted by "utility" was essentially limited to the economic study of the means to satisfy hunger and to provide necessary shelter or clothing. As Robert Cooter and Peter Rappoport noted, "utility sprang from conditions associated with physical survival and development," leading them to naturally "believe that people were fundamentally alike except for an insignificant personal component, rather than that the personal component swamped the shared one."[34] This view again implied a strong and hierarchical conception of human needs. Pigou himself did not hesitate to assume quite normative visions of human nature, distinguishing socially valuable desires from what he saw as vacuous satisfactions. "Non-economic welfare is liable to be modified by the manner in which income is spent," he argued in 1920, "different acts of consumption that yield equal satisfactions; one may exercise a debasing, and another an elevating, influence." As he saw it, "the reflex effect upon people's characters of public museums, or even of municipal baths, is very different from the reflex effect of equal satisfactions in a public bar."[35]

From this perspective, not only did the utility of an increase of income for the rich decrease general welfare, but the very needs they could choose to satisfy, "such as gambling excitement or luxurious sensual enjoyment," could affect the general welfare, depending on their consumption choices. The point of social policy was not just redistribution, but also about the kind of needs that would be satisfied under a demand "controlled" by the rich.[36] Inversely, "resources transferred to poor persons, in the form of command over purchasing power," added Pigou, could "from the point of view of the national dividend be wasted" by allowing uninformed consumption choices.[37] Transfers in cash could then bring the risk that the poor would use the money to satisfy different needs than those defined as collectively important. In this sense there was little doubt that "material welfare economics," as Lionel Robbins called it, was also motived by a normative vision of the "good society."

This consistently utilitarian vision pushed thinkers like Pigou to advocate redistributive measures. But unlike guaranteed income schemes, since he assumed normative views of needs and a certain homogeneity in utility functions, the idea of transfers in kind was often seen as preferable. In Pigou's purview the state could still take on a larger role in economic life, providing its population with basic goods such as public health care, education, social housing, leisure, or even food.[38] As Peter Sloman notes, not only did "benefits in kind [have] less impact on incentives" to welfarists, but they could also "improve workers' efficiency"[39] in ways that cash transfers could never accomplish. Through Beveridge and other welfare bureaucrats, Pigou's primacy of material needs was to become a crucial component of postwar welfare states.

By the late 1930s, however, a series of hard-hitting attacks had severely shaken the foundations of this "older" welfare economics. With this came a skepticism about states' capacity to be an effective social planner. Its perspective was cast as too normative and was based on false assumptions about the possibility of interpersonal comparisons and maximizing utility. The most important intervention on the matter was made by Lionel Robbins, who by 1932, in a series of lectures at the London School of Economics, had made the case that the assumption of "equal capacity for satisfaction" was in fact external to economics and rested essentially on ethical concerns rather than scientific ones.[40] Drawing from Pareto's principle of optimality,[41] by which an allocation of commodities was deemed optimal only if no person could be made better off without making someone else worse off, he argued that there was no scientific basis for the idea that redistribution increased general welfare.[42] A favorite example of Robbins's was the story of an Indian official who tried to explain the logic of the Benthamite model to a high-caste Brahman. For the Brahman, as Robbins recalled, the Benthamite idea just could not "be right." "I am ten times as capable of happiness as that untouchable over there,"[43] he argued. For Robbins this was an unsettling thought. While he felt no sympathy for the elitist view, it seemed obvious to him that "if the representative of some other civilization were to assure us that we were wrong, that members of his caste (or his race) were capable of experiencing ten times as much satisfaction from given incomes as members of an inferior caste (or an 'inferior' race), we could not refute him."[44] Robbins also argued for a radical skepticism toward our ability to engage with "other minds" and therefore "know" a priori individual needs.[45] While the argument Robbins advanced probably had more to do with recusing the political and ethical framework implied by the work of more radical economists like J. A. Hobson and R. G. Hawtrey[46] than with thinking about humanity's epistemic limits, it became extremely popular among economists intent on building a "value-free" science.

Robbins's idea also demonstrated that there was in fact no way to dispute the idea that someone's subjective satisfaction could be larger than someone else's. It was impossible to claim *objectively* that the rich would experience less satisfaction from an increase of income than would the poor. Such a claim relied on a classification of needs that was purely an *ethical* postulate. For Robbins and other neoclassicists, in turn, interpersonal comparisons of utility and notions of "objective needs" were beyond the feeble reach of economic science.[47] The only function of economics was to "enable us to make choices with full awareness of the consequences,"[48] to inform us about the choices rather than choosing for us. Allowing choice was then a condition, he argued, for "delimiting the neutral area of science from the more disputable area of moral and political philosophy."[49] "There is nothing in economics," he added, "which relieves us of the obligation to choose." By 1934, with the Hicksian ordinalist revolution[50] in full swing, the modern theory of consumption, with its rates of substitution between goods, replaced interpersonal comparisons. While the different solutions to the problem of welfare remained contested by the period's main economists until the mid-1950s,[51] it became clear that "ethical judgments" or normative visions of human needs could not remain part of the program of "positive economics" (as opposed to "normative economics").[52] This important shift implied that transfers in kind—what Richard Musgrave would later call "merit goods"[53]—were now cast as deeply suspicious,[54] since preferences—a term economists began to prefer to "needs"—and satisfaction differed widely. In a sense they were not even knowable unless, as Samuelson would put it, they were "revealed" as choices on a market.

The welfare debate strongly influenced Friedman as a young economist. Very early in his career he had understood that the "attitude toward all public policies will be affected by our ideas concerning wants."[55] While questioning the very relevance of the idea of "utility,"[56] Friedman agreed for the most part with critics of Pigovian economics and put "freedom of choice" rather than the "maximizing aggregate utility" at the forefront of his work. In the first draft of his review of Abba P. Lerner's *Economics of Control*, for instance, Friedman openly criticized Lerner for seeming to "uncritically" "accept as obvious Bentham's illogical 'greatest good for the greatest number.'"[57] In his most renowned work, Lerner had famously offered an elegant defense of equality as "the maximum of probable total satisfaction" using Robbins's argument against him.[58] Even if we assumed that people had unequal capacities for satisfaction, Lerner argued, there was "no way of discovering with certainty whether any individual's marginal utility of income is greater than, equal to, or less than [that] of any other individual."[59] Every individual, like the Brahman Robbins had encountered, "could declare that he has exceptionally high capacities for satisfaction"; but if, as Robbins pointed out, there was no way to dispute it, there neither was a "way of testing the validity of such claim."[60] It was therefore impossible to "maximize the total of satisfactions," but it would still be possible to maximize the probable total satisfaction through income distribution. If giving too much to an individual is worse in terms of aggregate satisfaction than giving too little (because of Lerner's assumption of diminishing utility of income), an unequal division of income would always lead to a smaller total satisfaction than could be achieved "by dividing income evenly."[61]

This line of argument left Friedman unconvinced, however. "Eliminate the ignorance" of an individual's capacity for satisfaction, he wrote, "and the same analysis immediately becomes a justification of inequality."[62] Most of the argument was, he thought, "empty talk," filled with "verbal looseness and ambiguity," "neglecting almost completely the numerous questions that have been raised about that formulation in the course of a century's discussion."[63] Lerner, like most of the figures in the canon of welfare economics, had failed to demonstrate "how the satisfaction experienced by an individual can be measured" or even if "the satisfactions of different individuals were simply be added to get a total for society."[64] Interpersonal comparisons simply seemed misleading, assuming what a "good society" should look like without really providing a strong case for implicitly normative views.

In fact, as Friedman claimed a few years later, it was the very idea of utility "as a neutral concept"[65] that had to be contested. "Science is science" he argued, "and ethics is ethics; it takes both to make a whole man; but only confusion, misunderstanding and discord can come from not keeping them separate and distinct, from trying to impose the absolutes of ethics on the relatives of science."[66] As he himself argued in his plea for a Humean "positive" economics, the economist need not inform citizens about the ends that should be pursued ("what ought to be"),[67] but only about the means of getting there. It had to be "independent of any particular ethical position or normative judgments" and to offer us rather "a system of generalizations that can be used to make correct predictions about the consequences of any change in circumstances."[68] This also had clear policy ramifications. The solution Friedman envisioned to this crisis explained his emphasis on cash and market exchanges rather than in-kind transfers. As he responded in a letter to economist Earl E. Rolph (who would later become a vocal supporter of the NIT), rather than assuming the "implicit" and "unattractive" goal of "maximizing some kind of aggregate utility," economists should replace it with "the end of maximizing effective freedom of individuals."[69] This aim—maximizing freedom rather than welfare—would naturally shape his views about poverty. Without the normative framework of welfare economics, equality was soon to be replaced by, first, a more targeted struggle against poverty and, second, a less prescriptive definition of needs. The reasons for focusing on a floor of income instead of reducing inequality were, however, less economic than political. "Even with a completely competitive order," Friedman argued at the 1947 Mont Pèlerin Society conference, there would always be a "problem of poverty" and "no democratic society is going to tolerate people starving to death, if there is food with which to feed them."[70] The same year, in a letter to economist Robert de Fremery, he argued that "almost no matter how you would define a free market, it will imply inequalities at the bottom of the scale which you, like I, would find socially intolerable."[71] This skepticism about laissez-faire was in fact characteristic of the neoliberal project from its very inception. As argued by Niklas Olsen, during the 1930s and 1940s many of the neoliberal network's members were "deeply suspicious of nineteenth-century capitalism" and associated unregulated markets with both widespread poverty and monopolies. In that sense, most of them thought the market had to be organized and sustained and viewed a certain degree of state regulation and redistribution as "essential to a liberal society."[72] Therefore such a plea was made not in the name of an abstract notion of welfare, but rather as a condition for a market economy to function. Friedman himself had been deeply influenced by Henry Simons's 1934 *Positive Program for Laissez-Faire*, which advocated a more extensive role for the state in organizing and preserving the market mechanism. When it came to the question of poverty or destitution, this meant thinking out ways to guarantee, as Hayek had himself advocated in *The Road to Serfdom* in 1944, some "minimum of food, shelter and clothing, sufficient to preserve health."[73]

In Friedman's view, however, such a minimum could not be given in kind to the poor, but had to be reached through the poor's own decisions. To guarantee what he called a "minimum standard of living,"[74] cash transfers rather than in-kind public programs seemed more appropriate to expand the recipients' freedom of choice. Part of the argument of the piece stemmed from exchanges concerning the question of poverty that Friedman had with Swedish Nobel Prize–winning economist Gunnar Myrdal at Columbia University in the late 1930s.[75] But his more conscious defense of cash transfers can be traced back to an unpublished piece Friedman drafted in 1939 shortly after working within the newly opened National Resources Committee to calculate a cost of living index for the Department of Agriculture and Labor.[76] In those years the New Deal administration was in desperate need of more data on consumer purchases, spending, and incomes and launched in summer 1935 a nationwide survey reaching a million families.[77] But given the almost Kafkaesque discussions he went through when working on consumption indexes—for example, deciding whether or not wine had to be counted as food[78]-he quite rapidly moved away from a perspective that would define "objective needs" and what *should be* "rational" consumption choices. Once the "minimum standard of living" was *determined* (through scientific measures of food consumption essentially) it had to be insured, he argued, through an equivalent income rather than by collective provision. "In a democracy at least," Friedman wrote, "it is a fundamental premise that in general the individual's choices are to be accepted; that he is the best judge of what he wants, and of what is 'good' for him."[79] "The standards" provided by the nutritive science he followed must be combined with those "set by the individual's own choices, not substituted for them." To escape acts of coercion on behalf of the state and of a priori definitions of needs curtailing freedom, money appeared to be the ideal solution for letting individuals choose *how* they wanted to sustain their own lives. Within this first cash-based proposal, built on the ruins of the older welfare economics, Friedman's "minimum standard of living" could seem an attractive alternative to the New Deal's service-based programs and the state's inefficiency in responding to the wide variety of each set of preferences. After disqualifying any "normative" or politicized idea of needs defined by the majority, only a policy organized around cash transfers could guarantee freedom of choice. Cash grants given to the "indigent," Friedman would later write, should be spent according to each citizen's personal "values."[80]

Such a commitment to freedom of choice also pitted Friedman against a contractual vision of rights, obviously open to the same objections Pigou had about how the money would be spent by individual consumers. Indeed, if citizens had the right to choose for themselves through a guaranteed income rather than being coerced into specific choices reflecting politically defined needs, how could one guarantee an "optimal" allocation of resources? How could one guarantee that the choice would not produce catastrophic economic outcomes? In his paper, Friedman perceived that without any conditional clause, people *might* indeed use some of the money unwisely or inefficiently. In that case the smallest amount of money needed to reach a minimum level of calories (as it would be provided by calorie count) would not suffice. One could not simply translate the minimum calories required into the minimum income needed. Since consumers' choices varied, the composition of the diet itself could not defined uniformly. "Even though potatoes and beans" are probably the "least expensive nutritionally adequate diet,"[81] Friedman observed, it would be justifiable for those receiving such a diet to complain at having it imposed on them. The relevant question to ask was not "What is the least amount of money that would purchase an adequate diet if nutritional adequacy is the sole end?" but "Given that individuals are to be allowed to make their own choices, what is the least amount of money an individual spend[s] and receives a nutritionally adequate diet?"[82] Rather than opting for potatoes and beans alone, individuals might believe an adequate diet would include meat once a week or wine.

Friedman's response to this analytical puzzle was a "failure coefficient." This was the proportion of persons who, given the liberty to make their own consumption choices, would fail to achieve a sufficient diet. If Friedman's "failure coefficient" was placed at 5 percent, the level of income necessary would then be calculated in relation to the consumption choices of 95 percent of the target population. This coefficient might suffice for citizens buying meat once a week. Similarly, if one based the amount of income on the most efficient and rational diet—potatoes and beans every day—one would have to assume a much steeper failure coefficient. In any case, as Friedman wrote, the proportion of failure would decrease with income. Yet, he added, it "might never reach 100 per cent."[83] Since choices differed greatly "from individual to individual" and since "at any given income, some will obtain adequate diets while others will not," we have "to recognize individual variability and the resultant fallibility of any single figure and to reconcile ourselves to a certain percentage of failure."[84] The justification for using this "failure coefficient," he thought, "follows from the basic premise that the choices of individuals are the final standard. The "failure coefficient" could then be viewed equally as a "freedom coefficient" defining the degree of freedom one wanted to grant individuals. Thinking through the primacy of individual choice rather than contractually creates space for a form of social policy freed of any contractual duties and willing to act only on the incentives.

This antipaternalist feature would also become a key dimension of the guaranteed income proposals launched in the following decades. Rather than trying to constrain individual choices, policy makers would have to transform the environment in which these choices were made, altering the *structure of incentives* without projecting any paternalist views on subjects as such. The sole decision the economist had to make was to define the "optimal" failure/freedom coefficient. Challenging the idea that governments could define social needs, Friedman and his contemporaries began to see the market as an antiauthoritarian tool that would allow citizens to decide how to sustain their livelihoods and fulfill their wants. This approach to welfare would also explain the future traction Friedman's proposal would receive among liberals. States could simply adjust the "rules of the game"[85] and, maybe, imagine a higher level of basic income to render it more egalitarian. Future versions of the proposal therefore differed not so much in nature as in the architecture of incentives built around it.

Equality and the Price System

The rising primacy given to market consumer choices would only intensify in the following decades with the slow generalization of a narrowly income-based conceptualization of poverty and the increasing centrality of the price system within economic theory. If needs were not "knowable" through the centralized action of the state, the price system appeared as the best tool to reveal individual preferences. For thinkers such as Pigou, Marshall, Keynes, or Richard Tawney, despite their important differences, the question of equality was generally bound up with a criticism of the dominant role the market had taken in the organization of society as a whole. The discrediting of nineteenth-century liberalism was profound and shaped an understanding of equality embedded within the larger ideal of a "post–laissez-faire" society. As British sociologist T. H. Marshall wrote in his famous *Citizenship and Social Class* (1950), "basic equality" could not be "created and preserved without invading the freedom of the competitive market."[86] Since the market had failed to guarantee the material reproduction of the population, it was now up to the government to act through ambitious programs of public housing, rent and price control, public investment, and services. This implied a set of institutions that, as Marshall claimed, would not be meant merely to "abate the obvious nuisance of destitution in the lowest ranks of society," but would assume "the guise of action modifying the whole pattern of social inequality." "It is no longer content to raise the floor-level in the basement of the social edifice," Marshall continued, "leaving the superstructure as it was. It has begun to remodel the whole building."[87]

There was no stauncher advocate of this line of argument than socialist economist and historian Richard H. Tawney. As he argued in *Equality* (1931), the best strategy on poverty consisted not in "the division of the nation's income into eleven million fragments, to be distributed, without further ado, like a cake at school treat, among its eleven million families"

but rather, through "the pooling of its surplus resources by means of taxation, and the use of the funds thus obtained to make accessible to all, ir-
respective of their income, occupation, or social position, the conditions
of civilization which, in the absence of such measures, can be enjoyed only
by the rich." We cannot, he added with a degree of irony, calculate "the
contribution to culture of the reading room of the British Museum" by
simply "dividing the annual cost of maintaining it by the number of ticket
holders."[88] "High individual incomes," Tawney argued, "will not purchase
the mass of mankind immunity from cholera, typhus, and ignorance, still
less secure them the positive advantages of educational opportunity and
economic security."

In a similar vein, William Beveridge argued in *Full Employment in a
Free Society* (1944) that the increase of "spending power of consumers"
was hardly the best way to abolish the "five giants" (Want, Disease, Ignorance, Squalor, and Idleness). "Money spent on drink," he noted, "does
not give employment to the miner, but to the brewer; money spent on
milk does not help to solve the problem of the unemployed engineer. It
may be said that consumer's demand should be supreme, and that, if the
consumer ordains, the miner should become a brewer and the engineer
a dairy farmer."[89] "Such ends," he argued, "cannot be brought within the
scope and calculus of competition," and they "presuppose a social choice."
"Many vital needs," Beveridge added, "can be met only by collective action." In place of a price system and sovereign consumers, he argued for
the empowerment of a "democratically controlled state" to secure the allocation of goods "in accord with the wishes of the citizens."[90] In its most
radical form, this view implied that the state as a collective decision maker
could replace a posteriori adjustment of production resulting from market exchanges by an a priori political assessment of needs and economic
planning.[91] This commitment to equality was therefore strongly embedded within the more general framework of social rights and citizenship
rather than the narrow area of income distribution.

In the United States, this line of reasoning was palpably present in
what Margaret Weir and Theda Skocpol termed a tradition of "social
Keynesianism." American Keynesians such as Alvin Hansen or, later, John
Kenneth Galbraith advocated not only fiscal policies and "automatic
stabilizers" to reach full employment but also "massive public welfare
projects" and the expansion of the role of "the federal government in the
economy."[92] Hansen in particular was convinced that even if full employment could be reached "through private enterprise," it would still "not

solve the gross deficiencies which we have in education and public health or in the slums and blighted areas of our cities."[93] Galbraith's 1958 best seller *The Affluent Society* similarly argued that "the line which divides the area of wealth from the area of poverty . . . is roughly that which divides privately produced and marketed goods and services from publicly rendered services."[94] In other words, poverty emerged when there was no adequate balance "between the supply of privately produced goods and services and those of the state."[95] For a high-profile Keynesian like him, "poverty [was] self-perpetuating partly because the poorest communities are poorest in the services which would eliminate it."[96] Galbraith's "attack on poverty," Alice O'Connor noted, required "a complete reordering of economic priorities, away from growth for its own sake and towards redistribution for the sake of 'social balance.'"[97]

Although this conception retained relative dominance until at least the early 1960s, mainstream economists would progressively center the preservation of the price system at all costs. This growing worry emerged with the famous "socialist calculation" debate of the interwar period.[98] While the debate pitted the views of Austrian economists like Ludwig von Mises and Friedrich Hayek against market socialists like Oskar Lange and Abba P. Lerner, all participants showed a common concern for the necessity of a price mechanism. The latter would be famously reframed by Hayek as an ingenious decentralized system to use dispersed information between economic agents.[99] The information needed to allocate scarce resources, Hayek argued in his seminal piece, "never exists in concentrated or integrated form but solely as the dispersed bits of incomplete and frequently contradictory knowledge which all the separate individuals possess."[100] This argument was an obvious reference to the possibility of an assessment of social needs, but more important, it strongly delegitimized the state as a social planner in favor of the aggregation of individual consumer choices. By the late 1940s cash transfers gained traction among economists as a more suitable alternative to collective provision or price controls and heavy-handed state interventions in the market. By the 1950s, as Peter Sloman has shown, a vast majority of neoclassical economists had become convinced that "market pricing was normally more efficient than collective provision,"[101] laying the foundation for Samuelson's later "neoclassical synthesis." James Meade's 1948 *Planning and the Price Mechanism* proposed and his " liberal-socialist solution" was probably the most explicit statement of this perspective, stating that the price system was probably "among the greatest social inventions of mankind." While equality was worth pursuing as a goal, the means to get there had to be market friendly. State planning was "bound to be clumsy, inefficient and wasteful as compared with a properly functioning price system."[102] The best way to tackle poverty was through "an extension of the use of the price mechanism to promote the more efficient use of resources associated with a socially desirable redistribution of income."[103]

Throughout his career, Friedman would rely on Meade's principle when advocating his views. Indeed, his main criticism in the 1930s and 1940s concerned not the fact of redistribution per se, but the paternalistic tools used to reach it. While he admitted to "strong egalitarian leanings" and thought through "an egalitarian ground"[104] until the mid-1940s, he always remained consistent in defending the centrality of the price system. A striking example of this line of thought can be found in a 1946 pamphlet about the housing question that Friedman cowrote with George Stigler. In this small brochure they argued that if they wanted "even more equality," "not only for housing but for all products it is surely better to attack directly existing inequalities in income and wealth than to ration each of the hundreds of commodities and services that compose our standard of living."[105] Of course, neither Friedman nor Stigler ever really advocated a strictly egalitarian distribution of income: they were generally focused on building floors rather than ceilings. But their main concern at that period was not exactly redistribution per se. "The major fault of the collectivist philosophy," Friedman argued in one of the few texts where he refers to neoliberalism, "is not in its objectives" but rather "in the means." "Failures to recognize the difficulty of the economic problem of efficiency," he continued, "led to readiness to discard the price system without an adequate substitute and to a belief that it would be easy to do much better by a central plan."[106] Postwar developments increasingly seemed to corroborate Friedman's hypotheses. As the members of the 1947 Mont Pèlerin Society conference put it, what was needed was "the possibility of establishing minimum standards by means not inimical to initiative and the functioning of the market." The NIT was here understood as a solution to a crucial problem for neoliberals in this early period. "Progressive negative taxation" could work as "a substitute, not as an addition, to present social policy."[107] The idea was received with skepticism by some attendants, but it was also cast as "an attractive alternative to socialism,"[108] in Karl Popper's view—a way to deal with the poverty capitalism generated while preserving its fundamental tenets.

A few years later, during a series of lectures he gave at Wabash College, which would form the basis of his later international best seller *Capitalism and Freedom*, Friedman restated the line of argument. The event itself was made possible by a grant from the Volker Fund, created in 1932 to promote free-market ideas. The series was to give particular attention to the topic of inequality and redistribution. The program for the conference—settled after lengthy discussions between Friedrich Hayek, Frank Knight, Ludwig von Mises, and Friedman himself—would devote considerable attention to the amount of inequality Americans should expect "from the operation of a genuinely competitive free enterprise economy." The main question was to what extent the state could "reduce the degree of inequality without serious adverse effects in other directions."[109] Whether it would concern housing, minimum wage, or social security, Friedman always opposed what he saw as a distortion of the operations of the market. In his view, all the New Deal policies were directed "against the symptoms,"[110] but "the real problem" was poverty as such—not the market. This argument was trenchant and utterly inverted commonsense notions about poverty. While policy makers were accustomed to the idea that poverty was a symptom of low wages, bad housing, and precarious employment, Friedman had managed to argue that it was in fact the other way around. As he wrote in an exchange with Keynesian economist Don Patinkin, "the social costs that are ordinarily attributed to poor housing are really the social costs of poverty." "What they justify," he added, "is a program of establishing a minimum income and seeking to eliminate at least certain kinds of poverty."[111] Friedman's conjecture was simple: rather than working through the categorical order of the New Deal that dissolved the category of the "poor" to create new categories in interaction with the labor market, he advocated "a program directed at helping the poor" "as people not as members of particular occupational groups or age groups or wage-rate groups or labor organizations or industries."[112] While any free market economy would imply "socially intolerable" "inequalities at the bottom of the scale,"[113] the solution could not be to restrain the market through rent controls or public housing, which would only worsen the situation.[114] The point was rather to always rely on "the price system for distribution of goods" and only afterward, if confronted to undesirable outcomes, "achieve changes in the distribution of income by general measures superimposed on the price system."[115] For Friedman and other early neoliberals, the price mechanism was here elevated as the civilizational benchmark for efficient organizing of economic activity and, perhaps more important, a check on individual freedom. Indeed, a great part of the problem came from the fact that "welfare arrangements limit the personal freedom of the recipients."[116]

Friedman's plea for a negative income tax was also part of a broader redefinition that the concept of freedom underwent in the mid-twentieth century. Whereas classical ideals of freedom, as Annelien De Dijn has shown, "called for the establishment of greater popular control over government, including the use of state power to enhance collective well-being."[117] neoliberals redefined freedom as the visible absence of state coercion. In the field of social policy, the very notion of defining needs politically and satisfying them through collective provision would be strongly contested in the name of greater individual freedom. From this perspective, the market and the choices made by individuals quite rapidly appeared to Friedman, in Béatrice Cherrier's words, to be "the best protection from the coercion of the majority," providing coordination "without standardization and a 'check' to political power."[118] This was a view that he would consistently put forward during his career by depicting the market as a genuine "system of proportional representation" protecting the diversity of individual preferences. In the market, "each man can vote" "for the color of tie he wants and get it; he does not have to see what color the majority wants and then, if he is in the minority, submit."[119] "The ballot box," he wrote, "produces conformity without unanimity; the marketplace, unanimity without conformity."[120] The market was turned into a framework to coordinate different and maybe opposing aims (or "preferences") by peaceful means, a way to escape the "coercion" of the majority rule. In his review of Friedman's *Capitalism and Freedom*, even the market socialist Abba P. Lerner, who had advocated for a "social dividend" at the same period, admitted he found himself "in enthusiastic agreement [with the book] some 90 per cent of the time." While this claim might be surprising from an economist who was on the other side from Friedman in the socialist calculation debate, their objections never really touched the centrality of the price system. "The book powerfully demonstrates," Lerner argued, "an impressive number of ways in which both freedom and welfare could be increased by a fuller utilization of the price mechanism."[121] Not surprisingly, Lerner, with many others, would endorse Friedman's NIT by the mid-1960s, when it set off a nationwide debate. More than just a technical matter, reducing social policy to income concerns "hollowed out" the idea of equality of democratic content and defined the price mechanism as "noncoercive," in contrast to democratic institutions. Under the surface, the very foundation of *how* modern economics thought about equality and its relation to politics and the market had changed.

Friedman's vision hardly pitted itself against these egalitarian concerns. The NIT could in effect be more or less egalitarian depending on the height of its income floor. It concerned the *means* deployed to reach an egalitarian aim. For Friedman, and for an increasing number of economists of his generation, relying on the price system by promoting cash transfers had become the centerpiece of any ambitious policy agenda. Within such an analysis, the attraction of the NIT was unsurprising: as Friedman himself argued, not only was such a program "directed specifically at the problem of poverty," but "while operating through the market" it did "not distort the market or impede its functioning,"[122] as did earlier New Deal programs. The new line of "poverty" below which a citizen was to receive the NIT, then, operated *under* the market rather than *within* the market, preserving the impersonal power of the price system against the categories of the welfare state. The end goal was to be free *in* the market rather than *from* the market.

The Rise of Mass Taxation

Intellectual shifts were hardly sufficient to explain the later success of Friedman's proposal. Instead, his scheme was also made possible by a more profound transformation in the American government. It was indeed during the war that the US federal government shifted from class taxation to mass taxation. By 1945 two-thirds of Americans were paying taxes, whereas before the war the government reached only 4 to 8 percent of the working population. As Gary Gerstle observed, to finance the war the government had to extract revenue from a large percentage of the population, helping to "fundamentally alter the landscape of possibility for federal government activity."[123] During the five years of the war, the US government spent $304 billion on defense alone, more than double the other expenditures of all the preceding budgets since the Declaration of Independence in 1776.[124] By 1942 the Revenue Act would bring nearly all working Americans into the tax system. As Dennis Ventry has noted, "before World War II, the idea of negative income taxation was inconceivable."[125] It was the war effort, overall, that brought more than fifty million new taxpayers onto the rolls and made it seem that, when thinking about the distribution of income, it would be more efficient to use negative rates of taxation rather than to deal with complex welfare schemes. For the first time the tax system was regarded as a proper tool for social policy and economic stabilization.[126] When Heller, Vickrey, and Friedman discussed the scheme in the early 1940s, however, they rapidly considered it "too innovative and experimental"[127] and dropped a project that never made it into any of the reports or studies.[128]

The idea survived, however. It fizzled among fiscal economists in small circles clustered around state administrations and in seminar rooms. In 1946, while Friedman, Stigler, and Heller were all teaching at the University of Minnesota, the scheme finally achieved references in published pieces. Stigler argued for a tax "with negative rates" in "The Economics of Minimum Wage Legislation,"[129] and Heller advocated the system in his courses.[130] Although it did not immediately reach the broader public, during the following years the idea rapidly attracted an increasing number of economists as an interesting alternative to welfare programs and state regulations. For example, during the 1950s, several economic and public finance textbooks mentioned the scheme proposed by Juliet Rhys-Williams and Friedman's negative income tax, arguing for the "amalgamation of direct taxation with social insurance."[131] But what is perhaps the most clearly articulated version of the idea was given by economist Robert R. Schultz in 1952.[132] In his dissertation Schultz argued that the postwar welfare state and its "categorical relief" had become an "oppressive administration," "often highly inequitable and inadequate for the relief of poverty" and a "waste" of money affecting "morale and incentive" among beneficiaries.[133] To "replace" New Deal programs, Schultz advocated what he called "continuous taxation." The idea was similar to Friedman's, but instead of receiving the negative income *after* taxes, "every person" would receive *up front* "a minimum subsistence income" and only then pay taxes "above this subsidy," making it similar to our present notion of basic income. But depending on where the "break-even point" was set, both systems could lead to exactly the same outcome in terms of income distribution. The difference was significant from a political point of view, but not from the standpoint of economics. As Friedman himself later argued, "a basic or citizen's income is not an alternative to a negative income tax. It is simply another way to introduce a negative income tax if it is accompanied with a positive income tax with no exemption."[134]

*   *   *

Although the idea of a negative income tax attained relative popularity among economists and policy makers in the 1940s and 1950s, it took another decade for it to transcend the outer borders of the New Deal consensus. By the mid-1940s, thinkers such as Oskar Lange, Abba Lerner, Jan Tinbergen, William Hutt, Juliet Rhys-Williams, and Milton Friedman had already offered approximate versions of the current basic income. Most of these theorists took part in the socialist calculation debate, pitting market socialists against neoliberals. Although the idea was raised in debates under different names—"national dividend," "social dividend," "negative tax," "guaranteed income," "basic income"—all these schemes shared an emphasis on grants to maintain markets. All of them also saw the basic income as a market-friendly welfare proposal. As an economist, Lerner could not "'adjudicate' the correctness or legitimacy or 'goodness' of such an end." Even as a socialist, the "maximization on such lines is completely in the spirit of socialist ideals."[135]

Lerner's cash grant also found some cautious followers in the "new welfare economics" of the 1930s.[136] Economist William H. Hutt, for instance, revived his own "liberal socialist" version of the proposal in 1944. This idea was to acknowledge the failures of laissez-faire but refuse the interventionist bent of the Beveridge plan, which impinged strongly on market principles. Hutt viewed the system as the "purest democracy," since no "dictator's or bureaucrat's arbitrary" decision would be at the base of "irksome changes of employment." Instead, "market demand" would be "the ultimate commanding force."[137]

Like Gregor Mendel's evolutionism, however, these visions had little purchase in the welfare worlds of the 1930s and 1940s.[138] Lange and Lerner's decade was an era when planning states undertook major interventions in their economy during a global war effort and when the ranks of the industrial workforce swelled. Underneath, mass parties, often on the left, pushed states for specific need fulfillment. European politics testified to the same problem. Dutch economist and policy adviser Jan Tinbergen's 1934 attempt to introduce a *basis-inkomen* into his socialist party's platform did not pass muster.

By the late 1950s, however, some key parameters had already begun to shift. The death of the welfare consensus was also presaged in the economics profession: by the early 1930s, Beveridge's and Pigou's views came under aggressive attack in the "second neoclassical revolution," which recast the price system as a more efficient allocator than the postwar planning state. This new world also implied a different view of human needs than the one seen by More, Proudhon, Paine, Charlier, Fourier, and Marx. Rather than being politicized and constituted through a democratic process, needs now could simply be "revealed" as individual choices on a market.[139] In this world, older arguments for cash transfers suddenly acquired irresistible urgency.

Milton Friedman occupied a key position in this shifting landscape. Although his 1939 proposal for cash-based welfare failed to catch the attention of policymakers, after his 1962 *Capitalism and Freedom* became an unlikely best seller, his ideas were taken up by forces across the spectrum. As happened with Mendel, Friedman, Lange, and Lerner's generation had to wait several decades for their vision to find a willing audience. Only by the early 1960s, with the spectacular outbreak of the "poverty-issue" following the publication Michael Harrington's *The Other America*, would the proposal be seriously considered. Along with rising concerns about the effects of automation, Friedman's proposal captured the country's anxious imagination. The very contexts that had led him to drop the idea in the early 1940s were now radically different: to his surprise, his monograph defending the proposal would sell more than a million copies—and nearly every economist of his generation would come to back it in an "age of affluence."

CHAPTER THREE

Cash Triumphs

America after the New Deal Order

It is not till it is discovered that high individual incomes will not purchase the mass of mankind immunity from cholera, typhus, and ignorance, still less secure them the positive advantages of educational opportunity and economic security, that slowly and reluctantly, amid prophecies of moral degeneration and economic disaster, society begins to make collective provision for needs no ordinary individual, even if he works overtime all his life, can provide himself.
—Richard H. Tawney, *Equality*

Being poor is simply another way of saying that one lacks purchasing power. — Arthur Kemp, "Welfare without the Welfare State"

In summer 1963, Wilbur H. Ferry, cofounder of the Center for the Study of Democratic Institutions—one of the most influential liberal think thanks of the period—met with close friends and fellow activists in the Princeton office of Robert Oppenheimer, father of the atomic bomb.[1] They planned to draft a statement that would challenge the way Americans thought about the future of work, social policy, or human rights in an "age of abundance." Besides Oppenheimer and Ferry, figures in the room ranged from economist and futurologist Robert Theobald to Todd Gitlin and Tom Hayden, leaders of Students for a Democratic Society (SDS), who had released the Port Huron Statement just a year before. What would later be published as the Manifesto for a Triple Revolution emerged in part from the group's shared concern about the possible "disappearance of work" and the specific challenge it constituted for liberal thinkers. Now, the entirety of the postwar "industrial productive system" appeared to be "no longer viable."[2] The left, as they saw it, needed to "form a new consensus" centered on the realization that "the traditional link between jobs and incomes [was] being broken."[3] An "unqualified right to an income," inspired by Milton Friedman's negative income tax, now had to "take the place of the patchwork of welfare measures" and ensure "that no citizen or resident of the United States actually starves."[4] The idea Friedman had devised in the early 1940s to ensure "a floor below which no man's income ... could fall"[5] suddenly captured public attention far beyond the seminar rooms. "New circumstances" Ferry and his colleagues recognized demanded "radically new strategies."[6]

With no fewer than thirty-four signatories—including Nobel Prize winners Linus Pauling and Gunnar Myrdal, socialist Norman Thomas, writer and social critic Dwight Macdonald, and such major figures of the New Left as Michael Harrington and James Boggs—the statement was sent to President Lyndon B. Johnson and immediately made it onto the front page of the *New York Times*. In the following months proposals for a guaranteed income appeared in more than five hundred editorials in the country, making the idea a national topic of discussion. The debate opened by the memorandum far exceeded Ferry's expectations. In the following years, guaranteed income schemes would receive substantial popular support, including from civil rights leader Martin Luther King Jr.

Ferry attributed this phenomenal media attention to "sheerest luck," since "nothing [was] happening in D.C." that weekend.[7] Retrospectively, his interpretation is, of course, unconvincing. What had changed since Friedman formulated his initial proposal in the early 1940s? What transformations gave a fringe idea such resounding popularity, even within leading liberal and socialist circles? Here the rise of guaranteed income cannot be understood without examining the profound economic, political, and intellectual transformations that affected the New Deal order. The rising skepticism toward social security expansion and public spending as a way to tackle poverty and increase employment in the light of new conceptions of poverty created a more welcoming environment for income-based strategies. Wilbur J. Cohen—one of the key architects of the American welfare state—would perceive this shift as an increasing "fiscalization" of social policy, uncoupling poverty from issues of inequality and market dependence. It also captured basic income's emergence as an elegant response to the changing views on matters such as welfare, race, inequality, unemployment, and the role of the state. As Brian Steensland has argued, without these evolving conceptions, the social turmoil of the 1960s "would likely have yielded reforms that were in keeping with the existing New Deal philosophy of social provision—public jobs, social services, and the like—and which worked within the existing categorical structure."[8] The growing aura of basic income as an inevitable policy solution, then, was part of a wider transformation of the categories that had shaped postwar policy making and Americans' understanding of their own economic system. From Milton Friedman to James Tobin, Michael Harrington to Robert Lampman to Robert Theobald, there was increasing agreement that postwar remedies had lost their effectiveness in the face of persistent poverty while the acceleration of automation and rising turmoil in American inner cities were crucial in turning basic income into a central aim to welfare reformers.

The Fiscal Revolution and the Collapse of the Welfare Consensus

Above all, the unexpected popularity of the negative income tax was intimately tied to the "rediscovery" of poverty after Michael Harrington's *The Other America* was published in March 1962. Harrington's book—which was to kick-start a nationwide discussion on the extent of "poverty amid plenty"—was itself a sign of a profound shift in the way Americans conceived social policy. The outbreak of the topic of poverty eroded the belief that the commitment to social security expansion could be successful in the war against poverty in favor of a concept more focused on establishing an absolute "floor" of income to eradicate extreme poverty. While this idea became relatively popular among economists and policy makers during the 1950s, it took another decade to overcome the dominant vision shaped by Franklin D. Roosevelt. Indeed, the income-based approach contrasted with some of the assumptions on which the postwar Keynesian programs were founded. New Deal policies were organized around the idea that the inherent failures of the market stipulated the need for an interventionist state capable of reducing market dependency. It would do so by providing constant public services and by shrinking income gaps to increase economic growth and reach full employment. Services, labor market regulation and full employment policies were thus widely preferred to direct cash transfers. Until the early 1960s, as Alice O'Connor has argued, "poverty, as such, was not yet seen as a distinctive social problem, much less as the target of a concerted government attack."[9]

Seen through this lens, the remedy to a problem like poverty was a further extension of social security programs, sooner or later ending in its eradication. A representative example of this incrementalist strategy was Wilbur J. Cohen, a central figure in the creation and expansion of the American welfare state who served as welfare secretary under Kennedy and Johnson. What was needed, he argued at a 1957 conference at the University of Wisconsin, is "more schools, more roads, more hospital beds, and more housing. We want more teachers, more doctors, nurses, social workers."[10] The state, using ambitious service-based programs, had to guarantee a "minimum level of living" that would in turn increase the national product. Cohen's remedy proposed to "gradually and categorically expand the foundations of the social security program"[11] until poverty was completely eradicated. "It might be counseling, it might be referral to a job, it might be the mother going back to high school or a job," he argued in the late 1950s, always favoring employment schemes over cash.[12]

This view was widespread in the administration. In 1955 the *Economic Report of the President*, prepared for Eisenhower by the Council of Economic Advisers, already underlined the "small and shrinking" but "still significant" number of poor families. Yet the report never cast "poverty" as a segmented social problem, instead pointing to raising low wages and public works employment or improving the pension system to prevent old age poverty. In the early 1960s publications on poverty such as the 1962 study by the Conference on Economic Progress, *Poverty and Deprivation in the United States*, was strongly shaped by postwar orthodoxy. While recognizing the rising importance of the topic of poverty (the report cited a number spanning two-fifths of Americans), the text drafted by Leon Keyserling, principal drafter of the Wagner Act and former chairman of Truman's Council of Economic Advisers, advocated a policy essentially organized around government spending and the pursuit of full employment.[13]

Even at the height of the 1960s poverty debate Johnson himself always strongly opposed this wholesale reorientation around cash transfers. This was a president who had been deeply influenced by the legacy of the People's Party, whose grandfather had run on the Populist ticket in the 1890s, and who described himself as a Roosevelt New Dealer.[14] His program against poverty, Walter Heller recalls, was filled with bulldozers, tractors, and heavy machinery, a services-and-goods program rather than cash-based one.[15] Johnson grew up poor in a small Texas farmhouse and had been an active New Dealer; he always thought of antipoverty measures in terms of government programs. Even the situation in the Appalachians, where by the late 1950s almost a third of the population lived in poverty, was generally understood as the result of a lack of infrastructure, jobs, education, and other services. Expectedly, employment and educational programs characterized Johnson's "unconditional war on poverty." "Our chief weapon," he declared in his 1964 State of the Union message, "will be better schools, and better health, and better homes, and better training, and better job opportunities to help more Americans, especially young Americans, escape from squalor and misery and unemployed rolls." "Very often" he added, "a lack of jobs and money is not the cause of poverty, but the symptom. The cause may lie deeper—in our failure to give our fellow citizens a fair chance to develop their own capacities, in a lack of education and training, in a lack of medical care and housing, in a lack of decent communities in which to live and bring up their children."[16] Within this framework, it was clear that the postwar welfare architecture was not yet perceived as a problem. Its legacy, as Leslie Lenkowsky argued, "seemed above politics."[17]

Although this vision retained relative prominence until at least the mid-1960s, by the late 1950s the social policy climate had already begun to turn. The "drastic slowdown in the rate at which the economy [was] taking people out of poverty"[18] and the unexpected increase of the recipients of Aid to Families with Dependent Children raised doubts about established postwar remedies.[19] Policy makers steadily followed its trail. An increasing number of younger social scientists like Robert Lampman, generally trained in economics rather than social work, would progressively collect data giving a grimmer prospect for the efficiency of the existing institutions.[20] Although it was largely anticipated that assistance programs would disappear with economic growth and the further expansion of social security, statistics appeared to prove the contrary. The number of welfare recipients continued to increase over the 1950s, swelling the camp of skeptics in the welfare debates.[21] Among these was Lampman, whose work since the early 1950s reflected an extreme pessimism about postwar hopes of an upcoming "people's capitalism" in "a classless homogenized state of affluence."[22] Focusing very early on the study of income distribution, he thought that Simon Kuznets's conclusions concerning the decrease of inequality were misleading.[23] In 1958 his claims began to draw attention after the public success of *The Affluent Society*, where John Kenneth Galbraith argued that poverty was now "insular," composed essentially of urban ghettos and isolated islands in rural areas.[24] Struck by what they felt was an overly optimistic view, several economists began to collect more systematic data to measure the extent of poverty in an affluent America. Leon Keyserling, for instance, gathered evidence that more than a quarter of all Americans were living in poverty "by any standards that should have meaning for us today."[25] The next year Illinois' Democratic senator, Paul Douglas, commissioned Robert Lampman to write a report challenging Galbraith's narrative.[26] The results showed that the "exit from poverty" had considerably slowed since the late 1950s, calling into question the efficacy of existing welfare programs.[27] That same year Michael Harrington published his first piece on the topic in *Commentary*, initiating a change in American public opinion on poverty. While Lampman estimated that nearly 20 percent of the population was living in poverty (setting the poverty line at a $2,000), Harrington went as far as to estimate a third (with a $3,000 poverty line).[28] The claim was stunning, since more than twenty years earlier, in his 1937 Second Inaugural Address, Roosevelt had already informed the nation that "one-third" of the population was still "ill-housed, ill-clad, [and] ill-nourished."[29]

These numbers came as tremendous blows to postwar social policy aims. Poverty of this magnitude seemed to imply that not much had changed since the New Deal and that, if "new strategies" were not deployed, this hidden America would "irrevocably stay away from abundance."[30] For Lampman and many experts of his generation, "a redefinition of the contours of New Deal liberalism" was "essential to better tackle relative poverty."[31] This shift would be complete with the publication of Michael Harrington's *The Other America* in March 1962 and the January 1963 review of the book in the *New Yorker* by Dwight Macdonald, another signatory of the Triple Revolution Manifesto.[32] Macdonald's review in particular reached a wide readership, and allegedly pushed Kennedy to launch a specific program to address poverty.[33] The ensuing debate also crafted a bipartisan consensus that poverty was now a "specific" condition, detached from the question of inequality and the labor market. Using a tone very different from Lampman's dry statistical work, Harrington had captured the public imagination. He claimed that millions of poor families had in fact "scarcely been affected by the reforms of the past quarter-century."[34] More significantly, beyond these quite descriptive statistics, Harrington added a qualitative dimension to earlier conceptualizations of poverty. Rather than merely constituting a monetary problem, poverty had hardened into a segmented culture. This idea ran back to Oscar Lewis's culture of poverty, popularized through his 1959 book on Mexican slum dwellers.[35] For Lewis poverty was not only a material situation shared by very different groups, but a "sub-culture of its own" with "its own modalities and distinctive social and psychological consequences for its members."[36] In the same vein, Harrington postulated that poverty formed "a separate culture, another nation, with its own way of life"; it was akin to the experience of being "an internal alien, to grow up in a culture that is radically different from the one that dominates society."[37] In this framework the poor could now be "analyzed as a group."[38] That was, he thought, "the most important analytic point" of his book.[39]

Lewis's segmentation of poverty was also rather new. During the 1950s no specification existed of a group of poor citizens separate from society as a whole. When "poverty" was used it mostly referred to the modest standard of living of the working class, not to a distinct social stratum they belonged to. Not incidentally, the words "inequality," "socialism," and "market" did not appear in Harrington's best seller, openly breaking with progressive thinkers, who rarely segmented these questions. Addressing inequality was steadily sidelined as an aim. "Inequality of wealth is not necessarily a major social problem per se," Dwight Macdonald wrote in his seminal 1963 review, yet "poverty is."[40] For Macdonald, it was clear that the main concern now was to provide a floor, not a system like social security that, he thought, perpetuated the inequalities that kept "the poor forever poor."[41] After his recruitment to the Council of Economic Advisers, Lampman drafted his first report for the president's antipoverty agenda, and he carefully noted that such a program "must avoid completely any use of the term 'inequality' or of the term 'redistribution' of income or wealth."[42]

Naturally, if poverty "form[ed] a distinct system," outside the categories of the postwar welfare order, it also required a specific policy approach.[43] As Leslie Lenkowsky argued, the new framework implied that "traditional welfare policies seemed unlikely to be productive and, some thought, cause social and political problems of their own."[44] By the early 1960s the controversial approach that Milton Friedman first began to advocate in the 1940s became consensual among reformers and policy makers. Lampman, Harrington, and even Oscar Lewis generally tended to see the dominant programs (social security, minimum wage legislation, unions, and labor laws) as institutions designed to protect the interests of organized workers but not those of the poor. The shift also spoke to a real insider-outsider dynamic created by the New Deal order, in which black workers took much longer to arrive in industrial jobs. Beneath this institutional reality, however, lay a discursive shift. The new outsiders were now no longer considered to be waiting for integration into the New Deal order. Lewis, for instance, did not hesitate to speak of a group that "do not belong to labor unions, do not participate in the benefits of the social security system, make very little use of the city's museums, art galleries, banks, hospitals, department stores, concerts, airports, etc."[45] He was hardly alone in this assessment. The "other America" was composed, as Harrington wrote, of those "who are beyond the welfare state."[46] The alleged "cultural traits" enabling poverty to reproduce itself were also a direct challenge to the presumed efficiency of traditional macroeconomic approaches. "These people," Lampman claimed, remained "remarkably untouched by the New Deal welfare state measures" and were "well beyond" the reach of "unions," "co-operatives," and federal programs in "farming, housing and urban renewal."[47] A similar argument was put forward by economist Robert Theobald, also a signatory of the Triple Revolution statement, who claimed that the need for social reform came precisely from the failures of the postwar framework.[48] In his 1963 best seller *Free Men and Free Markets*, Theobald argued that "since the passage of the Social Security Act in 1935 we have assumed that the basic maintenance needs of people will be met by public welfare," yet it was now clear that "our existing socio-economic system is outmoded by abundance."[49] He went so far as to argue that "the welfare services that were originally meant to help these people have really become a method of enslaving them."[50] What was required was to introduce "an economic floor," "economic basic security," that could guarantee a life free of poverty.[51]

More surprising was the *extent* of the agreement between progressive writers and neoliberals such as Milton Friedman in the early 1960s. When Friedman and Harrington discussed poverty issues at Cornell University in December 1964, for instance, the audience was stunned by the similarities in their diagnosis of the failures of social security and the need for "more innovation and experimentation."[52] "The world is full of surprises," wrote the *Cornell Daily Sun* the next day, since "the perspicacious observer at last Thursday's lecture . . . may have detected a strong area of agreement between the conservative, laissez-faire Friedman and the left-wing author of *Poverty in America*, Michael Harrington."[53] "Although these men approached the problem of poverty from diametrically opposite points of view," the student newspaper added, "they both agree that American welfare measures have benefited the middle classes and lower middle classes more than the abject poor."[54] Beyond obvious political differences, it was clear to both that poverty had become a problem sensitively separate from the labor market, inequality, and an inadequate public infrastructure, breaking both with nineteenth-century conceptualizations of the social question and with the New Deal approach.

This line of argument also marked a strong break with Galbraith's social Keynesianism and its earlier emphasis on the balance between public and private services and goods. The specificity of poverty as the problem of a segmented group had made expanding the welfare state obsolete as a remedy; the New Deal order was fracturing.

Basic income schemes enjoyed a natural boost in the wake of this shift. When Friedman republished the idea in his 1962 best seller *Capitalism and Freedom*, public responses to the proposal were strikingly different. His negative income tax now commanded widespread attention, reaching audiences beyond universities and government administrations. An idea he had thought ahead of its time in the early 1940s was now taken up in the highest echelons of Washington bureaucracy. The presidential circle, especially the Council of Economic Advisers, now comprised economists such as Walter Heller, Robert Lampman, James Tobin, and Joseph A. Pechman. These "commercial Keynesians"[55] converged on a fiscal understanding of social policy and depicted social security as simply another form of taxation—and a less efficient one. Walter Heller in particular—the most influential chairman in the history of the CEA—was emblematic of this abstract vision of the state promoted by young advisers who were often trained in top departments of economics. His commitment to the "new economics" movement launched by Paul Samuelson and Robert Solow was aimed at integrating Keynesianism into a neoclassical framework, and it tended to downplay the political and cultural dimension of social policy.[56] As James Tobin would later argue, this approach treated problems as "technical rather than ideological."[57] This was a vision disconnected from the transactional deals traditionally associated with social policy, made up of categorical expansions generally motivated by electoral agreements. Heller, as Nicholas Lemann has pointed out, through his background and intellectual formation, lived rather in "a clean, precise world of numbers and orderly concepts"[58]—viewing the world much the way his engineer father would. He was more attracted to the beauty of taxation incentives than to the muddiness and uncertainty of public spending that interested Galbraith. As Binyamin Appelbaum notes, "Heller's ideas marked a tactical break with the traditional Keynesian emphasis on increased government spending"; rather than borrowing money to spend on public plans, Heller claimed the state could simply "borrow money from the private sector and then give it back to the private sector to spend."[59] As one observer noted, the Kennedy generation had begun to shift American government from a "*doer* of public activities to a distributor of public benefits." Following such a shift from "bureaucrats to cybernetics," welfare was no longer cast as a "large-scale . . . bureaucracy with thousands of governments and millions of people." Instead, the state itself was to be "cybernated" and "[shift] to some form of guaranteed income, adjusted automatically as the income of the recipient" rose or fell, monitoring "the system and activat[ing] money-disbursing schemes." A New Left would become equally enamored of this rising "cybernetic welfare state."[60]

The New Keynesian emphasis on tax cuts also reflected a strong preference for private initiative and sovereign consumers, with a strong fear of inflation linked to state regulation of the labor market and wages. "Why cut taxes rather than go the Galbraith way?" Heller wrote to Kennedy in a memo from 1962.[61] The Wisconsin economist's main argument was rooted in a neoclassical theory according to which the expansion of public spending in that context would "lead to waste, bottlenecks, profiteering, and scandal" and would increase the opposition to the "expansion of government" and "over-centralization, [leading] to a 'power grab' and a 'takeover' of the cities, the educational system, the housing market."[62] Finally, "tax-cuts-induced deficits," Heller argued, were "also more acceptable to the world of financial community than expenditure-induced deficits."[63] This privatized Keynesianism offered a way to break with balanced deficits and the productive undercapacity that Kennedy faced when taking office while at the same time recognizing—as Heller noted—"the importance of working through the market system."[64] Within the Council of Economic Advisers, Heller shared this view with James Tobin, who similarly argued that if "jobs, more and better schools, are certainly the most appealing solutions" for poor families, a fiscal strategy transferring cash directly to people and businesses would be more efficient.[65] In this frame, he added, "private employers and free markets do much of the work of the war on poverty—without public expenditure and government bureaucracy."[66] The central tenet of this strand of Keynesianism was, then, as Major argues, "that when the economy falls into recession the government needs to prop up demand by substituting public spending for private investment and by bolstering the purchasing power of the poor and middle class."[67] In other words, classical Keynesians would address unemployment through public work programs, whereas modernized Keynesians focused on boosting private investment through tax cuts.

This generational gap between Keynesians only intensified in the ensuing decade. While the 1960s saw a generic Keynesianism triumph among economists, this shift constituted, as Aaron Major has argued, "a major departure from the basic policy paradigm of the 1950s."[68] While Kennedy was, as Jacqueline Best has argued, "the first Keynesian president, he was decidedly of a neoclassical bent."[69] "Economics," Heller wrote to Milton Friedman in 1961, "makes strange bedfellows." On the topic of tax cuts, he added, "I find Ken Galbraith fighting against me and you fighting with me"—"thank heaven, one can't identify economic positions by labels alone."[70] This marked a significant evolution in field of economics that would slowly, as noted by Herbert Stein, the future chairman of the CEA under Nixon, render "the distinction between Keynesians and non-Keynesians" less significant. "Within this general consensus," he added, differences existed, of course, but were essentially "of emphasis and of degree."[71] "In one sense," Milton Friedman claimed, "we are all Keynesians now; in another, nobody is any longer a Keynesian."[72]

The costly tax cuts of the Revenue Acts of 1962 and 1964 frustrated American labor leaders, since they disproportionally favored corporations, top incomes, and the middle class.[73] To compensate, the administration abandoned any major public works program that Kennedy had promised before the campaign. Instead he began to think about an antipoverty agenda. But in line with his tax strategy, income-based programs delivered through the fiscal system, like Friedman's NIT, seemed far more appropriate. "Social security," Heller claimed in 1963, "does not cover [the poor]," "government welfare unwittingly contributes to broken homes and illegitimacy.... School lunch programs have not nourished the communities that could not afford to transport the surplus food or the children who could not make even the token payments."[74] Because of its technocratic bent, this "fiscal revolution," as Herbert Stein termed it, was characterized by Aaron Major as a clear "transition period between postwar Keynesianism and contemporary neoliberalism."[75] And if "Kennedy was not Reagan" as Kim McQuaid noted, "his decision to buy popularity in business circles ... via conservative Keynesian tax cut nevertheless set the stage for the decades of economic conservatism that were to come."[76]

This "fiscal community"—as Wilbur J. Cohen, welfare secretary under Johnson, bitterly observed—analyzed social security systems as "an ordinary tax, and as a tax it constituted a dubious form of social policy."[77] What Cohen termed the "Harvard-Yale-MIT-Brookings economists" would later become the main proponents of Friedman's NIT within the

Democratic administration, reframing social policy in terms of efficient transfers.[78] Cohen's views of government, as Odin Anderson has argued, were "essentially organic," "government and society" always being "interrelated," while this new generation, especially Friedman, had a more atomic understanding of the relation between the state and society.[79] Social policy followed suit. By 1962 Lampman had already designed a concept of the "poverty income gap," in contrast to the concept of "rate of poverty," giving priority to the monetary gap. From such a perspective, the main question then became whether to close the gap with cash rather than expanding universal programs or restraining inequality.[80] While Johnson had explicitly requested removing "anything that could be construed as a reference to putting cash in the hands of the poor people,"[81] part of his administration seemed increasingly favorable to the idea. Even Galbraith, himself a strong advocate of the incrementalist perspective in the 1950s, seemingly changed his mind by the mid-1960s. Although in his original 1958 edition of *The Affluent Society* he had advocated "unemployment insurance at a rate near the average weekly wage as the policy recommendation," by the mid-1960s he was promoting a negative income tax instead.[82] After a long confinement in obscure economic textbooks, guaranteed income had finally reached a national audience and was now being promoted within the Johnson administration.

Automation Panics and the Fall of Full Employment

Underneath this changing policy climate deeper tectonic shifts in US political economy were under way. After a younger generation of policy experts and social activists questioned the legitimacy of New Deal welfare programs, the edifice of full employment—another central pillar of the New Deal order—was called into question. Rising concerns about automation would create a favorable environment for guaranteed income and less work-oriented schemes within a left that was traditionally labor-centered. The notion itself had been coined about 1947 by Delmar S. Harder, vice president of the Ford Motor Company, to describe the process through which mechanical and electronic devices replace human labor or, as management theorist Peter Drucker would write, "the use of machines to run machines."[83] Although the topic of automation already enjoyed considerable popularity in the 1950s, as a concern affecting the job market as such it rarely emerged in the professional literature and among policy makers.[84] In 1955 the *Baltimore Sun* castigated it as "the cliché of the year," and it was the object of numerous articles and discussions in newspapers and magazines across the United States, while congressional hearings on the topic were now held almost every year.[85] By the late 1950s, however, the chronic unemployment that had affected the country since the Korean War became a point of contention among policy advisers and economists. Especially in the Democratic Party, some were convinced that the "labor lump" was a different kind of problem than the issues social engineers encountered in the 1930s. Democratic congressman Clarence Long, for instance, argued in 1959 that this new type of unemployment could probably not be dealt with by operating through "the demand side, through spending and other devices."[86] Indeed, the persistent, chronic unemployment among certain groups (especially the young and the black population) led to a whole body of literature about this new kind of "structural" unemployment, defined by labor historian Philip Taft as "involuntary idleness which arises from causes other than changes in aggregate demand."[87] Uncovering its drivers became the holy grail of economic thinking and policy thinking alike.

For an increasing number of economists, the singular character of this "structural" unemployment was that it did not necessarily stem from a lack of jobs but came from a mismatch between workers' skills and employers' needs created by the displacements automation generated. In a Senate hearing on unemployment problems, influential labor economist John T. Dunlop argued that "mass unemployment of the thirties gave way to class unemployment of the fifties. It is the balkanization of the unemployment that is now of greater concern."[88] In his view, it occurred in "clusters and pockets in certain communities, occupations, racial groups, age brackets, and short time workers. It is less general but more concentrated in certain classes of our citizens."[89] This implied that the solution was to rely less on classical macroeconomic policies, making the economic structure less responsible, and to promote rather tailor-made programs of job retraining or relocation. This shift, prompted by the neoclassical revolution and the human capital theory in labor economics, would largely displace more structural explanations of power imbalances in society, reordering the agenda toward expanding "opportunity without massive redistribution."[90] By the early 1960s the idea had gained some traction, notably within the Kennedy administration, though without changing previous commitments to boosting aggregated demand through tax cuts.[91] This was notably strengthened by commercial Keynesians' general reluctance to use strong state intervention within the labor market to tackle persistent unemployment. As Adolph Reed has argued, this discussion, would strongly reshape how public policy should "respond to the relation of poverty, unemployment, and economic inequality" by increasingly putting aside structural factors.[92]

This development took off most spectacularly outside the administration, however. Economist Charles C. Killingsworth, for example, argued that automation was more than a mere problem of skills mismatch. For Killingsworth, although jobs were being created in new sectors, "the growth of employment in these new 'industries'" could not "offset the decline in the older, larger consumer goods industries."[93] To some commentators, especially within the nascent New Left, the diagnosis that automation was reaching a stage of uncontrollable acceleration cast into doubt the efficiency of New Deal liberalism and full employment itself, opening paths for new solutions such as guaranteed income. Of all the organizations that had a leading role in popularizing this view, the Center for the Study of Democratic Institutions was probably the most prominent example. Ever since its foundation in 1959—boosted with by a colossal $15 million grant from the Ford Foundation—the liberal think tank had been insisting on a more serious study of the automation question. The center (and, above all, its figurehead Wilbur H. Ferry) produced most of the major publications on the topic, and its seminal essays exerted a profound influence on the automation debate for over a decade.[94] In his youth Ferry had been a New Deal Democrat and had served as director of public relations for the Congress of Industrial Organizations (CIO), one of the main federations of US unions at the time, and he thought the developments in automation constituted one of today's formidable challenge for liberals. Indeed, since the early 1960s Ferry had been intensely occupied with a phenomenon that would come to be known as "cybernation."[95] This term denoted a combination of automation (machine power) and cybernetics (machine intelligence) that would drastically reduce jobs.

Ferry took inspiration from a variety of predecessors. The concept of "cybernetics," for example, derived from the work of MIT mathematician Norbert Wiener, who had first theorized the notion in 1948 as a discipline aimed at studying forms of communication and learning used by humans, animals, and machines.[96] In Wiener's view, humanity had entered an era where machines could learn and communicate, leading to a potential "replacement of human labor."[97] Wiener illustrated this thesis with a well-known elaboration on the idea of automated chess-playing machines. A

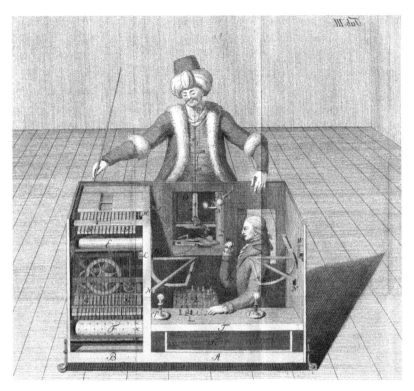

FIGURE 3.1. Wolfgang von Kempelen's automated chess-playing machine. Copper engraving from Karl Gottlieb von Windisch, *Briefe über den Schachspieler des Hrn. von Kempelen, nebst drei Kupferstichen die diese berühmte Maschine vorstellen*, 1783.

common view held in scientific circles at Wiener's time was that it was no less than a hopeless task to create or even imagine a machine that could prove itself as a chess player, capable of surmounting human intelligence and ingenuity, mainly since, as Wiener claimed, "such a machine would require too many combinations." Indeed, the combinations a machine would have to compute in order to play properly would swiftly run into the infinite, requiring an almost infinite time to set up the program. This view also found its roots in tales of an eighteenth-century illusionary act called "the Turk." This early automaton, engineered about 1769 by Hungarian inventor and author Wolfgang von Kempelen, was supposed to be able to play chess by itself and actually beat many of its contenders— including Napoleon and Benjamin Franklin—over decades in many European public displays. Of course, the automaton was just an extremely complex mechanical machine, with a complete lack of any intelligence except for the dwarf hidden by a complex set of mirrors. As it stood, the example provided a perfect illustration of the relation between "man" and "machine" in the first industrial age. As Wiener wrote, in the industrial age automation had "displaced man and the beast as a source of power, without making any great impression on other human functions."[98] Much like the chess-playing automaton, machines could replace human strength but not human intelligence, with its cognitive ability to apprehend, combine, and adapt. This very period, Wiener thought, was now nearing its end. Although he agreed that it would be impossible to create a machine able to beat humans from the start, recent progress in computer science made him confident that we could imagine a machine that could learn by itself. The machine would then "store on a tape every game it had ever played" and slowly turn into a master chess player. Wiener's conjecture, although highly contested in the early 1950s, would turn out to be rather prophetic when, only forty-seven years later, in 1997, the IBM chess computer Deep Blue beat the world champion Garry Kasparov for the first time, in a highly publicized contest. The computer had indeed learned how to play by itself, after analyzing no fewer than 700,000 games by master players.

In Wiener's view, these evolutions in cybernetics would soon have major impacts on society as a whole. In the not so distant future, he claimed, American society would evolve to "a more completely automatic age" in which one could imagine an automobile assembly line "controlled by something like a modern high-speed computing machine."[99] Its economic effects would be far-reaching; such a radical transformation, yet to arrive in Wiener's time, would "produce an unemployment situation, in comparison with which the present recession and even the depression of the thirties will seem a pleasant joke."[100] While the topic of unemployment remained rather peripheral in Wiener's book, he was already keenly aware of the implications his theory might have for the labor process as a whole. If work came to disappear, it would imply that the society should use these new modalities of production to benefit all humans, by increasing their leisure and enriching their "spiritual life," rather than just "for profits and the worship of the machine as a new brazen calf."[101] If not deployed carefully, he warned, these new methods of automation could easily lead to an even more dualized society, in which the profits of cybernetic innovation would have dramatically unequal effects. Of course, Wiener rarely came close to advocating a fleshed-out social policy to respond to the evolution he prognosticated (or any type of guaranteed income). His remarks on automation and work, however, did not go unheeded in scholarly circles. Although his vision remained marginal in the next decade, by the early 1960s major figures within the American left steadily began to radicalize his theory.

"The acceleration of technology," Wilbur Ferry argued in 1961, meant that in the near future there would "not be enough jobs of the conventional kind to go around."[102] This evolution, he claimed, would ultimately lead to a worrying impasse: although Americans would have enough resources to provide a decent standard of living to everyone, a lack of conventional jobs could polarize society between those who reaped the benefits of abundance and those it structurally sidelined. "The national economy was booming," he wrote "and produced more than enough goods and services for all, yet five million people were jobless and thirty million Americans lived below the poverty line."[103] As such, cybernation could kick-start a "major crisis" that would push large chunks of the American population onto the unemployment rolls. Whereas in the past there had evidently been periods of accelerated automation (such as in world agriculture), the central difference from these previous episodes was the *speed* at which these accelerations would happen.

This catastrophist view reached an even larger public with the publication of the Ad Hoc Committee for the Triple Revolution's Manifesto in 1964. In their letter to Johnson, they argued that these developments invalidated the mechanism that guaranteed "people's rights as consumers" "on the basis of contributions to production."[104] Not only was the "income-through-jobs link" utterly outdated, but existing welfare schemes were "less and less able to disguise a historic paradox: that a growing proportion of the population is subsisting on minimal incomes, often below the poverty line, at a time when sufficient productive potential is available to supply the needs of everyone in the United States."[105]

One solution naturally imposed itself here: a guaranteed income. Solving the matter through such a scheme was appealing, since it responded to the needs of a rising New Left long eager to dispense with work as a central category for human emancipation. The committee's 1964 memorandum also sought to project a society that could "set the citizen free to make his own choice of occupation and vocation from a wide range of activities not fostered by our value system and our accepted modes of 'work.'" Directly inspired by Ferry's work, Robert Theobald's 1963 *Free Men and Free Markets* would grab national attention. His book anticipated most of the ideas that would later shape the liberal case for a guaranteed income and the concern about the changing nature of work in a "cybernetics era."[106] Such an era, he thought, could unfold in two ways: either disconnect work from income to provide what Theobald called an "economic basic security" through a guaranteed income, or crumble into a more dualized and dehumanized society where abundant resources would be extremely unequally allocated. "The goal of full employment is dead," Theobald added, and Americans should now "be talking about how to provide income for people when there are no jobs for them."[107]

The most enduring example of such a "postworkerist" shift was the work of James Boggs. Born to Alabama farmworkers of modest means, Boggs joined the exodus from the Cotton Belt of the South to the Rust Belt of the North in 1937, at age eighteen.[108] This journey, undertaken by millions of other rural black Americans at the time, led him to industrial Detroit, where he become an auto worker at Chrysler in 1940. He was soon captivated by the powerful labor movement and a series of great upheavals stemming from the latest industrial disputes. During most of the following decade he remained an ardent union activist and a member of the Socialist Workers Party, a Detroit-based Trotskyist group.

Boggs would nonetheless become increasingly skeptical about the aims of the postwar labor movement. His own experience with processes of accelerated automation in Detroit and the sharp rise in unemployment led him to question some of the key socialist views about the working class as the elemental agent of change. Indeed, when the debate on the topic started to spark in the popular press—more as a point of celebration than as a concern—Boggs's experience in Detroit proved rather difficult. Thousands of jobs were lost at Ford, at Chrysler, and at Boggs's own plant throughout the 1950s. From 1954 to 1960 alone, Detroit's East Side lost over 70,000 jobs.[109] In his view, the labor movement had failed to grasp the extent of the challenge automation posed and how it could prompt new political and theoretical strategies. By the end of the year, he had compiled "State of a Nation: 1962," a comprehensive report that was widely circulated among liberal intellectuals and later published in the *Monthly Review*. It was rapidly reissued by Leo Huberman and Paul Sweezy as *The American Revolution: Pages from a Negro Worker's Notebook*, then widely translated. The book was received to great critical praise from figures such as Bertrand Russell and Todd Gitlin, who saw in Boggs a great way of "transmit[ting]" a "new cultural standard" aimed at freeing men from "the Protestant ethic."[110] Although often underestimated in its importance, his work was "one of the earliest critical leftist contributions to an American post-industrial literature"[111] and would influence later publications like Harry Braverman's *Labor and Monopoly Capital* or André Gorz's *Adieu au prolétariat*.

The most striking aspect of Boggs's analysis, however, was its specifically political reading of automation. His personal experience of mass redundancy led him to a more radical understanding of its consequences, explaining, by the late 1950s, his "growing disengagement with the worker-centered" politics found on the Left.[112] For Boggs, as Stephen Ward notes, "automation represented a new stage of production that was causing the reduction rather than expansion of the industrial workforce, thus compelling a rethinking of Marx's scenario of revolution."[113] "How can the labor movement speak for the Negroes," he argued, "in this age of automation when, for example, 76 percent of Negro youth in Detroit are unemployed and therefore completely outside the control of organized labor?"[114] The labor movement, now mainly a privileged faction of the class, was in danger of turning into a reactionary "interest group," utterly disconnected from its militant incarnation in the 1930s New Deal coalition. Since then, Boggs claimed, "Marxists have continued to think of a mass of workers always remaining as the base of an industrialized society," and "they have never once faced the fact that capitalist society could develop to the point of not needing a mass of workers."[115] If in the 1930s, he argued, "the struggle was principally over conditions of work," "today the struggle must be to force the power structure to utilize all the ingenuity which has been created by men's labors to free men from the slavery of being forced to work in order to live." "Automation and cybernation" he added, "is the frontrunner of man's ultimate quest not only to produce more efficiently but to be relieved of the vast burden of producing altogether."[116]

Boggs's political conclusions were clear. Any project clinging to full employment or the extension of existing welfare programs appeared breathless at best: it was clear that "the American labor movement" and its concomitant industrial strategy had "reached the end of the road."[117] Welfare politics had to reckon with this cul-de-sac. Boggs even argued that for this new generation of "workless people," especially black workers, "the simple formula of 'more schools and more education and more training' is already outmoded."[118] "To talk about full employment," he added, is "reactionary."[119] As such, the old socialist vision found itself turned upside down. What was required instead, he argued, was a declaration that "everyone has a right to a full life, liberty, and the pursuit of happiness, whether he is working or not."[120] Within that framework, the central figure of social progress was no longer the worker but the "human being" as such. What America needed, he added, was "a new Declaration of Human Rights to fit the new Age of Abundance."[121] Almost spontaneously, this step outside the laborist frame pushed Boggs toward the idea of a guaranteed income.

This turn would also have serious implications for the future of the civil rights movement. Until the mid-1960s, a more mainstream view within the movement remained strongly committed to a broadly New Dealer or industrial-democratic philosophy. Such a strategy found its emblematic expression in A. Philip Randolph, together with labor organizer Bayard Rustin, the main instigator of the 1963 March on Washington for Jobs and Freedom. A generation older than Martin Luther King Jr., Randolph was a union organizer of great stature, to the point that the Justice Department had called him "the most dangerous Negro in America."[122] Staunchly convinced of the importance of the labor movement within the civil rights struggle, he began as an early socialist and had already run for office under the Socialist banner twice in the early 1920s, explaining his commitment to full employment and the expansion of the existing social policies. "No greater wrong has been committed against the Negro," Randolph argued in 1944, "than the denial to him of the right to work."[123] After the passage of the Civil Rights Act in 1964 and the Voting Rights Act in 1965, however, his strategy seemed in retreat. Of course, "Jim Crow had been dealt a deathblow," as Adolph Reed argued, but "it was clear that the great problems of poverty and inequality persisted in the South and nationally." Yet "how the movement should go forward," and "what foci and strategies it should adopt to attack those problems, was a matter of considerable debate."[124] For Rustin it was clear that the movement now needed to move "beyond race relations to economic relations" and could not succeed "in the absence of radical programs for full employment, abolition of slums, the reconstruction of our educational system, [and] new definitions of work and leisure."[125] This was an aim that required, more than ever, the very same kind of strong political coalitions that had "laid the basis for the Johnson landslide" and that would further transform the socioeconomic foundations of the country, refashioning its political economy.[126]

This view was challenged by a new generation of activists like Boggs. As he had noted, automation would of course not immediately displace labor in general but would first hit minorities at the lower levels. And if cybernation was eliminating "Negro jobs" in particular, it was also rendering obsolete the very aim of the civil rights coalition. Indeed, by destroying these jobs, Boggs argued, it was "also destroying the process, the ladder, by means of which white workers moved up, the bottom on which they rested."[127] As a consequence it was "absolutely absurd," he argued in a 1965 conference on cybernetics and automation, "to think that the Negroes, having been economically deprived for so long, will catch up economically with the whites, and achieve equality with them on a vocational basis." "Integration, at best," he added, "will be only a token, not a solution for our old problems."[128] As Ferry would argue two years later in a lecture at Stanford University, "racial integration in the United States [was] impossible," finally ruling out "the liberal dream."[129] The strategy of integration through coalition building with unions, religious groups, and white workers was losing traction in light of the imminent disappearance of work. Following this path, Martin Luther King would also steadily reorient his policy agenda from "jobs" to a "poor people's campaign." Indeed, in the last years of his life King became an advocate of a guaranteed income. While he was increasingly critical of capitalism and moving toward a certain idea of a democratic socialism, he grew increasingly skeptical about the centrality of work. As Christopher Lasch saw it, while he was "more and more" convinced that "the main issue" was "economic," King began to advocate a guaranteed income and to argue that "our emphasis should shift from exclusive attention to putting people to work [to] enabling people to consume."[130] This now famous endorsement of the idea came by 1967 in several speeches he made and in his last book, *Where Do We Go from Here: Chaos or Community?*[131] and marked a sensitive distance from his earlier commitment to full employment. This strategy contrasted with the March on Washington and the 1966 *Freedom Budget for All Americans* drafted by Randolph, Rustin, and Leon Keyserling.[132]

As with the poverty question, guaranteed income emerged here as an interesting alternative both to full employment and to service-based social policies. Social crises were no longer about welfare's "technical" ability to tackle poverty, but rather concerned its deepest political and moral foundations. This slow intellectual shift would make Friedman's perspective very attractive in comparison with the labor-centered Keynesian policies. Although Friedman of course never went by the label "postworkerist," he did teach a generation to relate to the work imperative in a novel way — through incentives rather than contractually. The conceptual elegance and antipaternalist design of the idea did, in Friedman's view, explain its appeal "to the left."[133] The negative income tax approach, for example, never made any reference to essentialist accounts of poverty or special theories of anomie. Instead, it saw poverty and unemployment as pure products of the welfare state and minimum-wage legislation. Poverty and unemployment, seen through this prism, were therefore no longer the result of personal or social pathology but rather were a rational decision based on how welfare states created disincentives to work. On the employer's side, they resulted from a rational decision to abjure hiring new employees because of excessive labor costs.

Rather than trying to constrain individual choices, an NIT would change the environment in which they are made—*the structure of incentives*. A "direct federal payment" of this type, Robert Lampman noted, "would be an innovation not only technically but conceptually as well," since it "would establish a right to minimum income without prior contract and without determination of blame."[134] Thinking through supply and demand curves rather than in terms of duties was an original maneuver for the reluctant New Dealer. It was also of interest to an increasingly experimental New Left, which naturally sought to increase income yet make it less labor oriented. What would be required was an adjustment of the "rules of the game"[135] and, possibly, a higher level of basic income to decrease the demand for labor. The difference in future versions of the proposal—especially those launched from the left—therefore reflected not a difference in kind but a difference in the incentive structure. Indeed, when Theobald, Hazlitt, Tobin, and Friedman gathered in Washington for a debate in front of a thousand businessmen, under the auspices of the US Chamber of Commerce, they elegantly converged in their opposition to full employment, mainly differing on the amount to be granted as guaranteed income.[136]

Precisely this feature appealed to Theobald. At a 1967 conference talk titled "Towards Full Unemployment," he would argue that Friedman's main concern was to "increase the efficiency of the economic system" rather than to obtain "full employment."[137] Friedman's idea, he thought, was original to the extent that it was required only to "supply money rather than moral uplift, cultural refinements, extended education, retraining programs or make-work jobs."[138] It would also make it "unnecessary to worry about certain types of people who cannot find income-producing jobs."[139] An initially conservative idea was germinating into a fruitful framework for New Left experiments.

Black Poverty and the Triumph of the Income Strategy

Driven by mounting deindustrialization, cybernation, and newly fiscalized social policy, the mid-1960s witnessed an unprecedented proliferation of guaranteed income proposals. These were sent off from all points on the political spectrum. It took a while for this enthusiasm to reach the government, however. Kennedy and Johnson had repeatedly refused to consider the income strategy. As head of the newly created Office of Economic Opportunity—created in August 1964 to launch the president's War on Poverty—Sargent Shriver instructed Johnson to live by the slogan "No Doles." A year later Shriver had been promoting the idea of a negative income tax and included it in his 1965 antipoverty budget,[140] but Johnson, as Lampman recalls, "wanted no part of it from the outset."[141] Things began to change only with the patent failure of the Community Action Program as urban unrest in inner cities increased after the 1965 Watts riots and budget restraints imposed by the escalation of the Vietnam War further limited the president's options. These programs, directed through the Office of Economic Opportunity, included job training, educational remediation for poor youth, child care, community jobs, and a vast number of local initiatives.[142] This created a flurry of conflicts between administrations and coordination problems[143] between federal government and local authorities, which generally had to manage the programs themselves. As Edward Berkowitz has argued, "by the end of 1967 the euphoria of 1965 had been replaced by a feeling close to despair."[144] Mounting criticism of the efficiency of the government action and the continuous growth of welfare rolls; rising dissatisfaction with the expansion of the federal government and bureaucracy; and, perhaps most important, the increasing "culturalization" of poverty—especially "black poverty"—granted guaranteed income the momentum its proponents craved.

One of the most striking factors driving the proposal's popularity was an increasingly culturalist reading of black poverty. The idea that poverty in ghettos was to be understood as the result of cultural factors such as the disintegration of the family structure rather than of macroeconomic dynamics was not without precedent. Alvin Schorr, who worked within the Social Security Administration in the late 1950s before joining the Office of Economic Opportunity in 1965, had already argued that Aid to Families with Dependent Children incited black men to leave the household, reinforcing the matriarchal structure of poor African American families. His polemical report had even influenced legislation in several states like Louisiana, where benefits for women who had children while divorced were restricted, and in Newburgh, New York, where the city manager had cut off welfare to several families in a highly publicized conflict.[145] In his 1962 best seller Harrington also did not hesitate to describe "Negro poverty" as "unique in every way," growing out of a "subculture" that could easily, if no targeted measured were introduced, "reproduce itself for years to come."[146] As for poverty in general, Harrington's understanding of "black poverty" made him a skeptic on welfare state expansion. He rather thought that within the New Deal order "the Negroes were being asked to help to build a welfare state that would discriminate against them in a double sense, that would not really benefit them because they are so poor as to be beyond the reach of the new benefits, and that would continue and reinforce the racist pattern of all American society."[147] For this surplus proletariat, integration into the New Deal Order was at best a distraction and at worst an illusion.

The definitive blow to the integrationist perspective came with the publication of Daniel Moynihan's 1965 report *The Negro Family: The Case for National Action*. Moynihan's conclusion was also unexpectedly radical, suggesting, as Touré Reed notes, that the welfare crisis was now divorced from unemployment and economic factors.[148] This "new kind of problem," Moynihan argued, could not be alleviated by a mere expansion of public service provision or full employment but only through the "establishment of a stable Negro family structure."[149] As he claimed,

> At this point, the present tangle of pathology is capable of perpetuating itself without assistance from the white world.... In a word, a national effort towards the problems of Negro Americans must be directed towards the question of family structure. The object should be to strengthen the Negro family so as to enable it to raise and support its members as do other families. After that, how this group of Americans chooses to run its affairs, take advantage of its opportunities, or fail to do so, is none of the nation's business.[150]

Moynihan ventured further than mere culturalization: his book not only sought to blame the black family structure's pathology as such, but also castigated the existing welfare system, which, in his view, encouraged the disintegration of the black family in the first place. The incentive structure built in the AFDC program, he claimed, literally tore apart African American families. Since Roosevelt, New Deal social engineering was eroding black self-reliance. Ironically, such culturalist analyses also explained Moynihan's interest in guaranteed income schemes, including his later conceptualization of Nixon's Family Assistance Plan (FAP). The income framework provided not only innovative ways to think about welfare, but also a way to restore "some sense of individual responsibility for outcomes" to African American families. As he noted, "Where a services strategy tended to locate in government blame for services that do not succeed, an income strategy would tend to implicate the individuals, who would make their own choices in the market."[151]

Moynihan's message found an unlikely cross-partisan audience. In the same vein, a 1965 article by economist James Tobin—at the time a member of the Council of Economic Advisers—titled "On Improving the Economic Status of the Negro" praised the idea of a negative income tax as the solution to the "specific character" of black poverty.[152] Deeply influenced by Moynihan's writings, Tobin argued that "public assistance encourage[d] the disintegration of the family, the key to so many of the economic and social problems of the American Negro."[153] The existing structures of social assistance, he claimed, created a situation where "he, or likely she, is essentially forced to be both idle and on a dole."[154] Tobin even went beyond environmental factors, pointing at more profound cultural traits "related to a matriarchal tradition inherited from slavery and to the submergence of the nuclear family in the extended rural agricultural settings."[155] In these circumstances, he argued, close to Boggs, that even if the economy "prosper[ed] and labor become steadily more productive as in the past," "the other America," especially blacks, "will be stranded." The postwar framework, he added, "no longer operates."[156] Poverty could no longer be solved by public jobs or better schools, or "by minimum wage laws, trade union wage pressures, or other devices which seek to compel employers to pay them more than their work is worth."[157] "The biggest issue the nation face[d] in the war of poverty," he thought, was to establish a "system of income supplementation and maintenance" that would integrate "public assistance with a vastly simplified and reformed system of income taxation" in order to preserve the "incentives to work," encourage "maintain[ing] stable families," and provide a decent income.[158] The racialization of the poverty question seemed to favor only the cash-based approach.

For Tobin, a negative income tax could also be a useful device to break "the barriers to competition" that restrict[ed] black workers' entry into the labor market—barriers that in Tobin's eyes were in fact "created by public policy itself, in response to the vested interests," reflecting the "concentration of economic power in unions and in industry."[159] The "privileges" and "advantages" of white workers become another way through which they "purchase[d]) their standards of living and their security at the expense of unprivileged minorities."[160] Tobin was no newcomer to this argument. Friedman had been arguing in favor of it since the mid-1950s,

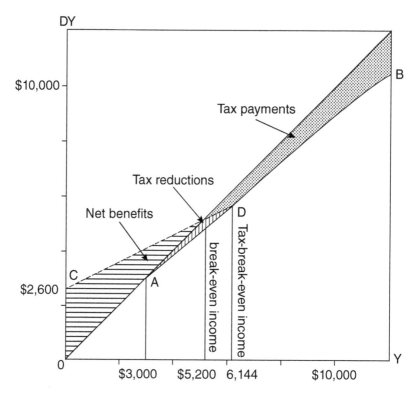

FIGURE 3.2. Tobin, Penchman, and Mieszkowski's 1967 plan for a guaranteed income. *Source*: James Tobin, Joseph A. Penchman, and Peter M. Mieszkowski, "Is a Negative Income Tax Practical?," *Yale Law Journal* 77 (November 1967): 7.

claiming that the NIT would be a simple device to create effective "equality of rights" and "equality of opportunity." Friedman had been consistent in arguing that the minimum wage legislation that Johnson saw passed in 1966 was actually "anti-Negro" and was instrumental in creating poverty and ghettos. Young blacks who were "less productive" owing to their lower levels of education would then be less likely to be hired when minimum wages were increased.[161] Tobin's proposals gathered traction within the maelstrom of the Johnsonian War on Poverty and reinforced the conviction of Sargent Shriver, head of the Office of Economic Opportunity, to push the income strategy within the administration.[162] Whereas only a few years earlier Wilbur Cohen had conceived his commitment to expanding welfare and training programs as a decisive "contribution to the civil rights movement,"[163] by the late 1960s Cohen's view had already lost its appeal among liberals.

This shift was particularly marked within the civil rights movement itself, which "was no longer pushing integration" in social policy.[164] Movements born in the mid-1960s, as scholars like Adolph Reed and Cedric Johnson have shown, would favor racial autonomy instead of the expansion of what Stokely Carmichael termed "welfare colonialism," which locked African Americans in an unequal class compromise. Carmichael electrified some civil rights activists with his plea for black power, coining a new phase for the movement. For him, as Boggs had argued before, what was needed was a "question[ing of] the middle-class values and institutions of this country," moving away from the New Deal coalition building of the preceding generation to focus on "the dignity of man." As Reed argued, black power rhetoric symbolized a shift within "the civil rights movement's conventional understanding of the political."[165] Whereas classical figures of the movement such as Bayard Rustin and A. Philip Randolph, for instance, "saw politics as fundamentally institutional, embedded in the interest-group system, a strain of radicals approached it as more expressive and hortatory, with black cultural integrity as a central normative commitment."[166] Appealing to younger activists, this new approach, Reed adds, "propounded a new political metaphysic in which integration was not a tactic, strategy, or even an institutional goal for a just society."[167] This birthed a different relationship with politics, less concerned with organizing the labor movement or creating large coalitions on specific demands. And while some of these new activists in principle endorsed the ideas of Randolph's and Rustin's Freedom Budget, they rejected the strategy necessary for organizing to advance it.[168] The pursuit of institutional expansion was then seen as paternalistic, inevitably leading to "sell[ing] blacks out," and an obstacle to the "proper goal of black liberation," which was "racial autonomy."[169] Within this framework, guaranteed incomes became an attractive alternative for organizations like the National Welfare Rights Organization (NWRO), which was slowly breaking with the coalition politics of the former generation.

The NWRO was founded in 1966 in the wake of the "Cloward–Piven" strategy and would come forward as the most vocal supporter of the cash strategy. Political scientists Richard Cloward and Frances Fox Piven first formulated the tactic in a piece published in the *Nation*, "A Strategy to End Poverty," that would become a catalyst for grassroots welfare organizations across the country. The two professors at the Columbia University

School of Social Work had imagined a plan aimed at dramatically increasing the number of poor people on welfare rolls, since many who were eligible usually did not claim their benefits. The outcome was a bureaucratic and budgetary nightmare that would force the Democratic Party to reform public welfare. "The ultimate objective," they argued, would be to "wipe out poverty by establishing a guaranteed annual income."[170] The idea prompted the unification of welfare rights activists from all over the country, gathering in Chicago in August 1966 to create the NWRO. Among the best-known figures of the newly created movement were George Wiley, a former associate director for the Congress of Racial Equality (CORE), and Johnnie Tillmon, who had founded the Aid to Needy Children (ANC) in 1963, one of the first grassroots welfare mothers' organizations. The NWRO would then include in its goals establishing a "system that guarantees enough money for all Americans to live dignified lives above the level of poverty." Guaranteed income programs were becoming the object of mass activism.[171]

The argument's attractiveness mainly stemmed from the degree of autonomy that guaranteed income schemes would grant to recipients. This would allow women to invest themselves in the community, for instance, rather than in an increasingly jobless labor market. To a certain extent, Moynihan's argument about family structure and the lack of work for males had charmed welfare activists. This question would notably be the subject of a small conflict between Beulah Sanders and George Wiley, vice president and president of the NWRO, on one side and Martha Griffiths, a feminist Democratic congresswoman on the other, during a 1968 congressional hearing about Johnson's Work Incentive Program. For Griffiths there was something deeply upsetting about enrolling people in welfare without granting them a prospect in the labor market. Keeping "a group of people who are on welfare" "forever," she argued, "maybe that is all right for the country, but it is not all right for the people on welfare. Those people have a right to participate in the economy of this country. They have just as much right to have a job as anybody else has." The vast majority of women drawing welfare, she added, "wanted to work if they had a place to put their children."[172]

Sanders and Wiley, on the other hand, proposed an argument strikingly close to Moynihan's. "If you are going to give us jobs," Sanders argued, "give our men the jobs; let us stay home and take care of our children."[173] As she would later frame it, Sanders wanted "mother power." "The important thing," Wiley added, "is that the men, that the people who are able to be

FIGURE 3.3. Pamphlet produced by the Greater Cleveland Welfare Rights Organization, criticizing President Lyndon Johnson's 1967 Work Incentive Program (WIN) in which welfare mothers were required to enter a job training or job placement program. May 1969. Cartoon is uncredited. *Source*: Western Reserve Historical Society.

heads of households or ought to be legitimate heads of households be the
ones that get those jobs."[174] Women could then do what they are the most
"valuable" for, "out into the community," "mixing with the people, finding
out what their problems are, and trying to help solve those problems."[175]

Following this line of argument, a guaranteed income became the natural solution to female and industrial joblessness. First, Wiley argued, because "income supplements" were more efficient than raising minimum
wages "to avoid the problems [it has] caused in a number of industries,"
as Friedman and Stigler had argued since the 1940s. And second, because
"if the department can pay a tremendous amount of money for people to
live in slum houses," Sanders argued, "they can pay that money for people to live in a decent apartment." "The main problem for poor people,"
Wiley added, "is money."[176] Rather than subsidizing poor and inefficient
public housing or public jobs, welfare activists began to push for female
autonomy through cash.

Antistatist Government

This antistatist tone was very much in line with the increasing hostility
among liberals and socialists toward an "administrative state," or what
Herbert Marcuse, following Theodor Adorno, referred to as the "administered society."[177] From the late 1950s onward (with the work of Columbia professor Robert K. Merton and his students Peter Blau and Alvin
Gouldner) scholars in the humanities and sociology in particular had moved
the question of bureaucracy to the center of public attention. Rather than
an efficient and democratic institution, bureaucracy was now commonly
seen as absurd and irrational, constructing a dangerously constrained society. As Reuel Schiller has noted, one component of "this revolution
was the emergence of a broad consensus that the state was something to
be feared and that administrative bureaucracies were agents of corrupt
power, not well-meaning experts pursuing the public interest."[178] Even
Ralph Nader, who would later be known as an advocate of increased state
regulation, began as an open critic of the state bureaucracy in the 1960s,
in favor of freeing individuals as consumers from the self-interested federal bureaucracies. Nader was hardly alone in this antiadministrative mood.
As Niklas Olsen has argued, during the 1960s "many leftist intellectuals
and politicians" radically "abandoned their belief in the role of the state
as a necessary regulator of the market"[179] in favor of extolling the virtues

of the civil society and individual autonomy. Theodore J. Lowi, who in the early sixties was one of the leading American political scientists, argued in his highly influential *The End of Liberalism* (1969), that the "democratic state" had "drained away" with the rise of a technocratic "administrative power," turning the "citizen into *administré*."[180]

This antistatist turn was particularly visible in the way Robert Theobald envisioned activity in a society that would guarantee an income floor. "The guaranteed-income proposal," he claimed, "is based on the fundamental American belief in the right and the ability of [the] individual to decide what he wishes and ought to do."[181] In Theobald's view it also offered an attractive alternative to public jobs and would "lead to the revival of 'private enterprise,'" meaning, he added, that "the individual should have the right to obtain enough resources to do what he believes to be important."[182] Theobald's ultimate goal was not so much the creation of a new, collectively defined sphere of activity, but the spontaneous revival of private activities made obsolete by the market because they would require too high a financial cost. A guaranteed income would render wages largely irrelevant; productive groups would spontaneously appear and "produce the 'custom-designed' goods that have been vanishing within the present economy," making it "market-oriented but not market-supported."[183] Guaranteed income would then rely on market principles about how to think about work but would subvert its coercive aspect by getting rid of the labor market.[184] A new division of labor would emerge out of the decentralized actions of truly free, autonomous individuals. This approach would allow for a curious convergence with what Arthur Kemp and Chicago economist Yale Brozen called "welfare without the welfare state."[185] If "welfare statists" always seek the expansion of the federal government to tackle poverty, the task of the liberal was "much more difficult" and consisted in moving "away from the welfare state without [a] decrease in welfare."[186] Both on the left and on the right, the aim became welfare without the welfare state, freed of the administrative, gendered, and political structures of the New Deal order. This task, Kemp thought, could be achieved precisely through a guaranteed annual income in the form of a negative income tax.

Within the administration itself the income shift came by the late 1960s, with Daniel Moynihan as chronicler. "The antipoverty program enacted in 1964," he argued, "came to embody many of the ambiguities and uncertainties of an ambitious services strategy directed to the problems of poverty. A good deal of money was being expended [and] it was going, in large degree, to purchase services, which could not be shown to benefit the poor."[187] In this context, he added, "an assertion came forth, labelled conservative but in historical terms almost classically liberal, that government administration did not work, while the market did."[188] Only then did the idea of an income strategy gain appeal in Washington, offering a perspective on tackling inequality but without expanding the federal government in a political climate that was turning increasingly antistatist and antiadministrative. The final turn would come with the publication of two reports related to welfare matters. First came a research report published by the Department of Health, Education, and Welfare that directly attacked the government's strategy to end poverty. The report claimed that under the current system 60 percent of Americans living below the poverty line did not benefit from the existing programs, casting doubt on the effectiveness of on the Great Society strategy.[189] The second was the highly anticipated 1968 report of the Kerner Commission on Civil Disorders, established by President Johnson to investigate the causes of the 1967 urban riots. The report received an exceptional amount of public scrutiny and notably recommended a guaranteed income as a "long-range goal" to fix a broken welfare system and provide a "basic floor" "for all Americans."[190] The proposal would have the advantage of providing both for "employed persons working at substandard hours or wages" and for those who "cannot work," like "mothers who decide to remain with their children."[191]

By the late 1960s the legislative momentum for the guaranteed income already appeared unstoppable. In January 1967 President Johnson finally established a Commission on Income Maintenance Programs. While he warned that the scheme was being pushed "by some of the sturdiest defenders of free enterprise" and that it was "almost surely beyond our means at this time," he added that "we must examine any plan, however unconventional, which could promise a major advance."[192] That same year, the Office of Economic Opportunity, driven by a Sargent Shriver initiative, launched the first of several large-scale experiments in boroughs of New Jersey.[193] Finally, by 1968 more than a thousand economists, across the spectrum and from some of the nation's most prestigious institutions, signed an open letter to the president supporting a guaranteed income.[194] As Paul Samuelson argued in his *Newsweek* column, "Any plan that simultaneously commands the allegiance of professor Milton Friedman and John Kenneth Galbraith must have a lot going for it."[195] At that point the question was no longer *whether* the idea was going to be adopted, but *when*. Even Republicans were now considering implementing such a measure. And after Hubert Humphrey's defeat in the 1968 presidential election, Nixon felt some urgency to solve the "welfare mess" with radical measures such as a negative income tax, especially in the face of continuing social and urban unrest.[196]

The idea's most notable propagandist within the administration was Moynihan. The policy maker had left the Johnson administration in 1965—never having the ear of the president—only to be hired as Nixon's chief adviser on urban affairs. Unlike Johnson, Nixon never took a keen interest in domestic affairs and remained unwilling to gamble political capital on welfare matters, since his true area of interest remained foreign policy. Moynihan pushed for a Family Assistance Plan (FAP), a version of guaranteed income supposedly aimed at eliminating the "disincentives to family formation that were built into the AFDC."[197] When he argued that the plan would eliminate a lot of social workers' jobs, "Nixon's eyes lit up."[198] Although he had opposed the general principle during the campaign, the idea of his administration's embracing an "'income strategy' against poverty to replace Johnson's 'service strategy'"[199] persuaded him to go ahead with the idea in April 1969. As Lemann has noted, this was an attractive framework for conservatives too, since it did not require "promoting integration or expanding the federal bureaucracy" and would "cost only 2 billion a year and cut back on the size of government."[200] Part of the motivation to reform also came from an increasing consensus among conservatives that unequal benefit allocation between states (Illinois gave four times as much as Mississippi, for instance) was partly driving the great black migration from the southern states.[201] "The welfare system," Nixon stated in one of his speeches, "has helped draw millions into the slums of our cities."[202] Moynihan was also convinced that the service strategy had transformed the "black middle class" into "providers of social services to the black lower class," allowing them to blackmail government into inflationary social demands and usher in a general civilizational crisis of inflation.[203] The way this middle class had benefited from the jobs created by the Office of Economic Opportunity, and the power it had gained over the federal government, grew into an even more vexing problem. Choosing the income strategy, he then argued in a memo to Nixon, would "deprive 'the militant middle class' of the ability to make an ongoing 'threat to the larger society, much as the desperate bank robber threatens to drop the vial of nitroglycerin."[204] As Lemann notes, this gave the income strategy a strategic advantage as "a gesture towards the ghettos that would simultaneously take the play away from the militant middle class."[205] Indirectly, transferring money also became a way to disempower the newly created class of welfare workers and bureaucrats, loosening its grip on the poor and, by extension, on the federal government. This would allow a distribution of cash rather than an alteration of power relations.

Sticking to this cash-based approach, Nixon began in 1969 by abolishing taxes for those living below the poverty line. He then rapidly moved toward the FAP. Although the plan was approved in 1970 in a Democratic-controlled House, it would face backlash in a Senate worried about its effect on work incentives. The proposal's centrist inflection, transcending party lines, dissatisfied most of its natural constituency. The left, and in particular the NWRO, thought the amount of $1,600 a year advanced in the plan was too little for single mothers. The US Chamber of Commerce, which initially pushed for the income strategy, would also oppose the plan on the basis that the FAP structure would reduce the incentive to work. Even Friedman, who had written numerous essays and given talks on the topic for several decades, ended up castigating Nixon's proposal along the same lines as the Chamber of Commerce.[206] Politically, the NIT ran into a dilemma that would return with a vengeance in all later contexts: adequate basic incomes were unaffordable, while affordable basic incomes remained inadequate.

By 1972, after a round of heavy revisions, the Nixon plan was again definitively defeated in the Senate. The year after the defeat of Moynihan's plan, however, Nixon was able to introduce two more modest plans that would become his lasting legacy for social policy. The first was the Supplemental Security Income (SSI) that would provide a federally guaranteed income to the blind, aged, and disabled. Second, and perhaps more important, was the Earned Income Tax Credit (EITC), patterned after Friedman's NIT but restricted to those who worked. These policies, as Brian Steensland has noted, "partially attained some of the goals of GAI proposals" by expanding the income strategy, yet without having been able to definitively erase the symbolic boundaries between the "deserving" and "undeserving" poor that would remain a crucial aspect of welfare policy in the United States.[207] Thus there was victory in defeat; as Lemann notes, in the field of welfare "the specific program failed politically," yet its "general principle succeeded." "The Nixon administration," he added, "in effect did implement the income strategy by greatly increasing the payment levels of welfare, food stamps, social security, and disability pensions while allowing government social welfare employment to level off."[208]

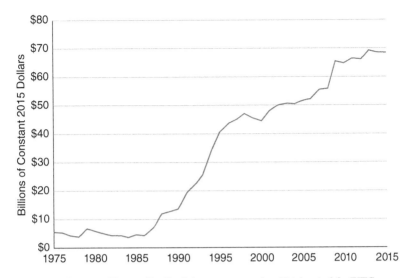

FIGURE 3.4. The Earned Income Tax Credit has grown over time: Total cost of the EITC, 1975–2015. *Source*: Gene Falk and Margot L. Crandall-Hollick, "The Earned Income Tax Credit (EITC): An Overview." Congressional Research Service Report, January 19, 2016.

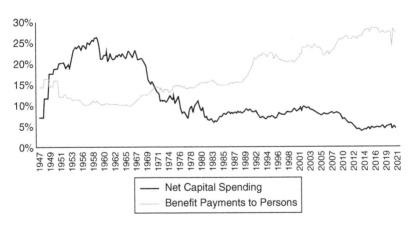

FIGURE 3.5. Spending by state and local governments, expressed as a percentage of current receipts. *Source*: Federal Reserve, T. S. Lombard.

The move toward cash proved premonitory for later administrations. Even during the two Reagan administrations, income support programs like AFDC, unemployment benefits, and food stamps were generally spared from hard cuts, unlike housing policy. The shift here would be exemplary of the income turn in social policy. Reagan dramatically reduced the budget of the Department of Housing and Urban Development (HUD) and substituted it with a new scheme of housing vouchers. Privatizing and cashifying also seemed to go hand in hand. The overall shift "from subsidizing 'bricks and mortar' to subsidizing people," as Paul Pierson has noted, reduced the number of new projects by 80 percent and strongly pushed for privatizing the existing ones, giving cash to targeted poor instead.[209] Reagan would then considerably expanded Nixon's Earned Income Tax Credit through the Tax Reform Act of 1986, increasing its budget from $2 billion to $7 billion a year. The scheme would then be expanded under the Clinton administration and its budget would systematically increase with each subsequent presidency, reaching $70 billion in 2019. The shift would accompany the American developmental state's transformation into a less activist transfer state. While capital spending declined severely during the late 1960s, benefits payments to citizens continued to increase, feeding the broader turn to cash transfers.

* * *

When a twenty-seven-year-old Milton Friedman, concerned about the poverty generated by the game of free markets, began to think out techniques to eradicate it, he could hardly have anticipated the success of his income-focused strategy. His negative income tax ended up capturing one of the enduring shifts in the field of economics that occurred during that period: the state's decline as an economic agent and its focusing instead on shaping the incentive structure of an economic game composed of sovereign consumers rather than citizens. This shift, the starting point of what British economist John Kay terms "redistributive market liberalism," would cement an approach to social policy by which "the state must have a dominant role in matters of income distribution but should discharge this responsibility with as little interference as possible in the workings of the free market."[210] Beyond political labeling, the negative income tax Milton Friedman had advocated since the 1940s seemed to be an elegant, practical, and policy-neutral tool, capable of transcending classical oppositions between left and right but also offering an alternative to the patronizing views of classical liberalism and the worker-centered welfare policies of the "Old Left." Robert Theobald provided an apt summary of this paradox in 1963 with his insistence that the basic income idea could be reconciled with the desire to achieve *both* the freedom of the individual and the "necessity of free markets." This was a system that could provide the individual with "enough resources to live as a member of society" without "government interference in the market mechanism."[211] Such a "capitalism with a human face," as Samuel Brittan similarly envisioned it, could reconcile the pursuit of self-interest with egalitarian concerns.[212]

In the United States the idea of a guaranteed income—conceived in its strict, policy-oriented sense—did not survive the legislative brokering of the early 1970s. With the demise of George McGovern's proposal of a "demogrant" of $1,000 a person in the 1972 presidential race,[213] the American debate on guaranteed income seemed to reach an anticlimactic close. In 1973 Nixon dismantled the Office of Economic Opportunity—a key agency in Johnson's War on Poverty—and the results of the New Jersey experiment were received with relative indifference.[214] But while America's welfare debate was assuming an increasingly conservative bent, on the other side of the Atlantic, from France to Belgium to the Netherlands, the career of basic income and its cash transfer cousins was just beginning. As Theobald wrote in the epilogue of his best seller *Free Men and Free Markets*, the conditions that had favored the rise of guaranteed income in the United States were destined to "emerge in Europe in coming years."[215]

CHAPTER FOUR

The Politics of Postwork in Postwar Europe

The day of work, are you kidding? The day of workers celebrating themselves. I never got it into my head what workers' day or the day of work meant. – Nanni Balestrini, *Vogliamo Tutto* (*We Want Everything*), 1971

The society of labor . . . no longer exists and willnot return. – André Gorz, *Misères du present*, 1997

On April 30, 1983, a group of Dutch radicals in Amsterdam's Pijp quarter prepared for their annual May Day observance.[1] The date certainly was symbolic. As the anniversary of the global workers' move-ment—the initial "holiday outside all calendars," as Eric Hobsbawm put it—May 1 still was one of the proud marks the global labor movement had left on the human calendar.[2] In 1884 the American trade unionist Samuel Gompers—later head of the American Federation of Labor—called for a demonstration for an eight-hour working day on May 1, 1886. After vio-lent clashes between police and protesters, the first, unofficial May Day demonstrations on May 3 ended with a bomb attack in Chicago's Hay-market Square, killing twelve and maiming dozens.

In 1983, however—almost a century after Gompers's clarion call—the Dutch group thought the term Labor Day obsolete, if not positively dam-aging. They proposed rebaptizing it as the "Day against the Work Ethic" (*Dag tegen het arbeidsethos*), celebrating the advent of a world in which

FIGURE 4.1. Nacht tegen het arbeidsethos (Night against the work ethic), 1982. *Source*: Dutch National Archives.

humanity would be exempt from labor altogether. Members of the collective gathered in the Amsterdam Rialto movie house to found a consortium that would represent what they called the "conscientiously unemployed" under the name Dutch Council against the Work Ethic" (Nederlandse Bond Tegen het Arbeidsethos). The night featured talks, documentaries, poetry readings, and a screening of Charlie Chaplin's classic 1936 film *Modern Times* following a lecture by Dutch philosopher Hans Achterhuis on the topic of "postwork."[3] The mood was easygoing but excitable.

Founded by Dutch pacifist Bo "Bingel" Baden, the antiwork group-let was first conceived in "an empty space, with two old bureaus placed against each other."[4] Ironically, Baden's first meeting was underattended: not a single outside member showed up for the launch event. This was not to last, however. When Baden took to the local airwaves, a larger squadron of squatters (*krakers*) and former hippies had already trickled in, filling the vacant offices the organization occupied. Soon journalists showed interest, while angry members of the Labor Party (PvdA) and unionists expressed their discontent. Despite its status as a union of the "jobless," figures in the mainstream labor movement disagreed with plans to halt the reintegration of the Dutch "army of unemployed." Work was to remain central, the laborites claimed, and the Council was playing a dangerous game.[5]

Opposition from the established left, however, did little to cool Baden's ambitions. "We refuse to accept," proclaimed one of the first issues of his *Luie donder!* (Lazybones), "that labor, however dignified for man and his environment, can ever be humanity's highest value."[6] The front page of the issue bore the slogan "Desecrate Labor!" (Ontheilig de Arbeid!), and the Council claimed that "as long as we live in a society in which wage labor is central, there will always and by definition exist large groups of people who will opt out and who will be degraded to a societally inferior position."[7] Bingel also urged policy makers to experiment. In a piece titled "Duty to Labour—Yuck!" (Arbeidsplicht—Bah!), for instance, Council members looked at the possibility of replacing the current social security system with a more streamlined version.[8] Disgusted by the "obligation to look for work," they called for a "right to autonomy vis-à-vis one's own labor and life" and insisted on seeing their current unemployment benefits as a substitute for a continuous grant.[9] The "permanently unemployed," they claimed, "have much to benefit when we transcend the society of the '*Animal laborans*' and abolish wage labor . . . we have to decouple labor and income."[10] The text finished: "Long live the basic income!"[11]

The Council's 1982 plea was not the first Dutch call for a basic income. Dutch socialists in the 1930s had already drawn on French and English precedents to think out a grant system that could remedy the country's roiling economic crisis. The word *basisinkomen* (originally *basis-inkomen*) was first introduced into Dutch vernacular sometime in the middle of the

decade. Its inventor was the Dutch Nobel Prize–winning economist Jan Tinbergen, then a member of the Dutch Social Democratic Workers' Party.
In a 1934 commentary on the party's "labor plan" (*Plan van de Arbeid*),
Tinbergen had tried to persuade colleagues to include a version of the
permanent grant in the program, probably based on his earlier readings
of G. D. H. Cole and C. H. Douglas.[12] The absence of a work requirement
worried other members: they felt it could alienate socialist electorates
with a strong work ethic. Personalist writers such as Alexandre Marc and
Emmanuel Mounier had tried to devise a proposal for a "vital minimum"
in the 1930s as an alternative to socialist currents.[13] While such authors
anticipated advocates of universal basic income in the mid-1960s, their
theories also remained intimately tied to the centrality of "work" as the
basis of human flourishing.[14] In this welfare world, the sovereign consumers celebrated by Tinbergen, Lerner, Lange, and Friedman were a
hard sell.

By 1983, however, the grip of workerist dogma had become much weaker.
Beginning in the late 1960s, social reformers, politicians, and activists had
begun rethinking parts of the Dutch social security system to ease the
work-centered features inherent in previous versions. By 1983, intellectuals like Jürgen Habermas and Claus Offe were diagnosing "the end of the
work-based society" (*Arbeitsgesellschaft*), a trend marked by a weakening
link between income and employment across European economies.[15] Italian radical Nanni Balestrini described his generation's workers as "ideo-
logically estranged from work and from any professional ethic."[16]

The founding of the Council against the Work Ethic also came at a
time of retreat for the frail Dutch labor movement. Two years earlier, the
Dutch government and several representatives from the union movement
had sealed the "Wassenaar Accords" (Wassenaar Akkoorden), in which a
reduction of salaries was agreed on to combat the country's inflationary
crisis.[17] Hailed as the beginning of a new North European consensus politics (known as "polder politics" [*polderpolitiek*]), the accords inaugurated
a further weakening of the trade union movement.[18] Although the measures contributed to a "Dutch jobs miracle" in the years to come, the accords left behind a splintered left, split between workerist, ecological, and
Christian factions. In 1980 public television station Tros broadcast a Dutch
reworking of Milton Friedman's *Free to Choose* under the title "Aan ons
de keuze," with his plea for the negative income tax.[19] As the long American debate on basic income was ending in the late 1970s, the European
basic income debate was just gathering steam.

The Dutch debate acquired particular gravitas in the early 1980s. Unemployment skyrocketed to over 10 percent in the opening years of the decade, coupled with spiraling inflation, pushing a significant portion of the workforce onto unemployment rolls. (The situation was particularly acute in cities like Amsterdam, the Council's base, which over the decade earned the name "Amsterdamned.")[20] The effects of the slump were compounded by the city's ongoing housing crisis, which led to squatters' riots in 1980.[21] Ad hoc remedies were put forward, including public works programs, job sharing, reduced working hours, and schemes for municipal job guarantees. Crisis fighting could never secure a permanent solution to joblessness, however. Mainly younger workers remained permanently locked out of employment circuits and became indefinitely dependent on unemployment insurance, driving up social security costs. When profit rates recovered at the close of the decade, the effects on the overall employment rates appeared minimal and unevenly distributed. "The economy might be getting out of its slump," a policy adviser diagnosed in 1983, "but the effect on employment is nil."[22] Instead, "guaranteeing an income to everyone" now appeared a better solution, disregarding people's place in the labor process.[23]

A distinctly new vision of emancipation was also at the root of the basic income proposal the Council defended in the early 1980s. This vision has gone by many names—the "postlabor thesis," "cybernetic socialism," "'73 thought," "anti-Fordism," or "postproductivism."[24] All participated in a broader revision of "the supremacy of labor in Western Marxist theory in the twentieth century."[25] Two parameters here allowed for a new UBI to take root—a left-wing antistatism and a new postwork sensibility. Both these currents destabilized the centrality of the "producer" in the socialist tradition in favor of other models and pitted themselves against a commandeering state. They shared clear roots within the American basic income debate of the 1960s. Owing to the comparative weakness of its labor movement and its developed assistance tradition, the Netherlands was one of the first countries to experience a national debate on the valences of a basic income, with the proposal making it into governmental advisory organs. Most prominently, however, the groundwork was laid in the period after 1968, when a generation of French thinkers influenced by cybernetics rethought received notions such as "labor," "state," and "welfare." And just as Milton Friedman had to wait until 1962 for his ideas to gain traction, early European defenders of a basic income had to wait until the early 1980s for a more welcoming environment.[26] Both bureaucracy and labor, the New Left argued, would be severely redrawn by the cybernetic revolution. Leftists thus carried out a double maneuver against both an "Old Left" and an "Old Right," which had supposedly entered an unholy "statist" alliance in the 1970s. It was this dual revolution—exemplified by thinkers such as Herbert Marcuse, Michel Foucault, Ivan Illich, Bram van Ojik, Roel van Duijn, Félix Guattari, Toni Negri, André Gorz, and Philippe Van Parijs, many of whom ended up as basic income sympathizers and proponents—that laid the groundwork for the European UBI wave.

Work versus Labor: The End of Producer Sovereignty

The Dutch Council against the Work Ethic held its first "anti–May Day" in 1983. Nearly a decade earlier, however, a French group had already held a remarkably similar anti-event: on May 1, 1975, the French Union ouvrière circulated a pamphlet titled "Down with the Festival of Alienated Labor" among workers in Paris who were gearing up for their annual May Day celebration. "Mandatory planning, collective ownership of the means of production, proletarian ideology," the organization claimed, had simply "nothing communist about them."[27] Industrial unions in turn had become "just the tools of the bosses," and workers were "bone-headed to think that one in your thousands would demand to lose your life."[28] As the leaders saw it, "union strategists" were "not saying 'Death to labour, never work, let's abolish wage slavery, right to laziness, death to survival.' "[29] Instead, they were out to strengthen the class compact, locking the proletariat in its corporate cage.

With its call to antiwork insurrection, the Union ouvrière was only part of a broader radical ecosystem. In the late 1960s, northern Italy's industrial centers had already experienced a similarly convulsive wave of strikes, in which workers refused to honor the productivity promises of the postwar settlement. In works such as Nanni Balestrini's 1971 novel *Vogliamo Tutto* (*We Want Everything*), for instance, protagonists called on colleagues to "fight so there is no more work" and "battle against the state built on labor."[30] Inspired by Italian precedents, 1970s German radicals then organized TUNIX-collectively ("Do Nothing") under the slogan the "Great Refusal," hosting speakers such as Michel Foucault, Gilles Deleuze, and Félix Guattari.[31] Later, members of TUNIX joined so-called Happy Unemployed groups, who set up action committees ridiculing the "love of labor" of social democrats.[32] Both in Amsterdam and in Berlin, radicals read Ivan Illich's 1977 *Le chômage créateur* (Creative unemployment), which offered a stinging critique of the family wage celebrated by conservatives and socialists alike.[33] Former members of TUNIX also became enthusiastic proponents of the basic income in the 1980s, explicitly contrasting it to classical unemployment schemes.[34] In 1985 the Council thus joined a lively European scene made up of French unemployment unions, British claimants organizations, Belgian ecologists, German anti-workists, and Italian postoperaists.

All these organizations served as representatives of a new "postindustrial left" that had sprung up in the 1960s and 1970s.[35] They also discerned the profoundly destabilizing consequences that new cybernetic techniques had on received notions of state and labor. These proved handy tools for undermining the Fordist order first conceived by postwar planners.

More than a mere method of production, Fordism was here conceived as a comprehensive *social theory*, a technique for producing goods as much as for producing subjects.[36] With the family and the workplace as two nodes, postwar Fordism centered on the "breadwinner and family man" who "circulated his wages and other social benefits back into the family as a basic social reproductive unit," which then served as the "basis for state policy in matters of employment, welfare, and development."[37] The Italian thinker Mario Tronti saw this postwar period as one of "dynamic stabilization" in which the aims of capital and labor converged in a rare cross-class consensus.[38] By the late 1960s, however, with students in the streets and workers marching on the factories, the Fordist contract was disintegrating; in its interstices, a new basic income movement would flourish.

The United States again set a consistent precedent for these debates. It was within Ford's own Detroit factory, overall, that post-Fordism's first symptoms manifested themselves in the Automation Department.[39] In 1946 Henry Ford's eldest grandson, Henry Ford II, took the reins at the Detroit plant and began to move away from his grandfather's charismatic corporation.[40] Rather than center productivity in a populist vein, Ford brought in Harvard specialists like Robert McNamara and management gurus à la Peter Drucker.

Social science paid close attention to all these developments. In 1957, German social scientist Friedrich Pollock surveyed the wave of robotization sweeping the American industrial landscape.[41] He extended his 1938 "integration thesis," which had first proclaimed the unification of the masses into "the authoritarian state."[42] In Pollock's "postliberal" economy, the market had been abolished and planning had been generalized, mainly through mergers, price controls, and cartels. But freedom under capitalist integration was an illusion. This process was only intensified with the spread of automation in the postwar period, when increases in productivity could be used to buy off pacified working classes. The result was an increasingly "administered society," as Theodor Adorno called it, in which the state used its regulatory powers to "ratify industry policies" using "government coercion in the name of the 'public interest' to hide tensions between workers and business . . . [and] further maintain the status quo of big ownership."[43] In Detroit, global capital of Fordism, James Boggs, the primary theorist of postwork, had already witnessed the devastating effects of automation on the black workforce. Soon, he claimed, this mass redundancy would hit European labor markets too.[44]

Pollock's and Boggs's writings on automation and deindustrialization inspired the most eloquent proponent of the postwork philosophy in the 1960s, Herbert Marcuse. His *One-Dimensional Man* (1964) kept a keen eye on the recent effects of the "cybernetic" revolution and the way it restructured labor practices. Marcuse's reconsideration of Marxian views of labor went back to the 1930s, drawing on the writings of Lewis Mumford and other technocratic futurists.[45] It was mainly in the 1950s, however, that he began to reconsider socialism's emphasis on the dignity of labor.[46] His formulation was analogous to what his colleague Hannah Arendt — with whom he had studied under Martin Heidegger in the 1920s — called distinction of labor as a purely "reproductive" activity (labor) and spontaneous and self-determined "action" (work), although Marcuse cast an even wider net for his notion of "labor."[47] *All* of human activity, he thought, deserved this label, erasing the boundary between "work" and "play" prevalent in the previous tradition.[48] It was this ontological notion of labor, above all, that capitalist societies seemed incapable of satisfying, even though its tendencies constantly pushed toward obsolescence. European working classes slaved under the yoke of a "welfare-warfare state" in which Keynesian demand management cooled their revolutionary fervor.[49]

Automation would undo this delicate balance, however. The robotizing ushered in by the 1950s, as Marcuse saw it, led to the end of the working class as the "living contradiction of established society."[50] It also opened up space for new models besides the male wage earner. If machines could create machines, labor was no longer exclusively a human affair, and the working class lost its prerogative as the "making class." Marcuse thus interpreted the aggressive automation of the 1950s and 1960s as a cue for humanity's final jump from the sphere of "necessity" to a new "freedom," releasing the energy previously suppressed by the work ethic. Against the "automation hysteria" of the 1950s, Marcuse thought that automation itself was radically altering the balance between freedom and necessity.[51] The two terms had undergone a sudden dislocation; socialism would revert from Marx to Fourier.

In 1966 Marcuse's Frankfurt colleague Erich Fromm already claimed that this jump could be instantiated in the form of a universal grant—a policy that would sever links between income and work.[52] Although Marcuse never openly endorsed Fromm's proposal, his philosophy intertwined elegantly with the New Left's search for a form of welfare beyond the welfare state. "Freed from this enslavement," Marcuse claimed, productivity would shed "its repressive power and impel the free development of individual needs. . . . The more complete the alienation of labor, the greater the potential of freedom: total automation would be the optimum."[53]

The late 1950s witnessed a steady translation of this integration thesis into European contexts. Works inspired by American and British sociology, such as those of André Gorz or Jean Baudrillard's *The Consumer Society* (1969), were prominent examples.[54] Discussing Galbraith's work on the "affluent society," Baudrillard argued that the "fundamental problem of contemporary capitalism" was no longer between the "maximization of profit" and the "rationalization of production conceived from the point of view of the producer."[55] It had moved to a "contradiction between a virtually unlimited productivity" and "the need to dispose of the product," gnawing away at the centrality of the work ethic.[56] This implied a gradual fading away of the working class as the subject of history. "The idea of a transcendent exteriority of force to the system," Jean-François Lyotard noted in his *Libidinal Economy* (1973), now appeared "to be dangerously threatened by the actual state of capitalist production."[57] The new question for radicals thus became how to reawaken a quiescent working class by subverting their commitment to labor.[58]

How this could be tied to an antiwork ethic was spelled out most clearly by situationist Raoul Vaneigem in 1967. "The obligation to produce," Vaneigem claimed in *The Revolution of Everyday Life*, "alienate[d] the passion to create," while "productive labor only reinforced the forces of order."[59] "From the Nazi *Arbeit macht frei* to Henry Ford to Mao," he noted, the "cult of labor" had now become a universal fact in the communist and capitalist worlds.[60] The 1960s, however, would see automation cause "mass replacement of workers by mechanical slaves."[61] The rise of the new machines would reveal that labor was superfluous to reproduction, thereby betraying "its adherence to the barbarous procedures of the established order."[62] "The trickery of work has been exhausted," Vaneigem concluded in 1967, and "there is nothing left to lose, not even the illusion of labor itself."[63]

Cybernetics again proved a capacious tool to counter the pro-work consensus. Since the mid-1940s, a growing French literature had begun to fantasize about using cybernetic techniques to heighten France's industrial output. To writers like Jean Fourastié—inventor of the *trente glorieuses* meme—cybernetics could drastically heighten productivity and expand free time.[64] Others saw the advent of a "governing machine" that would dispense altogether with the need for human governance.[65] Vaneigem and other situationists took issue with the technocratic bent of this literature—"cybernetic scum" (*canaille cybernétique*)[66] was Vaneigem's expression for them.[67] "Humanity will not be free," proclaimed Vaneigem's colleagues in the Situationist International, "until the last bureaucrat has been hung with the intestines of the last capitalist."[68] This also required a deeper questioning of the socialist tradition as a whole. Tragically, the nineteenth-century workers' movement "ultimately gave birth to a vision of socialism which was in fact a more effective integration of the working class into capitalism."[69]

Like the sorcerer's apprentice, however, French technocrats had conjured up a spirit that would prove difficult to control. The new "science of systems" was not just detrimental to class consciousness, it would also allow for a drastic expansion of the sphere of leisure and open vistas to a world beyond work. "Snatched from its masters," Vaneigem claimed in his *Traité du savoir à l'usage des jeunes générations* (a tract crucial to the '68 moment), "cybernetics will liberate human groups from work and social alienation" and complete "the project of Charles Fourier in an age when utopia was still possible."[70] Countering the "cybernetic state" proposed by technocrats— "Stalino-cyberneticians," as Vaneigem called them—situationists instead hoped for a revolutionary repurposing of automation. This implied the creation of a rival "cybernetic welfare state" that could be wielded to revolutionary ends.[71] "In founding a perfect form of power," Vaneigem saw "the cyberneticians will promote and the emulation and perfection of refusal. . . . their programming of new techniques will be twisted by another organization—a revolutionary one."[72] Although the working class had missed its appointment with destiny, capitalism still produced new grave diggers.

Developments in Marx scholarship seemed to push in a similarly anti-work direction. In 1964 English historian Eric Hobsbawm had put out the first snippets from a box of Karl Marx's unedited manuscripts labeled "Pre-capitalist Economic Formations."[73] Four years later, Canadian Germanist Martin Nicolaus published a longer introduction to the writings in the *New Left Review*. He hinted at the newly assembled pieces as the "*Grundrisse*" (Soviet publishers first released a collection of the manuscripts in 1941, in a limited edition of two hundred copies, and Marcuse had already encountered parts in the early 1950s).[74] By the late 1960s, the manuscripts had already lost their esotericism: Marcuse cited the "Fragment on Machines" in his 1964 *One-Dimensional Man*, and Raya Dunayevskaya and Grace Lee Boggs began translating chapters for a wider audience.[75] As Mike Davis noted, the book "considerably levelled the playing field for non-German readers," also adding "900 pages of required study to the several thousand pages of the four volumes of *Capital*."[76]

The Marx material Nicolaus unearthed slowly sent creative shocks through the left milieu. The most important of these was the distinctly new vision of emancipation that the thinker seemed to offer in the manuscripts. In several passages in the *Grundrisse*, Marx appeared to predict the progressive elimination of the need for labor itself. "To the degree that large industry develops," Marx's text read, "the creation of real wealth comes to depend less on labour-time and on the amount of labour employed" than upon "the general state of science and on the progress of technology."[77] At this point the "surplus labour of the mass" would cease "to be the condition for the development of general wealth," just as "the non-labour of the few has ceased to be the condition for the development of the general powers of the human mind."[78] Time would be freed up for "the artistic, scientific etc. development of the individuals," and "the measure of wealth would then not any longer, in any way, be labour time, but rather disposable time."[79] In Germany the publication of the manuscripts kick-started the growth of the "New Reading of Marx" with interpreters like Hans-Georg Backhaus and Moishe Postone,[80] while in Italy the discovery of the "Fragment on Machines" in Marx's *Grundrisse* stimulated the rise of postoperaism.[81] In his 1978 *Marx beyond Marx: Lessons from the "Grundrisse,"* philosopher Antonio Negri already claimed that "non-work, the refusal of work becomes the worker's point of view, the basis from which the law of value can be inverted and the law of surplus value reinterpreted."[82]

More than anyone, the new Marx had a lasting impact on French Marxist André Gorz, the most prominent of antiwork writers in postwar Europe. Born in Vienna in 1923 to a Jewish father and a Catholic mother and named Gerhart Hirsch, Gorz had moved into existentialist circles in the mid-1950s.[83] He ended up on the editorial board of Sartre's *Les temps modernes* in the early 1960s. He quickly became known as the head of the "Italian tendency." Gorz himself had featured several passages from the *Grundrisse* in the course of the 1960s.[84] His primary interests, however, remained political. Amid a debate on the "society of affluence" and the "end of class," in the early 1960s he initially held steadfastly to a classical socialist line, questioning the "integration thesis" that was taking root in some left-wing circles. In a text titled "The Belgian Denial" ("Le démenti belge") published in *Les temps modernes*, for instance, Gorz claimed that the integration thesis had been debunked. If "high salaries and advanced social legislation should provoke the *embourgeoisement* of the workers, Belgian workers should be among the most gentrified all of workers in Europe."[85] But the mass work stoppage showed this was not the case. Gorz's piece was published after the "strike of the century," when Belgian workers struck for almost two months in the harsh winter of 1960–61 and mobilized 100,000 protesters in quasi-insurrectionist fashion.

In the late 1960s Gorz made a sudden about-face on the integration thesis. Visits to America awakened an interest in black power and American antipoverty activism. These organizations were forthright about their commitment to organizing the poor rather than the working class. In Europe, Gorz adopted a "new class thesis" that claimed industrial working classes were shedding their radicalism and yielding the way to new class actors: "[parts] of the working class which will survive cybernation."[86] Postmortems of the French May '68 had still been hopeful that a new educated workforce could carry the revolutionary torch.[87] By the mid-1970s, however, these revolutionary fever dreams already appeared to have been in vain. "More than anyone anticipated," Gorz claimed, "capital has succeeded in reducing workers' power in the productive process" while increasing "the technical power and capacities of the proletariat as a whole and the impotence of proletarians themselves."[88] As a consequence, the class "collectively. . . . responsible for developing and operating the totality of the productive forces" had become "unable to appropriate or subordinate" this totality.[89]

This shift also tied in with Gorz's evolving reading of the *Grundrisse*. Although Marx's "fragment on machines" had seemed to presage the coming of a polytechnical class of workers—able to tend production without managerial authority—this overlooked the idea that "hyperspecialization" might occur at the cost of deskilling lower ranks of the workforce.[90] As American labor sociologists had observed already in the 1950s, the postindustrial workforce was bifurcating into "the unskilled worker, the broom pusher, whose job may be too menial to automate" on the one hand and "the highly skilled worker, who designs, constructs, repairs and programs the machine" on the other.[91] The first layer had always had little to gain from work, Gorz noted in 1973. Instead they "had been promised a bourgeois privilege, they had gone into debt to acquire it, and now they saw that everyone else could also get it."[92] Drawing on Ivan Illich, Gorz noted that "a good part of each day's work goes to pay for the travel necessary to get to work," while it cut "a person into slices, it cuts our time, our life, into separate slices so that in each one you are a passive consumer at the mercy of the merchants," shutting out that "work, culture, communication, pleasure, satisfaction of needs, and personal life can and should be one and the same thing: a unified life, sustained by the social fabric of the community."[93] Gorz also inched toward a more skeptical attitude on the left's pro-work stance. The effects of the information revolution, he claimed, were creating an increasingly stratified workforce beyond the purview of the organized left. "Productive activity" had "been emptied of its meaning, its motivations, and its object simply to become a way to earn a salary. It had stopped being part of "life," simply to become a means to "earn a living."[94] As he noted in what would become one of his most influential books—*Farewell to the Working Class* (itself a slight mistranslation of *Adieu au prolétariat*)—this cast doubt on Marx's idea that salvation could be found in the "proletarian condition" itself:

> As long as workers own a set of tools enabling them to produce for their own needs, or a plot of land to grow some vegetables and keep a few chickens, the fact of proletarianization will be felt to be accidental and reversible. For ordinary experience will continue to suggest the possibility of independence: workers will continue to dream of setting themselves up on their own, of buying an old farm with their savings or of making things for their own needs after they retire. In short, "real life" lies outside your life as a worker, and being a proletarian is but a temporary misfortune to be endured until something better turns up.[95]

Gorz concluded that the "Marxist conception of 'liberation *within* work'" as "the necessary prerequisite for liberation *from* work," had become an "unsustainable utopia."[96] A class-for-itself had become a class-against-itself. "For workers," he claimed, it was "no longer a question of ... putting themselves in control of work, or seizing power within the framework of their work."[97] Rather, the point was now "to free oneself from work by rejecting its nature."[98] Socialism was to become properly postindustrial.

In the 1980s, Gorz's book steadily became a best seller in European left-wing circles.[99] It was quickly translated into English, German, and Dutch. Not surprisingly, Gorz also provided the main point of inspiration for a new Dutch postwork left. In a 1982 electoral pamphlet for his own "Political Party of Radicals" (PPR, or Politieke Partij der Radicalen), for instance, the Dutch politician Bram van Ojik came out as a supporter for a relatively new proposal known as the *basisinkomen*. He opened his pamphlet with the haunting question first posed by Gorz in his *Farewell*: "Will the third industrial revolution ... lead to a new golden age, where we shall work less and have a large mass of riches at our disposal, or will some be condemned to joblessness and others to over-productivity?"[100]

Founded in 1968, van Ojik's PPR had enjoyed relative success in the early years of the decade, drawing some disaffected voters from the mainstream left. Referring to the "little-known"[101] American thinker Robert Theobald, the party's head sought to demonstrate that the situation the Netherlands faced in 1982 was far from unprecedented. In the early 1960s, he claimed, Theobald had already detected a growing "chasm" between "fallow labor power" and a "variety of unmet needs."[102] Since "labor" and "income" were "to a very high degree already uncoupled in the Netherlands," van Ojik proposed a partial basic income without an obligation for job seeking.[103]

When he put forward his proposal in 1982, van Ojik already had a sizable Dutch literature to draw on. In the mid-1970s a fresh version of the *basisinkomen* was making headway in Dutch and European debates, spurred by the oil crisis and the advent of stagflation. This was inspired by American precedents, especially the 1967 Dutch translation of Theobald's work in Antwerp.[104] Milton Friedman's plan officially entered Dutch policy debates in 1970 when fiscal specialist Ferd Grapperhaus contemplated it as a more "socially just" response to labor market rigidity. "It is not unthinkable," Grapperhaus claimed in 1970, "that increasing automation will have the consequence that certain groups in the population ... will be permanently shut out of the labor process."[105]

Grapperhaus's report did not have any direct policy consequences. By the time of van Ojik's publication, however, the Dutch debate had already acquired a different protagonist. This was the Dutch former missionary and company physician Jan-Pieter Kuiper, who had read Theobald's tract in the late 1960s. "In the last couple of decades," he declared in 1977, "many attempts have been made to restructure work [*herijken*] and to give the negotiation between capital and labor [*arbeidsonderhandelingen*] more content."[106] Although he was "obviously sympathetic to these initiatives," he now asked himself "whether we were right to do so."[107] The debate concluded in 1981 with a call by a subsection of the largest union federation—the Voedingsbond FNV, charged with representing food-sector workers—who came out in favor of a provisional basic income. Its main argument was to alleviate budgetary pressures on unemployment. Although most socialists and union members were hostile to the measure, a New Left steadily rallied to its defense.

A representative spokesman for this New Left was the former "provo" writer Roel van Duijn, himself a later member of van Ojik's PPR.[108] As a student in the 1960s he predicted the declining militancy of mainstream socialist organizations, including their integration into the corporatist structures. "The masses," van Duijn claimed as a radical, were those "whom we can't and barely want to convince."[109] Instead of proletarian militancy, a diffuse group of new social actors—students, outcasts, bohemians—could take on a fresh mandate as the "provotariat." Van Duijn proposed replacing existing union structures with a network of self-managed firms that could organize production using cybernetic technology. "The new society," van Duijn claimed in a 1971 pamphlet inspired by American author Richard Brautigan, "has nothing do with the centralized socialism of yore."[110] Rather, it would be "decentralized" and "antiauthoritarian" and would leave all decisions to "people where they find themselves in councils."[111] Inspired by Peter Kropotkin's anarchocommunism, van Duijn fantasized about a society that would "be ungoverned" and "would direct itself" through "self-directing councils," doing away with a "formalistic, bureaucratic officialdom" that occupied the state.[112]

Throughout his career van Duijn also operated as a broker for French antiwork politics. In the 1970s he featured in collections with Guattari, Foucault, Deleuze, and French *autogestionnaires*.[113] Dutch social democrats and communists, in his view, "thought that automation was dangerous."[114] What followed were "atrocious attempts" to "workerize" the student into a "*jeune travailleur intellectuel*."[115] All these tendencies, however, were nothing but "branches on the tree planted by Marx himself," whose central idea was that "humans become humans only through their labor and that the alienation of labor was therefore humanity's greatest evil."[116] In contrast, van Duijn thought the "cybernetic revolution" would "rip labor out of the hands of the worker" and "blow the bottom out of work-based morality," leading to a world where "automatic factories" would "produce everything men needed."[117] As he put it, "Automation will give a new impulse to class struggle. The proletariat will be shaken from its apathy, since automation brings with it increasing unemployment; what the worker used to do is now done by the machine or the computer.[118]

"Increasing automation of industry through computers" was thereby leading to a "new society, with not just an abundance of foodstuffs and other material provisions but also an abundance of *free time*."[119] "When labor has been fully automated," van Duijn concluded, "man is finally able to live his entire existence in freedom" and an unprecedented "collective creativity which will be unleashed."[120] The incoming "cybernetic revolution," he claimed, "will make our work-based system of ethics redundant"—against Marx's "core thought that man becomes himself only through labor."[121]

Van Duijn's proposed alternative was the cybernetic utopia drawn up by the Dutch situationist Constant Nieuwenhuis in 1965 under the name New Babylon. Conceived as a city in which work and physical exertion would become superfluous, New Babylon served as a blueprint for a future in which cybernetics would do away with the need for authoritarian guidance.[122] "Let us suppose," Nieuwenhuis claimed in a presentation of the plan, "that all nonproductive work can be completely automated; that productivity increases until the world no longer knows scarcity; that the land and the means of production are socialized ... in other words, that the Marxist kingdom of freedom is realizable."[123] As with Milton Friedman's concept, the city's cybernetic technologies would "wipe away utilitarianism" and render "valuable" a whole set of activities previously thought unworthy of the label work. "A new set of values," he finished, would now "have to give content to human lives."[124]

In 1985—the year van Duijn made his demands—this clarion call was as divisive as it was rousing. Most Socialist Party members had stuck to a classical workerist line. In a 1982 preconference report, for instance, the Dutch Labor Party pronounced itself in favor of a rekindled full-employment strategy. "Labor," the report claimed, was an "irreplaceable part of human existence" and remained the "prime means for self-development."[125] Rather than giving handouts to the unemployed, the resolution insisted on reskilling and education reform, which would "raise possibilities for recurring learning [*wederkerend leren*]."[126] Politicians such as minister Jaap van der Doef then castigated basic income schemes as starry-eyed, claiming the party "ought not to accept that 500,000 people are placed beyond paid employment," "since work is much more than a means to employment for people."[127]

Van Duijn disagreed violently. Criticizing the "state-centrism" of socialists, he claimed that the state "took away the autonomy and rights" and the "increase in responsibilities of citizens toward the state decreased their mutual obligations and the possibility for reciprocal aid."[128] Beyond the debate about labor and cybernation, a different question had come into focus for the New and mainstream Left: rethinking labor required a deeper rethinking of the state.

Antistatism against Social Rights

The Dutch basic income movement could not have arisen without a powerful antistate current. As Provo radical Duco van Weerlee noted in his 1966 manifesto, the Provo movement's final main aim was to "provoke state authority" as "avant-gardist auto-legislators."[129] After May '68, the French filmmaker Chris Marker also noted that a new "kind of problematic" emerged in the wake of the revolt, "dealing blows in every field of the orthodoxy, right or left."[130] "There was the barrage of the police, which was one order," Marker narrated in his 1977 movie *A Grin without a Cat*, "and the security service of the union, that was another order." "In between" he added, "there was a space to capture."[131] For the '68 generation, this new mode of struggle also meant an escape from the old order. This was what leading figures of the French "Second Left" called the "social statism" of the postwar political setting. The "Second Left" acquired its name from a speech by the French socialist leader (and later prime minister) Michel Rocard at a 1977 congress of the Socialist Party, where he first drew a distinction between these two lefts. One was "long-dominant, Jacobin, centralized, statist, nationalist and protectionist" and the other, the "second left," "decentralized" and "refusing arbitrary domination" in all its forms, "that of the bosses as well as of the state."[132] To Rocard, both the "old left" and the old Gaullist right were part of the problem: a conception of social change always articulated through parties, unions, or collective entities that were to conquer state power.

"What do we gain by replacing an employer's arbiter by a bureaucratic arbiter?" André Gorz similarly asked in the mid-1970s.[133] This centrality of the state in political parties of the left and right was what Pierre Rosanvallon and Patrick Viveret referred to as the dominant "political culture."[134]

Such a culture—either "from the left or the right . . . and for which the central element is the state, considered at the same time as the object of the struggle and the space of social transformation." A shared enemy was now marked out: "the old social-statist political culture."[135] The goal of the Second Left became to "destateify French society."[136]

While Rosanvallon and Viveret took specific aim at the state, most French neoleftists singled out both the "state" and "labor" as part of the same nexus. In anthropologist Pierre Clastres's 1974 *Society against the State*, for instance, the ascription of "labor" to man as a central activity coincided with the violent incursion of the state into primitive societies. "Two axioms," Clastres stated, "seemed to have guided Western civilization from its very dawn." The first posited "that the real society takes place in the protecting shadow of the state; the second postulates a categorical imperative: one must work."[137] Prestate societies, he claimed, saw "no necessity to labor" and "worked on a pure subsistence basis." As Samuel Moyn notes, Clastres regarded such savage idleness as an antidote to the "production of desire" and the "endless work he considered to be characteristic of the modern economy."[138] It was only when the state was founded that it became "possible to speak of labor."[139] Clastres thereby overturned the famous Marxist dictum by which the state was the political outcome of society's economic division into antagonistic classes. Instead, the major and fundamental division in modern societies was the "new vertical relation between the base and the top." "The political relation of power," he stated, "presumes and founds the economic relationship of exploitation. Before being economic, alienation is political; power comes before work."[140] By focusing on economic exploitation, Marxists had downplayed the problem to "found all the others": the state.

In France this hostility opened space for what Pierre Bourdieu called a newly "anti-institutional mood,"[141] with the welfare state increasingly being depicted as an exclusively disciplinary tool. This critique turned social security systems and interventions in social services into "a true exercise in stigmatization for the behaviors and components of their situation, an authentic politics of disciplinarization and normalization."[142] This critique of "social control" attained widespread popularity in the 1970s and 1980s in authors such as Jacques Donzelot,[143] Jeannine Verdès-Leroux,[144] and above all Michel Foucault. In the late 1970s the latter was struck

by the attention that the state pays to individuals; one is struck by all the techniques that have been established and developed so that the individual escapes in no way neither the authority, nor supervision, nor control, nor the wise, nor recovery, nor correction. All major disciplinary machinery: barracks, schools, workshops, and prisons are machines that permit identifying the individual, to know who he or she is, what he does, what we can do, where to place him, how to place him among the others.[145]

To all these institutions, Foucault was careful to add the "mechanisms of assistance and insurance," because "in addition to their goals of economic rationalization and political stabilization," "they make life and existence of everyone, but they also define each person as a separate event that is relevant, that is even necessary and indispensable to the exercise of power in modern societies."[146] Foucault increasingly began to conceive social security as a tool meant to standardize the conduct of individuals. As he remarked in 1983, "Our social security systems impose a particular way of life that subjects individuals, and any person or group who, for one reason or another, does not want or cannot access this lifestyle, to marginalization by the same set of institutions." Instead, leftists had to update, disclose, and examine the "relationship between the operation of social security and different lifestyles."[147] Studies on governmentality would form a starting point for Foucault and some of his followers, such as François Ewald, to problematize the welfare state as "modern forms of power."[148] Behind this protective cover, these institutions obviously intended the perpetuation of power, to observe "day by day," to normalize the behaviors and identities that they shaped and to realize the dream of "biopower."[149] A system organized around unconditional transfers like Milton Friedman's negative income tax could instead subvert both state and society.

Friedman's NIT appeared in French public debates as early as 1973, mediated through Lionel Stoléru's book *Vaincre la pauvreté dans les pays riches* (Overcoming poverty in rich countries). In the early 1970s Stoléru, a high government official, was sent by Valéry Giscard d'Estaing to study guaranteed income schemes at the Brookings Institution in Washington, DC. He quickly decided to transpose Friedman's proposal to France. When Giscard was elected president of France, with him as economic adviser, Stoléru argued that a negative income tax would be a more efficient way to struggle against the problem of poverty amid capitalist plenty. In the same spirit as the American debate, Stoléru argued for tackling poverty instead of equality. For him "the doctrines . . . can incite to retain either a policy aiming at eliminating poverty, or a policy seeking to close the gap between rich and poor."[150] This decision occurred on the "border between absolute poverty and relative poverty."[151] The first simply referred to an arbitrarily determined level (to which the negative tax applied); the second corresponded to general differences between individuals (here referring to social security and the welfare state). While "the market economy is capable of assimilating actions to fight absolute poverty," "it is unable to digest overly strong remedies against relative poverty."[152] The quest for equality of the postwar period, Stoléru argued, only "removed from the competitive economy both the compass that directs it and the spring that pushes it forward, which meant that it is taken into the hands of the state."[153]

Stoléru's idea was not implemented during the Giscard presidency. Foucault himself, however, retained his interest in the proposal, mainly in academic settings. On March 7, 1979, he focused his lecture at the Collège de France on the proposal Friedman had first launched in the early 1940s. In Foucault's eyes, Friedman's and Giscard's proposals presented a stark break with classical models of welfare, which were too firmly centered on a notion of the "laboring subject" as its definitive normative model. The negative tax system, Foucault claimed, implied "the formation of an economic policy that is no longer focused on full employment" and that could "only be integrated in the general market economy by abandoning . . . centrally planned growth." Ultimately however, with the NIT it became "up to people to work if they want or not work if they don't," including "the possibility of not forcing them to work if there is no interest in doing so."[154]

Foucault's interest in the work-state nexus ran much deeper than policy questions. "Precisely because classical economics has not been able to deal with the analysis of labor in its concrete specifications and its qualitative modulations," he noted, "an entire anthropology, an entire politics, of which Marx is precisely the representative," had been "rushed in" for the laboring sections of society.[155] Not surprisingly, Foucault saw Marx and Hegel as the most important exponents of this "ergocentric" vision. "Marx said that 'labor' is the essence of man," he noted in a 1977 interview with a Parisian student, which was "a Hegelian vision."[156] It was only with the neoliberal turn, Foucault thought, that this "anthropologistic" reflex had been tempered.[157]

An even more harmonious marriage between French antiworkerism and antistatism became manifest in the work of André Gorz. In the late years of the decade Gorz went so far as to advocate a front between neoliberals and "neosocialists" against the combined forces of French statism, whether in its socialist, its communist, or its Gaullist incarnation. In a series of articles written for *Le nouvel observateur*, Gorz stated that the left might even benefit from coming to think of workers in terms of "enterprises" rather than heroic "producers." Social transformation itself now had to be conceived through the prism not of the revolution, but of "entrepreneurship."[158] As he said in a text of 1976, "it is clear that Giscard is on the right. But it does not follow from that that the liberalization of society is necessarily a right-wing project and that we should abandon that to the Giscardians."[159] Gorz insisted that "everywhere in Europe there is now, between neoliberals and neosocialists, exchange and partial osmosis."[160] Of course, the core of any exchange between the New Left and the New Right was not so much about increasing corporate power; it was certainly about struggling against a common enemy: the state. As Gorz argued, "If Giscard arrives at disengaging the central power and freeing new spaces where we can exercise collective initiative, why not profit from it?"[161] As Gorz concluded: "Does the left want a society where everyone relies on the state for everything: the pollution of the shore, food additives, architecture, abusive layoffs, work accidents, etc.? In that case we will only replace a private carelessness by an administrative carelessness, an employer's arbiter by a bureaucratic arbiter."[162]

In a 1977 conversation with thinkers such as Pierre Rosanvallon, Ivan Illich, Michel Rocard, and Jacques Delors, Gorz claimed that the "death-knell had sounded for the idea of revolution and for the invocation of the State."[163] From Russian Stakhanovism to the *métro-boulot-dodo* of the French *salariat*, everywhere the call was for more "work, work, work, guaranteed by the state."[164] This entailed a vision of a mature working class educated in self-management, capable of mastering its destiny.

By the mid-1980s, such sentiment was hardly confined to the political margins. In the left-wing mainstream, books such as Paul Kalma's *Alcoholically Preserved Socialism* (Socialisme op sterk water)—a pamphlet written principally for fellow socialists—also imported French Second Left arguments for a critique of an "overstatified" left that was to extend rather than constrain capitalist individualism.[165] Although hesitant about basic income, it did insist on the obsolescence of a welfare system premised on industrial employment, thereby laying a template for Third Way reforms. Yet while Gorz and other *autogestion* writers proved to be a consistent source of inspiration for this Dutch antistate left, the mainstream left also had more difficulty accepting the proposal. In that year the Dutch Socialist Party (PVDA) set up a working group on the topic, with prominent party figures such as Dutch minister Sicco Mansholt claiming that the "introduction of a basic income had become" nothing less than "a necessity."[166] In his view, a "reduction of labor time" was "impossible" without the introduction of a basic income, refusing a trade-off between both proposals.[167] Countering figures such as van der Doef, Mansholt stated that the claim that basic income would lead to idleness was "nonsense."[168] People, he saw, "would always want to perform labor," yet today, "not all available work was compatible according to existing wishes."[169]

Things took another interesting turn at the end of 1985. In the middle of the year, a prominent Dutch think tank put out a report on the institutional inevitability of a basic income. In a statement titled "Warrants for Security" (*Waarborgen voor zekerheid*), the Dutch Scientific Council for Government Advice or "WRR" (Wetenschappelijke Raad voor Regeringsadvies), proposed a partial and low basic income at 30 percent of the social minimum, pegging its proposal at 5,000 guilders per annum or 450 guilders per month.[170] In 1981 the group had already put out their first musings on the subject.[171] In 1985, however, a more strongly neoliberal accent became visible. The report proposed abolishing minimum wage legislation in conjunction with its basic income. As the text concluded, "to ensure a better functioning of the labor market," "an abolition of the legal minimum wage should be given due consideration." This, they claimed, would "stimulate employment" and would finally rid the Dutch welfare state of its "complexity."[172] The report was followed by a second wave of basic grant militancy in the late 1980s in the "Weerwerk" movement.[173] Like the Council, state control of the welfare system was here described as a "coup d'état," in which capitalists had delegated key tasks to a coercive welfare bureaucracy.[174] "If everyone receives 1,500 guilders in the Netherlands," Weerwerk's magazine claimed sardonically, "then all work at the union will cease, and no more arrangements would have to be made to discipline people."[175] The basic income would instead "desecrate labor" and turn the unemployed from "dependent lowlifes" into "respectable citizens."[176]

One thinker swiftly recognized the importance of this burgeoning Dutch debate for his own basic income movement. In a text written in 1988, Belgian philosopher Philippe Van Parijs surveyed recent developments in Dutch social policy. In his view, the Dutch had been trendsetters in the fight for a "vital minimum," visible in their early adoption of the assistance law in 1965 and in later debates about guaranteed income.[177] "There was no need," he claimed, "to adhere to unilinear evolutionism to see that the frustrations, uncertainties, hopes, and conflicts that have given rise to the

Dutch debate might come to prefigure those that are only coming into shape in other countries."[178] "What is at stake in this debate," Van Parijs finished in 1988, "is different [from] and much more than the choice of an 'adjustment strategy' of social security to our current 'crisis.' "[179] Rather, the question was whether the central socioeconomic objective of "progressive forces can and should be radically reformulated": a reformulation, he claimed, that concerned nothing less than the promise "to guarantee liberty to all through the installation of a maximal basic income."[180]

The Van Parijs Synthesis and the Birth of BIEN

In 1982, Van Parijs's idea had already traveled a long way. In December of that year the philosopher had compiled a short note to colleagues in the "Economics and Society" unit at the Université Catholique de Louvain. Scribbled on the back of a pamphlet for the francophone Socialist Party (PS), the philosopher drew a skeletal outline of a proposal he had been toying with for several months. Giving it the name *impôt négatif*,[181] Van Parijs had thought of an idea that could solve the "existing crisis of the welfare state."[182] It would offer a potent alternative to full employment and growth, especially in regard to the conclusions reached by the Club of Rome in 1972.

Van Parijs's *allocation universelle* was the outgrowth of various projects. Born in Brussels in 1951, he had studied philosophy and politics at the new French-speaking University of Louvain-la-Neuve in the 1970s. In the late 1970s he migrated to Oxford on a scholarship, studying under Leszek Kołakowski, meeting G. A. Cohen, and acquainting himself with the work of John Rawls.[183] These English excursions brought him into contact with a variety of "analytical Marxists" such as Cohen, Erik Olin Wright, and John Roemer, who set him off on a study of late twentieth-century class relations.[184] During a 1977 sojourn at Bielefeld University, Van Parijs began work on morality and markets. Based on "a close reading of *Das Kapital*,"[185] he then continued his investigations at Berkeley, only to return to Belgium in 1980. Back home he sought to rethink, as he put it, "radical strategies for fighting unemployment in Western Europe."[186] It was here that he "hit upon a simple idea," only later discovering "it had already been discussed and advocated by others under a variety of labels."[187]

Van Parijs inserted his proposal into a frenzied debate on the future of Belgium's social model. Its roots went back to the mid-1970s, when a growing part of the Belgian elite began to question the efficiency of the welfare state. Pleas were made to replace the existing social security system and public service with social programs focused on a "floor" of income, in keeping with the Christian antipoverty campaigns of the mid-1960s. As the organization ATD Quart Monde (ATD "Fourth World") wondered in 1974, "How is it that, throughout history, the situation is no longer that of the exploitation of one by the other, but that of the ex-clusion [*refoulement*] of the most disadvantaged by the whole surround-ing society?"[188] Belgian employers also proclaimed the need to limit "the principle of solidarity" and not to turn "social security into an instrument for the redistribution of wealth."[189] From the late 1960s onward, such initiatives culminated in a rediscovery of Milton Friedman's negative in-come tax as well. As proponents saw it, the proposal could dispense with bureaucratic welfarism, including the latter's excessively egalitarian am-bitions. In 1969 the *Revue belge de sécurité sociale* had already published a plea for a version of the proposal, claiming that NIT pilots "tended to provide a more effective distribution of aid to those who needed it" than did classical systems of collective provision.[190] One year later, the idea was taken up by researchers at the University of Ghent, who defended Fried-man's idea by which "authorities could co-operate more effectively for the prevention of misery."[191] As with Kuiper's in the Netherlands, many of these calls remained confined to policy circles and party platforms. In the late 1970s, a flourishing basic income movement was absent from the Belgian scene.[192]

The early 1980s slump, however, thrust the proposal back into the lime-light. This time pressure emanated from a left-wing camp, with the fran-cophone Greens (Écolo) in the vanguard. Founded in 1980, the party had immediately begun by setting out a new vision of the Belgian social se-curity system in its 1981 election manifesto "90 Propositions from the Ecologists—Another Way of Doing Politics." In the mission statement, the party presented itself as "oriented in the longer term toward the introduc-tion of a guaranteed social minimum paid to each during the entirety of their existence."[193] Such a minimum, they claimed, was to be decoupled "from any previous labor performed" and would "instantly resolve the prob-lems posed by the current 'nonproductives': retired, children, the handi-capped."[194] "In exchange" for this minimum, the manifesto continued, a set term of "civil service" would "allow citizens to participate in a form of democratic solidarity," retaining a sense of reciprocity against the idea of "something for nothing." In 1984 Agalev, the Flemish counterpart of

Écolo, adopted a replica of the proposal in its party platform, also hoping to break Belgium's "stalemate."[195]

Nearly a year after proposing first drafts to colleagues at the Université Catholique de Louvain, Van Parijs opened his idea to public scrutiny in a text written for his own "Collectif Charles Fourier." Van Parijs and his coauthors began their text with a controversial conjecture. "Why not," they proposed, "get rid of employment insurance, legal pensions, state benefits and aid, study allowances, temporary assignment and third-circuit labor, and state subsidies for ailing industries" and replace the entirety of these benefits with one single stipend known as the "basic income" (*allocation universelle*)?[196] This income, they claimed, should be "transferred monthly, constituting a sufficient sum to cover living expenses for an individual living on his or her own." Additionally, Van Parijs's sum was "to be transferred regardless of whether the person in question was employed or unemployed, rich or poor, whether the person lived alone, with family, in partnership, or in a wider commune and regardless of whether the person had ever worked in the past." Furthermore, states "should not alter the transferred sum except as a function of the person's age or the supposed degree of employability and should finance it with a progressive income tax on the other revenues appertaining to those actors."[197] All this sounded relatively radical for 1984. The most audacious part of the proposal, however, came at the end. The creation of such an income, the contributors claimed, should be coupled with the complete "deregulation of the labor market," "the abolition of all minimum-wage legislation," "laws stipulating the length of the working day," "an elimination of all administrative obstacles for temporary employment," "a reduction in the minimum age of schooling," and, at last, "a cancellation of the maximum retirement age." "Do all of this," the authors finished, "and simply observe what will happen."[198]

Later issues of the *Revue nouvelle* made clear just how controversial the proposal was. Economist Herman Deleeck, for instance, was "congratulatory" about the group's "noble intentions,"[199] yet he thought the proposal was in vain owing to its forbidding price tag. Other respondents were less diplomatic. One writer cast Van Parijs's proposal as "an inferno paved with bad intentions," about to "trash one century of social history and social struggle."[200] Sociologist Pierre Reman thought that the Greens hereby revealed their divergence from the labor movement, which sought "to reduce inequality through the introduction of social constraints."[201] One Marxist correspondent claimed the basic income seemed nothing but "a liberal economist's dream" and a "nightmare for workers."[202] "In the name of an antibureaucratic crusade," he claimed, the Collectif's plan would only "reinforce existing privileges in the salaried class" and leave existing property relations untouched.[203]

Van Parijs considered many of these complaints unwarranted. The attractiveness of the UBI, in his view, lay precisely in its capacity to unsettle notions of "left" and "right." In a 1984 article for *La revue nouvelle*, for instance, Van Parijs went so far as to admit to the proposal's compatibility with a new neoliberal sensibility:

> A coherent libertarian is not only an unconditional adversary of every act of moralistic repression, of every restriction on immigration and of all imperial aggression. He also favors a massive and necessary redistribution of riches, to the detriment of the beneficiaries of the market and standing squarely behind its victims. However, he also vehemently calls for a radical reduction of state activity. How to avoid, then, in such conditions, the result that the beautiful simplicity of the left-right axis is pulverized in front of our eyes?[204]

The proposal could assist a left dedicated to "destatification" while seriously reckoning with an emerging neoliberal bloc.[205] Both the Green movement and BI activists had to converge on "a radical project that could burst open the very left-right axis" and offer a politics that would "escape the customary polarity between a right favorable to a revamped market and a left preferring a stronger state."[206]

Van Parijs's journey to the basic income was also driven by a specific quandary—the "Assar Lindbeck dilemma."[207] In the 1950s and 1960s, professionally trained economists within the Swedish Social Democratic Party were increasingly taken with the centrality of competitive markets as indispensable for economic efficiency (a sensibility that was already visible with grant theorists such as Lerner, Lange, Hutt, and Tinbergen).[208] "Since efficiency required competitive pricing and market change" but "raw outcomes were . . . unacceptable," a solution squaring competition with material security had to be found.[209] Wedded to the insights of the neoclassical revolution in the 1970s, Van Parijs's books were littered with references to Phillips and Laffer curves, stipulating a trade-off between unemployment and inflation and between tax rates and growth.[210] This toolbox allowed him to deconstruct the socialist tradition from within. As a graduate student Van Parijs "read all of Samuelson's textbook" and studied Gérard Debreu's formulation of the general equilibrium theory.[211]

It was clear that one had to move closer to "technical approaches in this area."[212]

Reconciling this with Marxism was no easy task. An equality of resources could not "be defined without making use of some market or marketlike mechanism, which enables people's tastes to be expressed and aggregated."[213] These prices were driven by consumers. In a pluralistic society, these consumers should also have the freedom to buy goods no longer structured around a strict labor contract. This vision pitted Van Parijs against theorists of the "positive freedom" of the first welfare state.[214] Like his mentor G. A. Cohen, Van Parijs thought that socialists were instead better off accepting "negative liberty" as a benchmark: a freedom "from" external constraints, rather than the normative freedom "to."[215] This new socialism did not need to "assert the existence of an analytical link between freedom and civic virtue," mainly because a "free society is arguably rooted in the observation that people profoundly disagree about what counts as virtue or vice."[216]

Analytical Marxism offered some suggestive solutions to Lindbeck's puzzle. After attending several seminars on Samuelson, Kenneth Arrow, and Debreu in 1979, Van Parijs had "the most important meetings for the rest of my life" at Oxford in 1980, at G. A. Cohen's Oxford seminar with Charles Taylor.[217] Cohen's approach here appeared "as an extremely stimulating way of trying to make the critique of capitalism more rigorous," beyond poststructuralist "bullshit."[218] It also implied the application of the general equilibrium approach to Marxism itself—a method pioneered in 1980 by fellow analytical Marxist John Roemer.[219] Instead of assuming a rigidly humanist model of human action, it integrated rational choice models with Marx's focus on capital and labor. This fusion had its casualties, of course. Marx's crisis theory was declared "untenable" owing to inconsistencies in its theory of the tendential fall of the rate of profit. The Marxian theory of exploitation needed a reboot to account for the hoarding of jobs by skilled workers.[220]

At the same time, it implied a rapprochement with the neoclassical tradition espoused by Samuelson, Debreu, and John Hicks in the 1950s and 1960s, which had revolutionized the marginalist vocabulary and left behind Marshall's emphasis on social welfare. Later, theorists such as Arthur Laffer, Phillips, and Friedman also dealt "mortal blows" to the Fordist order, now blocked around the triad of unemployment, inflation, and pollution.[221] "Full employment" seemed like an unnecessarily utopian goal; it had always run counter to Van Parijs's "libertarian instincts."[222]

When Van Parijs encountered Gorz's work in the 1980s, he finally began to find some left-wing support for these anti-Keynesian instincts. Keynes was "dead," Gorz argued, and "in the context of the current crisis and technological revolution it [was] absolutely impossible to restore full employment by quantitative economic growth."[223] Abandoning full employment need not usher in antiquated laissez-faire or a "pure" capitalism." The alternative lay in "a different way of managing the abolition of work ... a society in which time has been freed."[224] As Van Parijs later admitted about Gorz's *Farewell*: "Of all the books I've read in my life, it's perhaps the one that had the biggest impact on me."[225]

Underlying Van Parijs's proposal also was a new understanding of antiwork politics. In a 1984 review for a Flemish Marxist magazine titled "Marx, a Green Fellow?," for instance, Van Parijs declared that Marx himself could be understood as an "antiwork thinker" for his own time, mainly based on the recent discoveries in the *Grundrisse*. "The disalienation of humanity," he claimed, "implied the progressive abolition of labor," "yet not of every activity," which in turn "implied a reduction in work" as the key objective of any New Left.[226] "If he were alive today," he finished, "Karl Marx would undoubtedly have subscribed to these conclusions."[227] Van Parijs repeated a similar line in a 1985 visit to the Dutch Council against the Work Ethic, where he attended several meetings and conversed with participants. In the same year he commented on van Ojik's comments in his *Basisinkomen: Over arbeidsethos, inkomen, en emancipatie* (Basic income: On the work ethic, income, and emancipation), published by the PPR's publishing house in 1985.[228]

In 1986 Van Parijs decided to gather these efforts and organize the first conference of his flagship for the global BI movement. The BIEN (Basic Income European Network) held its founding conference at Louvain-la-Neuve September 4–6. Sessions were chaired by the English academic Peter Ashby and the German sociologist Claus Offe, and the founding committee included figures such as Paul-Marie Boulanger, Hermione Parker, Guy Standing, and Dutch philosopher Robert van der Veen.[229] The ambition was to put the basic income on the public policy map.

The most strident series of comments came from Van Parijs himself. "Participants to this conference," he argued, "no doubt disagreed about many issues."[230] Some of them were liberals—such as Hermione Parker, who had worked with Rhys-Williams's son in the 1970s and hoped that a basic income could create "a more flexible labour market" in which "wage bargaining would concentrate on questions of profitability, competition

FIGURE 4.2. First BIEN conference at Louvain-la-Neuve, April 1986. *Source*: Collectif Charles Fourier, UCL.

and equity."[231] Others, such as sociologist Claus Offe, had a conditional commitment to the labor movement and most likely disagreed with Parker that wage raises were little but "inflationary nonsense."[232] Others saw themselves as part of a rising New Left. The most "genuinely universal controversial issue," however, was the need to get the "purely semantic matters cleared up from the start." Van Parijs's compared his current term with previous ones such as "universal grant," "social dividend," "citizen's wage," and "social income." "The introduction of a basic income," he noted, "constitutes an uncoupling of work and income."[233] This uncoupling could come in a variety of modes. The first stipulated that "the income guarantee is not implemented through guaranteed work," which Van Parijs saw as the doctrine underlying the 1834 reform of the English Poor Law, which decreed the construction of workhouses. This view, he claimed, was rejected "by all basic income proponents," since it implied a degrading view of assistance.[234] The second version *did* stipulate the introduction of a permanent basic income, but with conditional clauses "between an individual making himself available for work (when there is some) and society providing her/him with an otherwise unconditional income." This version was the one proposed by Juliet Rhys-Williams, who insisted her recipients must enter a "work contract." In the third version, mainly associated with thinkers such as Edward Bellamy in the 1880s and the French personalist Jacques Duboin in the 1930s, the granting of a basic income was to be seen in "counterflow to a substantial social service."[235]

The early 1980s had removed some key constraints. When Van Parijs discussed the proposal put forth from the mid-1970s onward—the one forwarded by the Dutch Food Workers' Union in 1981, van Ojik in 1982, the Dutch Scientific Council in 1985, and his own Collectif in 1984—a subtle difference on conditionality became visible. "In most of the contemporary discussion," Van Parijs stated, "'basic income' and related expressions refer to an income that is completely uncoupled from work in all three senses"—be it through a provision of guaranteed work, the signing of a social contract, or the performance of a social service.[236] As with Friedman's negative income tax, neither "current performance of work," "willingness to work," nor "past performance to work," as Van Parijs noted, qualified for inclusion in its clauses.[237] In contrast to Bellamy's idea that nonwork would be an act of secession, Van Parijs now chose to fully decouple payment from work. This was tied to a new but duly thinned out notion of republican freedom as independence, assured by the patrimonial right that every citizen would have to a society's assets.

This absolutism could also deter allies, however. In 1984 the philosopher began a long dialogue with André Gorz.[238] Van Parijs had first encountered Gorz's work in the opening years of the decade, when Gorz was still in the skeptics' camp on UBI. In turn, he had been quick to criticize the proposals for work reduction that Gorz put forward. Although he was sympathetic to the notion of "autonomy," he thought the French thinker underestimated the extent of state control these reduction programs brought with them. Arbitrary work quotas would not break the "oppressive" and "humiliating practices" of the current welfare regime.[239] In an exchange recorded in the Brussels journal *Virages*, Gorz countered this claim, stating that quotas need not be achieved "with heavy bureaucratic-totalitarian control."[240] In his *Les chemins du paradis* (1983), for instance, Gorz repeatedly objected that unconditional basic income would render work "optional" and "absolve society from concerning itself with the equitable distribution of necessary work."[241]

In 1985 the Collectif put forward its own defense of the *allocation universelle* in a piece with the same title. Gorz retaliated with a 1985 response titled *Allocation universelle: Version de droite et version de gauche* ("Two versions of the basic income—right and left").[242] In his right of reply, Gorz now drew a careful line between two versions of the basic income. The first sought to multiply "temporary and precarious labor" and to throw minor reserves at workers completely "subservient to their employers."[243] The second, more consciously "left-wing," would "correspond to an acceptable standard of living."[244] While backing off from this previous dismissive stance, however, he also worried that an integral decoupling of "labor" and "income" would widen the "break in society" between overworked professionals and surplus workers.[245] Although Gorz did think that Keynesian remedies were past their expiration date—evidenced by his skepticism on François Mitterrand's "Keynesianism in one country"—he worried that cash transfers would simply widen the "social fracture" he first detected in the 1970s.[246]

Time soon caught up with Gorz's skepticism, however. With escalating deindustrialization in the 1980s, the UBI began to find more durable support on France's left. Proponents of the proposal went from economists such as Yoland Bresson (who advocated an "existence income"—*revenu d'existence*—in his 1984 book *L'après-salariat*) and Nanterre anthropologist Alain Caillé.[247] Félix Guattari continued to support the proposal in the late 1980s, casting it as an antidote "against poverty in all its forms" and "for the defense and enlargement of alternative rights against the mechanisms of corporatist division."[248] In 1988 Gorz again made incremental room for a "left-wing" UBI in his *Métamorphoses du travail*, contrasting neoliberal and "left-libertarian" versions.[249] In this latter version, the BI still had to be coupled with a "substantive social service," coupled with a "radical critique" of society's frenzied search for work.[250] Gorz now thought that the performance of a socially necessary form of labor would provide compensation for an unconditional grant.

Only in 1996 did Gorz undertake his final, unconditional conversion to basic income. After founding the AECEP (European platform for citizenship and plural economies) with Alain Caillé and Toni Negri, he rallied to a full-throated defense of the unconditionality implicit in the proposal. Claus Offe's work on of "full employment" also seemed to open up new spaces for such an unconditional basic income.[251] More important, Gorz's reading of Italian postautonomist tradition became a key motive for his shift: the "crisis of measurability" inherent to post-Fordism meant that labor itself had become impossible to standardize and nearly all activities could now conceivably count as "work."[252] Since it was no longer possible to satisfyingly measure labor, a permanent grant would provide the only natural response to the subversion of the wage. This conclusion came

three years after Gorz had pronounced socialism "dead as a system," including its "philosophy of work and history."[253] If the left "stood for the
emancipation of the workers," he claimed, this would now simply turn
them into the spokespersons for the minority "who still define themselves
chiefly by their work."[254] Gorz's reconversion was followed by a membership card in Van Parijs's BIEN. "We welcomed him," Van Parijs would
later remember, "as one would a prodigal son."[255]

*   *   *

Gorz's change of heart indicated just how far Europe's basic income movement had traveled since the late 1960s. It had moved its flagship policy
from an exotic export product into a proposal for a postindustrial left.
This left was meant to disorder the Fordist consensus undergirding the
previous welfare state and undo its increasingly unrealistic promises of
full employment. Underlying this shift was a double conceptual revolution in European left-wing thinking—the entry of postwork politics and a
new antistatism. This revolution reoriented debates on social policy from
"inequality" to "poverty" and reclaimed civil society as an arena of liberty
beyond the state, driven by "the quest for . . . an alternative to both the
neo-liberal and the paleosocialist" visions of emancipation, as Van Parijs
put it.[256]

This dual revolution also had its critics, of course. As French philosopher Pierre Rosanvallon noted in his 1995 *La nouvelle question sociale*,
the basic income owed part of its popularity to a tacit pact crafted between neoliberals and neoleftists in the 1980s. To the French philosopher,
it represented "the pernicious and paradoxical aspect of the end of the
classical conception of the welfare state" and a "symptom of the increasing separation between economic activity and solidarity, and of a surprising convergence between libertarian and utopian-socialist viewpoints."[257]
By "dissociating the economic from the social" and their striving for a
"'postlabor' society," basic income schemes easily allowed "the issue of
employment to be pushed into the background."[258] Rather than opening
space for new subjects to flourish, the proposal would narrow the field of
battle. With the new version of Tinbergen and Friedman's proposal put
forward by the Council, van Duijn, Gorz, and Van Parijs started a retreat
from the "producer subject" so prevalent in the postwar labor movement,
transcending citizens' "work function." In doing so they offered a capacity for living outside the normative worlds built by the work ethic, while

also shying away from the overly "biopolitical" state and other authoritarian modes of politicizing needs. In 1993 an affiliate of the Flemish Green Party similarly described it as a "postutopian" utopia:

> The proposed model [basic income] is a middle way between two utopias. It leaves the market intact but deals with the consequences of market failure. At the same time, it limits state intervention to the creation of a framework wherein those who have become the victim of those failures receive a veritable and humane—but not utopian or ideal—solution for this failure.[259]

Certain critics found precisely this acquiescence alarming. Four years later, when the basic income movement was globalizing itself, English critic James Heartfield castigated the movement for its acceptance of the current "retreat from the sphere of production."[260] The "non-class of non-workers" that Gorz had seen as the new subject, he claimed, simply accepted the "stagnation of the productive sphere." The realm of "material production" was now "seen as a hangover from the past."[261] After neoliberals successfully redefined work as "disutility," Heartfield saw that the "conflictual character of the contest over needs that so heavily marked the first seventy years of the century" became "submerged in a civil peace where basic needs are no longer a matter of public debate."[262] The proposal locked in defeat. In "identifying a minimum," the basic income would not necessarily have the effect of forcing incomes upward.[263] Instead, it might simply induce "a downward pressure on pay-claims" and casualize the remaining Fordist jobs.[264] Similarly, George Caffentzis claimed that much basic income campaigning fell prey to "a failed politics because it trie[d] to convince both friend and foe that, behind everyone's back, capitalism [had] ended."[265] The new "precariat" looked frighteningly similar to the proletariat of yore, which had spent a century building up labor rights that were now being withdrawn across the developed and developing world.

With its plans for "activation" and private full employment, Third Way politicians barely paid tribute to the earlier grant wave. New Leftists and centrists also found little common ground on the necessity of disinflation and central bank independence. In the 1990s, discussions on basic income became "increasingly philosophical in nature," and the proposal had seemingly "fallen off the mainstream policy agenda."[266] In their focus on tax credits and individualistic welfare solutions, however, the spirit of the previous European BI wave still seemed omnipresent in the 1990s. Tony Blair, Gerhard Schröder, Frank Vandenbroucke, and Wim Kok's market-friendly variant of social democracy hoped to expand private initiative across society. As the 1990s dragged on, cash grants increasingly seemed to fill this hole in the leftist imagination, both north and south. A new welfare world began to converge on a "floor without a ceiling," in which citizens would receive adequate provision but capital accumulation could continue unabated.[267]

On a global scale, similar trends were afoot in antipoverty campaigning at the World Bank and the United Nations, which pushed developing nations to let go of their import-substitution strategies and adopt a narrower focus on alleviating poverty. Michael Harrington's "other America" was now becoming the "other planet," a "vast majority" of nonindustrial nations reminiscent of American decline. Basic income supporters might have lost a battle, but they were winning the war. By the end of the 1990s, European activists were proclaiming "the death of the century of laboring man" in the Third World and First World alike; in 2004, Van Parijs's BIEN felt comfortable changing its name from the Basic Income European Network to Basic Income Earth Network.[268] Yet as critics such as Heartfield and Caffentzis pointed out, few things would prove more dispiriting than "work" disguised as "leisure."

Ironically, the Dutch Council against the Work Ethic became the best example of this paradox. Founded in 1982, the group almost disbanded after no more than two years of public service. The reasons participants gave for the group's near dissolution were ungainly. The Council, one former observant claimed, simply found the whole endeavor "way too much toil."[269] Or as the Dutch philosopher Hans Achterhuis reported as an early contributor: "The campaigners were more firmly gripped by the work ethic than their constituency. Their working weeks occasionally exceeded the double of a regular working week, and their work discipline was exemplary. . . . It was for a worthy cause, they claimed, and it allowed one to be one's own boss."[270]

In their attempt to abolish "labor," the postworkerists had nearly worked themselves to death.

CHAPTER FIVE

Rethinking Global Development at the End of History

The poor nations cannot overcome their poverty without industrialization. — Julius Nyerere, "The Plea of the Poor"

The century of the labouring man is coming to an end. —Guy Standing, "From Labour to Work"

In the closing months of 1994, British development economist Guy Standing arrived in South Africa. As head of labor market research at the International Labour Organization (ILO), the longtime basic income advocate had kept in touch with the members of the African National Congress (ANC) exiled in London and Geneva in the early 1990s, particularly with its Macroeconomic Research Group (MERG), which had been working on a transition program for a post-apartheid South Africa. When the newly elected ANC government was finally sworn in in May 1994, Standing was commissioned to conduct a "comprehensive assessment of the labor market" and advance a set of reforms necessary to "the country's reintegration in the global economy."[1] After the collapse of the apartheid regime and Nelson Mandela's inauguration as president, expectations about the country's endemic inequality and poverty were astronomical. After a decades-long lag, universal welfarism had to come for all South Africans.

Standing arrived in the newly biracial democracy with decades of research experience on one topic: labor market reform. He was particularly renowned within the ANC leadership for his heterodox views on development and structural adjustment policies. Trained at Cambridge in the mid-1970s under James Meade and Joan Robinson, he dedicated his PhD dissertation to questions of labor supply. After his doctoral work he quickly transitioned to working as an economist in the ILO's Employment and Development Department. Early in his career he found himself relegated to the institution's margins, working on short-term contracts and seen as dangerous by the organization's leaders because of his critical views on modernization theory and what he saw as the rigid "laborism" dominating the ILO. Working specifically on labor force participation in the Global South, he began thinking out an alternative to what he saw as the "jobs-oriented" strategy widespread in development economics at the time. By the mid-1980s he had become convinced that "labour markets were going to become much more flexible, much more insecure," and it now seemed obvious that it was pointless to pursue classical full employment policies. Instead of public works through state-led investment, a calibration of the cash transfer apparatus had become all but unavoidable.

In 1994, Standing already found an eager audience for these heterodox views: Tito Mboweni, minister of labor under Mandela, asked him to head a commission on labor market reform. Although the leadership of the party was divided on the road to economic reconstruction, most members had already significantly departed from the state- and labor-centered vision of the 1955 ANC Freedom Charter. This document still looked for alternatives to the conservative economic policy that had guided the segregationist National Party. Adopted in 1955 in Soweto, the charter established the core principles and ideals that guided the struggle against the racist regime. Inspired partly by socialist ideals, it marked a watershed in the history of the ANC. Turning away from a strict civil rights perspective, the charter called for a far-reaching reorganization of the economic basis of the South African society from land reform to nationalizing the "wealth of our country" held by banks and monopoly industry: "all other industry and trade shall be controlled to assist the well-being of the people."[2] The charter—censored after the ANC was banned in 1956—also included demands for free education, free health care for all, and a large expansion of public services such as transportation, nursery schools, social centers, and housing. Finally, following its strong workerist bent, the charter argued that "the state shall recognise the right and duty of all to work," a "forty-hour working week, a national minimum wage," and for all citizens to be free to form trade unions.

In the decades that followed, economists within the ANC generally emphasized the state-led character of the project. As the antiapartheid and exiled economist Vella Pillay would argue in the late 1980s, an antipoverty policy required the state to determine the "overall direction of accumulation."[3] Mandela's 1994 election platform, the Reconstruction and Development Programme (RDP), was itself notably conceived in the tradition of the Freedom Charter.[4] The charter's rationale, as Stephanie Brockerhoff has noted, "did not rely on expanding cash transfers as a redistributive mechanism per se, but on restructuring the state and bringing people into jobs."[5] Rather than universal grants, a capacious composite of land reform, public works, and dirigiste state building for housing equipped with electricity and water, as well as health care and a reshaped industrial base, would lead the country out of an apartheid economy premised on racial inequity.

Part of the originality of Standing's reform program for the Presidential Labour Market Commission lay precisely in its departure from these "laborist" assumptions. While broadly supportive of most RDP content, Standing recognized from the outset "the limited capacity to implement an interventionist approach, whether through labour market training, employment services, public works or subsidized job creation efforts."[6] Instead, he focused his recommendations on providing an income allowance as such. Taking into account the decline of wage labor as a redistributive mechanism, the report also pleaded for a vast increase in cash transfers "that reach people with minimal transaction costs." Such policies, Standing added, had the advantage of allowing "low-income or unemployed individuals and low-income communities to make their own labour market decisions."[7] Rather than a steering state creating jobs to respond to socially defined needs, it should give people money so they could sustain themselves as they saw fit. His vision implied a radical expansion of the transfer state and a departure from a policy too narrowly focused on assessing needs from the bottom up and coercing people into jobs they might have not chosen for themselves. As anthropologist James Ferguson would later record, this line of thinking implied a clear distrust for planners' knowledge of the "nature of poor people's problems."[8] To policy entrepreneurs like Standing, cash transfers instead became "a way of enabling low-income people to access goods, and participate in livelihood strategies, in ways that are more responsive to their actual circumstances."[9] And while Standing kept mentions of basic income out of the official report, he would nonetheless find more informal routes to disseminate the idea in papers, op-eds, and policy seminars.

The post-apartheid climate also appeared ever more receptive to Standing's policy revolution. When he presented his report to the government in Cape Town in May 1996, Frederik de Klerk and the National Party had already withdrawn from the national government. This left the ANC alone in power. As the first person to address the full cabinet when it graduated into an ANC government, Standing recommended setting up an extensive universal cash grant scheme in the country. He would also present the study to Mandela himself at his home. While cautioning him that he should read the whole five-hundred–page document only if he "suffered from insomnia," he tried to persuade the iconic leader to "consider introducing a basic income."[10] In the following months, however, the government would adopt a far more conventional macroeconomic approach. While Standing continued to work as a policy consultant to minister of labor Titho Mboweni until 1997, his vision of an expanded transfer state initially failed to gain traction among the post-apartheid policy elite. In fact, the very same day that he presented his views to Mandela, another report, commissioned by the minister of finance, Trevor Manuel, and shaped by the more orthodox views of the World Bank and the International Monetary Fund, was already in front of the government. What would become the "business friendly"[11] GEAR (Growth, Employment, and Redistribution) strategy turned the economic policy more explicitly toward international competitiveness.[12] Concerned chiefly with rising inflation, the public deficit, and lagging productivity, Manuel, alongside Thabo Mbeki, chose orthodoxy. Half-jokingly, Mbeki—trained as an economist in England and later president of South Africa—urged critics to "just call [him] a Thatcherite."[13]

To followers of the South African scene, however, the ANC's shift hardly came as a surprise. Indeed, as it edged closer to power, the party leadership, as Grace Davie has argued, had slowly backed down from "the idea of dramatic state-led economic restructuring."[14] Nominally cited in the RDP, Mandela himself would abandon ideas of nationalization and of a strong macroeconomic policy as he gained his freedom. As Davie noted, when Mandela left Robben Island the Berlin Wall had fallen, the South African Treasury was depleted, and the word globalization was "on everyone's lips."[15] After a series of trips to the World Economic Forum consulting foreign leaders, Mandela steadily grew more cautious to accommodate the business elites. Striding toward the presidency, he began to embrace capitalism in "a 'commonsensical' manner."[16]

"The success of your entrepreneurs" Mandela told members of the US Congress shortly after his election, "and with it the capacity of your society to give work to your citizens, rests on the fact of the elevation of every person, anywhere in the world, to the position of a free actor in the marketplace."[17] The "imperative" of the marketplace, he added, would perhaps produce the "magical elixir" required to bring development to South Africa. Addressing an audience of foreign and domestic investors, he went so far as to declare that they should not be afraid, because the economic program of the government had been cleansed of "anything that will connect us with any Marxist ideology."[18] While the collapse of the Soviet Union had clearly birthed a triumphant free-market creed, the ANC proved more than willing to shape a market-friendly democratic transition, almost relying on newly postideological tropes. South Africa, Mandela explained, was "neither socialist nor capitalist, but was driven rather by the desire to uplift its people."[19] "Like the rest of the leadership of the ANC," novelist J. M. Coetzee would later write about the antiapartheid legend he was "blindsided by the collapse of socialism worldwide." Although Mandela's failure was "understandable if unfortunate," it was clear that his party "had no philosophical resistance to put up against a new, predatory economic rationalism."[20] As early as 1994, South African journalist Hein Marais prophesied the grim conclusion that "the left had lost the macroeconomic battle."[21]

GEAR would also mark the definitive turn toward economic orthodoxy within ANC circles. A new strategy, focused on privately led growth emphasizing trade liberalization, privatization of public enterprises, fiscal discipline, and deregulation would attract international capital. Exchange controls were slowly reduced, tariffs were lowered to increase international competitive pressure, and public spending was curtailed in programs such as the State Maintenance Grant. Focused on child poverty, the program itself was replaced with a less generous system because the government feared the fiscal implications of the deracializing of the apartheid welfare apparatus.[22] A strategy of "growth through redistribution" was replaced by a more orthodox "redistribution through growth." GEAR, as Stephanie Brockerhoff has noted, "no longer placed the emphasis on government changing things for the better, but on market forces solving the existing problems."[23] Far from Standing's recommendations, cash grants were not seen as developmental but were depicted as handouts favoring dependency rather than self-reliance. After a brief commitment to reconciliation and reconstruction, the ANC abandoned all its former commitments to a profound transformation of the economic order and opted for what Patrick Bond baptized "homegrown structural adjustment."[24]

With the political weather changing, Standing's ideas regained their plausibility. Since the moment he set foot in South Africa in 1994, he had actively promoted a basic income outside government circles through talks at universities, discussions with Zwelinzima Vavi, general secretary of the Congress of South African Trade Unions (COSATU), the main South African union, and public conferences to slowly assemble a broader coalition supporting the idea. Afterward, basic income would slowly emerge within civil society as an attractive alternative to the government's conservative economic agenda. In 1998 a Basic Income Grant coalition (BIG) was formed, demanding comprehensive reform of the social security system, including a basic income of 100 rands a month.[25] The disappointing results of the GEAR strategy in following years would further boost the legitimacy of cash transfers. Indeed, although reducing inequality and poverty had been an official aim of the ANC, between 1995 and 1999 most indicators deteriorated. Poverty and inequality grew, unemployment increased, and the expected growth of 6 percent never materialized.[26]

By 2000 a commission formed by the Ministry of Social Development itself, with the aim of imagining a comprehensive reform of the social security system, would endorse the key tenets of Standing's agenda. Cash transfers had slowly emerged as a useful complement to the government strategy for tackling poverty. The report, published in 2002 and led by Professor Vivienne Taylor, special adviser to the minister for social development, criticized the "relevance of welfare systems from the Global North," focused on "economies based around full, formal employment."[27] Instead, she sought to envision a social policy adapted to a highly informal and dualized labor market, less marked by industrialization and processes of Beveridgite formalization. As old work- and state-centered developmental strategies seemed out of reach for good, the prospect of expanding the safety net beyond the working population began to gain ground. The idea was that a guaranteed income could "encourage risk-taking and self-reliance" and serve as a "springboard for development."[28] Arguments in favor of the proposal took on an increasingly postcolonial aura. As Ferguson pointed out, it meant that rather than associating development with formal wage labor, it could work by boosting the "entrepreneurialism" dormant in the informal sector.[29] What would be referred to as the Taylor committee report galvanized proponents of basic income and made South Africa one of the first countries in the Global South where the proposal was given serious consideration. While members of the government would remain reluctant to consider the idea and the report itself stated that "the conditions for an immediate implementation" were not present, they nonetheless favored an expansion of the cash-transfer apparatus and defended the developmental character of the policy plank.[30] Although the BIG campaign failed to pass its basic income as policy, it effectively succeeded in radically expanding the cash transfer nexus across the South African economy.[31] In following years South Africa would become one of the most striking examples of cash transfers as ersatz development policy in the Global South. This shift would encourage Thabo Mbeki to be more open about the advantages of a transfer approach. More important, it also allowed the ANC to comply with the recommendations of the International Monetary Fund or the World Bank while still expanding social spending. Indeed, despite the quite orthodox macroeconomic policy that was applied, transfers in the form of child support, pensions, or disability grants would grow substantially by the early 2000s. The deracializing of the old system begun in 1994, compounded by later amendments to the age and income thresholds, procedures for assessing disability grants, and expansion of child benefits, would lead to a massive increase in the number of beneficiaries at the same time as public-owned companies were privatized and market-based provision of health insurance grew.[32] Whereas during the 1994 election about 2.4 million people received cash grants, by 2014 this figure had already risen to more than 61 million, covering more than half of South African households.[33] Rather than expanding channels for formal wage labor, South Africa was firing up its cash transfer apparatus. "For while we talk about creating jobs," a well-known South African analyst wrote after the election, "we have been doing something else—we have been handing out grants."[34] Following on the liberalizing of the economy, the creation of this "enormous system of non-contributory social benefits" turned into a "key domain of policy innovation."[35] A neoliberal program of "selective privatization and marketization," James Ferguson added, was "combined with a far-reaching expansion of programs of direct distribution . . . increasingly decoupled from issues of labour and labour supply."[36]

As with Van Parijs, Gorz, and van Ojik in the 1980s, there was victory in defeat for Standing's post-apartheid plan. In the ensuing decade, the further erosion of formal patterns of wage labor and of any attempt to decasualize labor relations provided ample fuel for debates about basic income in southern Africa. As Standing himself would write, "economic informalization is growing, not shrinking" and "the standard way of looking at the labour force in terms of a simple division into employed, unemployed and economically inactive is an inappropriate basis on which to build a social protection system."[37] His shift would become an exam-

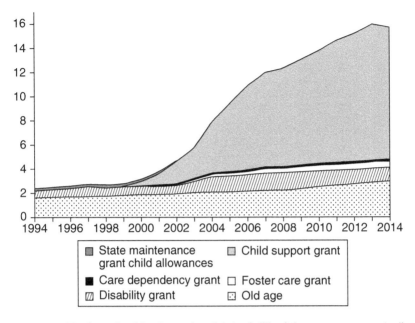

FIGURE 5.1. Numbers of social assistance beneficiaries (millions), by program, 1994 to April 2014. *Source*: Jeremy Seekings and Nicoli Nattrass, *Policy, Politics and Poverty in South Africa* (London: Palgrave Macmillan, 2015), 138.

ple for many countries in southern Africa and lead to a fast and popular growth of conditional cash transfers (CCTs) in the form of family allowances, pensions, disability payments, or child-care grants. The rapid expansion of those transfers shaped what Ferguson called a new politics of distribution.[38] While CCTs were still a substantive distance removed from a universal basic income, the positive emphasis they put on cash opened the way for new experiments and debates about unconditional cash transfers (UCTs), generating new ways of thinking about basic income itself.

As Guy Standing pointed out, "the growing interest in conditional cash transfers" in southern Africa naturally led to a further questioning of "the flaws of all forms of targeting, selectivity and conditionality, as well as their unnecessary costs."[39] Against previous pessimism, Standing now began to recognize the gathering momentum for his proposal. By the mid-2000s, new large-scale experiments would be financed by nongovernmental organizations in countries like Namibia, Kenya, and Uganda,

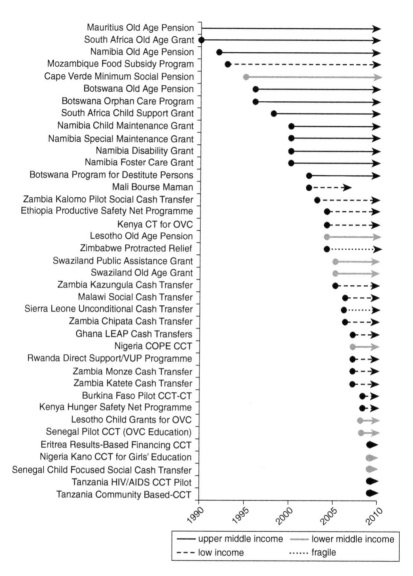

FIGURE 5.2. Start dates and durations of sub-Saharan African cash transfer programs, 1990–2010. *Source*: Marito Garcia and Charity M. T. Moore, *The Cash Dividend: The Rise of Cash Transfer Programs in Sub-Saharan Africa* (Washington, DC: World Bank, 2012), 47.

and major cash transfer programs implemented in countries like Lesotho, Mozambique, Ethiopia, and Malawi were strongly promoted by the African Union. By 2012, more than 123 transfers programs were in place all over southern Africa, slowly displacing the centrality that emergency food aid had taken on the continent during the 1990s.[40] International public opinion seemed to follow suit, as the top-down humanitarianism of the decade was slowly giving way to a more participatory market ethic by which Africans would decide their own world-historical fate through cash allowances.

In Namibia, Standing himself had established a conference in Windhoek with the Lutheran Church, bishops, and several NGOs to launch a UBI campaign in the country as early as 1996, trying to convince the government of the developmental properties of the proposal.[41] What would soon become the Basic Income Grant coalition[42] would succeed in making the government seriously consider the proposal, and in 2002 it was put into practice. In 2007, in the small villages of Otjivero and Omitara, a pilot partially supervised by Standing himself was finally launched.[43] For over two years, 930 residents under age sixty received a monthly grant of about twelve dollars with no strings attached, increasing the popularity of cash over food aid. And though Namibia had already implemented a fairly well developed grant system and never moved forward with a full basic income, the UBI would increase its child grant system ten times over by the late 2000s.[44] Behind the backs of the developmental elite, basic income had turned into the border of a new welfare world.

The impressively rapid rise of cash transfers on the global stage and among international institutions such as the United Nations, the International Monetary Fund, the International Labour Organization, and the World Bank[45] never followed a straight line. Its triumph in the field of development economics was part of a broader history of the way the Global South envisioned welfare and development. It was only through the gradual displacement of the conceptions of development focused on state-led industrialization and postwar full employment that the idea of a "transfer state" became more appealing. Indeed, as noted by the development economist Ha-Joon Chang, before the turn of the 1970s "there was a general consensus that development is largely about the transformation of the productive structure," mainly to "be achieved through industrialization."[46] With the demise of that view, shared by both advocates of modernization theory like Walt Rostow and more radical thinkers like Raúl Prebisch, poverty alleviation per se would acquire a newfound centrality in many development strategies. In a Global South that seemed increasingly unable or unwilling to decasualize labor, to direct investment, or to socialize resources, the development of a new cash nexus provided a market-friendly alternative to older postwar conceptions of welfare. It also formed the ultimate backdrop for the rise of basic income as a conceivable policy option in the former developing world. The rise of the transfer state in southern Africa is thus part of this wider story affecting countries like India, Mexico, and Brazil that underwent their own cash transfer revolution during the 2000s. In place of industrial policy and economic independence from northern metropoles, development was narrowly redefined as a commitment to supplying basic needs to everyone, within market exchanges. In a world where, as Guy Standing argued, the "century of the labouring man" was "coming to an end,"[47] development had to be reinvented outside the state-centered framework set up by postcolonial thinkers, Marxists, and modernization theorists alike. Here was a "radical and southern-driven change," challenging "the dominant view in the North that economic growth must come first."[48] Along the way, however, the very definition of development underwent an indelible change.

Industrialization as Development

The contours of the South's cash transfer revolution appear most clearly when contrasted with the preceding developmentalist period. Until the mid-1970s at the latest, most catch-up theories, from dependency to modernization theory, granted scant importance to poverty reduction *as such*. Development then, as Martha Finnemore argued, "was not poverty alleviation," "nor was it understood as poverty alleviation by those who were undertaking it."[49] Rather, growth and state-led industrialization were seen as the most efficient way to free the newly independent countries from want. The state was now responsible for "price and import controls," "the allocation of investments and much production, via parastatal companies formed by nationalizing colonial-owned enterprises."[50]

Industrialization stood as an economic sine qua non for this reordering. "The poor nations cannot overcome their poverty," Tanzanian president Julius Nyerere claimed in front of an American audience at Howard University in 1977, "without industrialization."[51] Nyerere's position was far from heterodox within postcolonial elites. For most, as historian Frederick Cooper has noted, state power was a crucial tool to enhance productivity, modernize, and industrialize what were seen as backward agricultural economies. Development had then to be rational and state-centered.[52] Questions of poverty were always embedded within broader macroeconomic and institutional issues related to the global division of labor. With the fall of the old empires, postcolonial states were driven toward theories of planned industrialization to get out of stagnation and poverty. In the South, as Gunnar Myrdal would recall in 1968, planning was truly "the intellectual matrix . . . of the modernization theory."[53] In fact, postcolonial economics, as Samuel Moyn noted, "were almost always presented as an alternative to capitalism."[54] Inspired by socialist ideals, decolonization leaders such as Julius Nyerere, Kwame Nkrumah of Ghana, and perhaps most significant, Jawaharlal Nehru of India, openly conceived their development strategy as an alternative to free market liberalism and imperialism alike. In 1902, J. A. Hobson's hugely influential *Imperialism* had argued that colonialism had an essentially economic base. In capitalism, he famously argued, "excessive powers of production"[55] resulting from wage restraint within industrial metropoles pushed governments to annex less developed countries in order to sell and invest the surplus commodities and capital. Famously taken up and criticized by Lenin, Hobson's theory would largely shape the view that development was not simply about poverty alleviation but more generally about political and economic independence. In *The Discovery of India*, the book Nehru wrote while he was imprisoned at Ahmednagar Fort from 1942 to 1945, he clearly framed the question of development within the broader problem of imperialism. "An industrially backward country," the future prime minister of India wrote, "will continually upset the world equilibrium and encourage the aggressive tendencies of more developed countries. Even if it retains its political independence, this will be nominal only, and economic control will tend to pass to others."[56] In the same spirit, Prasanta Chandra Mahalanobis, one of the main architects of the Indian development strategy in the 1950s and a pioneer of statistics in India, argued that "international rivalries and tensions arise from the desire to establish spheres of influence over under-developed areas." "The very existence of under-developed regions," he added, is "a continuing threat to world security and world peace."[57] For these postcolonial elites, poverty alleviation was only a small fragment within the mosaic of industrial development.

These views were strengthened by the early 1950s with the success of the "big push" model laid out in 1943 by one of the pioneers of development economics, Polish economist Paul Rosenstein-Rodan,[58] and the import-substitution industrialization (ISI) model, both justifying strong state involvement. The "big push" model was at the core of postwar modernization theories and assumed that, for mostly agrarian economies, only large-scale coordinated investment programs on heavy industries could lead to an economic takeoff.[59] Launched in isolation, investments in industrialization would be unprofitable and would need be done in different industries at the same time. The import substitution industrialization model came from a more radical strand of development economics originally developed separately in the 1940s by the Keynesian economists Raúl Prebisch and Hans Singer.

This Singer–Prebisch thesis would form the starting point of the dependency theory school of thought and call for an active industrial policy designed to replace dependence on northern metropoles with national industrialized products. Born in Argentina in a modest family of German descent, Prebisch had undergone a stellar rise among the country's elite and would become the most popular proponent of industrialization in the Global South. A self-described technocrat and economically orthodox in his youth, he had turned to heterodox views after the Great Depression of 1929 hit Argentina hard and as undersecretary of finance his own policies of austerity and wage moderation failed. He slowly began to adopt a more Keynesian perspective and, perhaps more important, started to question the classical views on the benefits of international trade, famously coining the terms "center/periphery" to analyze the unequal dynamics of the world economy.[60] Like Singer, who had been a student of Keynes's, Prebisch felt that the Cambridge economist had not pushed his model far enough and had misunderstood the specific challenges faced by countries outside the center. Keynes, he thought, had "ignored [the] role of structural social and power relations, and their negative effect on peripheral states."[61]

The publication that would truly propel ISI onto the global stage, however, was a paper Prebisch presented in Havana in May 1949 after the UN Economic Commission for Latin America (CEPAL) asked him to write an introduction to its *Economic Survey of Latin America*. His presentation, composed with passion in less than a week and later published as *The Economic Development of Latin America and Its Principal Problems*, electrified an audience immediately "caught up in an unexpected and mesmerizing collective experience."[62] It was as if Prebisch had given an elegant form to an intuition already shared by many policy makers on the periphery. In his fifty-nine-page analysis he offered a powerful study of the effects of price disparities between primary goods exported by the peripheral countries and manufactured ones imported from the center.

In his seminal report Prebisch rejected the view, largely inspired by Smith's ideas, of the comparative advantages of a global division of labor. "The enormous benefits that derive from increased productivity," he observed, "have not reached the periphery in a measure comparable to that obtained by the peoples of the great industrial countries."[63] The "obvious disequilibrium" and deterioration of the terms of trade that sustained or even widened the gap between the core and the periphery, Prebisch wrote, destroyed "the basic premise underlying the schema of the international division of labor."[64] A careful study of prices and the terms of exchange during the late nineteenth and early twentieth centuries demonstrated that prices did not fall and that decreases in costs due to technical progress in the core were absorbed in the form of an increase of the income of entrepreneurs and productive factors. Gains in the center were mostly transformed into higher wages for a unionized industrial workforce, while unorganized and casual workers in the periphery could not push for such increases. Any decline in income in the center would immediately be translated into a decrease of the prices of primary goods through a depreciation of wages at the periphery. Despite great technical advances in productivity, Prebisch observed, the benefits of global price coordination de facto "moved against the periphery."[65] "In other words," he added, "while the centers kept the whole benefit of the technical development of their industries, the peripheral countries transferred to them a share of the fruits of their own technical progress."[66]

From this diagnosis followed a knockdown case for peripheral industrialization. "Industrialization is not an end in itself," Prebisch warned, "but the principal means at the disposal of those countries of obtaining a share of the benefits of technical progress and of progressively raising the standard of living of the masses."[67] Under that assumption it was clear, as he added, that industrialization became "the most important means of expansion."[68] Poverty was then understood in the broader framework of the international division of labor and the macroeconomic dynamics that division created between countries. What Prebisch and Singer offered, then, was more than a criticism of the former colonial powers; it also provided, as Nils Gilman has noted, "a path forward": "International trade needed to be managed to prevent the deterioration of the terms of trade, and governments and corporations from the north had to be compelled to provide capital, technology, and expertise to enable the south to develop its own industrial base."[69]

Growth and inward-looking industrialization were here seen as the best way to develop Third World countries. This generally implied trade barriers, import tariffs, price controls, and a policy favoring investment in heavy industry over the agricultural sector.[70] His strategy, initially encapsulated in what would be called the "Havana manifesto," would then become a sensation and attract widespread support among southern nations but also vehement critics both in the United Nations and among those in the US development community who understood its political consequences. He had formalized a feeling that was to guide policies implemented in the Global South in the aftermath of decolonization.

India, for example, had followed its own version of such a strategy after 1947. In the aftermath of independence, if the long-term aim of development was, as Nehru himself argued, to "get rid of the appalling poverty of the people," the means to achieve such an objective were very different from the contemporary emphasis on cash. For Nehru, one of the central figures of the Non-Aligned Movement, it was clear that industrialization was "the instrument not only for achieving narrow economic objectives such as income growth and poverty alleviation, but also for achieving much broader objectives, such as social change, modernization, national security and international peace."[71] As early as 1929, the party of Gandhi, the Indian National Congress (INC), had held its general assembly in Bombay and adopted a resolution stating that only "revolutionary changes in the present economic and social structure of society" could alleviate "the great poverty and misery of the Indian people." For the party that Nehru led until his death in 1964, the postcolonial Indian state had to secure full employment and living wages, limit working hours, and guarantee union rights, but also "own or control key industries and services, mineral resources, railways, waterways, shipping and other means of public transport."[72]

Nehru's and Mahalanobis's postcolonial vision sprang from English Fabian socialism through their student years at Cambridge University. They both, as Galbraith recalled in his memoirs, "belonged to the world of Sidney and Beatrice Webb, George Bernard Shaw, R. H. Tawney, G. D. H. Cole, Harold Laski and the Fabian Society." "It was a world," he added, "in which decency, compassion and wide-ranging intelligence were combined with the belief that the nature of the economic order is, above all, a matter of moral commitment."[73] While Galbraith was ambassador in India, Nehru once even joked that he would be the "last Englishman to rule India."[74] Mahalanobis also took on a crucial role in shaping India's path to industrialization. Born in Calcutta in 1893 into a wealthy family, he became one of Nehru's closest advisers on economic questions, notably relying on the Indian Statistical Institute that he directed. Created in 1932, the Institute had relatively great autonomy and notoriously financed numerous visits of socialist economists such as Charles Bettelheim, Paul A. Baran, Joan Robinson, Michał Kalecki, and John Kenneth Galbraith and scholars such as Norbert Wiener to provide advice and help the government build its planning strategy.

Within this framework, concern for "poverty" always remained secondary to larger developmental priorities. For example, when the National Planning Committee was formed in October 1938 to prepare a "comprehensive industrial plan for the whole of India" and lay the groundwork for the postcolonial strategies of development, it famously established that

> the problems of poverty and unemployment, of national defence and of the economic regeneration in general cannot be solved without industrialisation. As a step towards such industrialisation, a comprehensive scheme of national planning should be formulated. This scheme should provide for the development of heavy key industries, medium scale industries and cottage industries, keeping in view our national requirements, the resources of the country, and also the peculiar circumstances prevailing in the country.[75]

National development and, perhaps more important, building a world beyond empires, implied that former colonies would attain "national self-sufficiency"[76] through state-led industrialization. "I am convinced," Nehru wrote in his timely history of India, "that the rapid industrialization of India is essential to relieve the pressure on land, to combat poverty and raise standards of living, for defence and a variety of other purposes."[77] And for that, only "the most careful" state-led "planning and adjustment" was required to "reap the full benefit of industrialization."[78] This approach would probably find its most coherent form in the 1955 Second Five-Year Plan, marking a significant turn toward a data-driven, scientific approach to economic planning.[79] What would later be referred as the "Nehru-Mahalonobis strategy"[80] was partially inspired by communist models but shared a lot with Prebisch's and Singer's initial inward-looking strategy. The "techno-futurist"[81] path Mahalanobis chose consisted precisely of a centralized "big push" to manufacture capital goods within the country rather than to import them.

Beyond India, this approach would provide the general framework within which most developing countries conceived their development strategy.[82] Indeed, Prebisch's Havana triumph did not go unnoticed. The year after his presentation he became executive secretary of CEPAL and would assemble a team dedicated to further promoting and elaborating the conceptual framework of his model. Soon CEPAL's policies would gain strength on other continents and open new doors for him. Notably at the United Nations Conference on Trade and Development (UNCTAD), where he became the founding secretary-general when it was created in Geneva in 1964, he was able to broaden his program to a global scale. By then he had more or less abandoned a narrow conception of ISI and began to think globally about the changes required for a more equal international trade. The inward-looking strategy had its shortcomings and could lead to its own crisis, as Brazil and India would experience by the late 1960s.[83] In fact, as Poornima Paidipaty and Pedro Ramos Pinto have noted, most postcolonial elites and developmental coalitions were beginning to recognize that the modernization framework had failed, in particular when it came to inequality.[84] Moreover, in most low-income countries adopting ISI, apart from Mexico, the manufacturing share of employment did not grow substantially between 1950 and 1965. Lack of domestic demand, uncompetitive manufactured goods, and overvaluation of currencies made the model difficult to sustain.[85] In India, where the strategy of import substitution had probably been strongest, growth rates in manufacturing were about 7 percent by the early 1960s, but they dropped to 4 percent by the end of the decade.[86]

Prebisch's attempt to find a solution to this problem at UNCTAD never implied a decline of world trade; he expected its expansion within a radically modified international framework. Import substitution industrialization was then slowly displaced by a more global criticism of the international division of labor. Moreover, for a certain number of small, newly independent states whose economies "were deeply tied to the global economy," delinking never really appeared as "a viable political option."[87] As Adom Getachew has noted, postcolonial states steadily thought out a more radical program requiring them to restructure international relations "to create a more equitable distribution of both the profit and employment global trade generate." If the "international division of labor might not be escaped," she added, "it could be remade into an egalitarian economy that could undo the relations of dependence and secure the economic dimensions of international nondomination."[88] Development was being globalized, dictating to both industrialized and nonindustrialized countries an imperative to reorganize their economies. "An essential element of such action," stated the final 1964 Act of the UNCTAD, "is that international policies in the field of trade and development should result in a modified international division of labor, which is more rational and equitable and is accompanied by the necessary adjustments in world production and trade."[89] For the newly created agency, it could even imply "the reallocation of certain industries or processes in favor of the developing countries,"[90] leading to redrawing the terms of trade globally. Within that framework, as Johanna Bockman has noted, structural adjustment was a global program that required "the reorganization of production and services worldwide."[91] Prebisch's view saw its climax in the 1974 UN General Assembly resolution for the establishment of a New International Economic Order (NIEO). Strongly shaped by his work during his CEPAL and UNCTAD years, the NIEO's resolution asked for the "full permanent sovereignty of every state over its natural resources and all economic activities," "regulation and supervision of activities of transnational corporations," "right to nationaliz[e] or transfer ownership to its nationals," large "transfers of technology" between the North and South, and "accelerated development of all the developing countries," intending to end "prevailing disparities in the world" and to secure prosperity for all. Together, the somewhat heterogeneous proposals that composed the NIEO envisioned not an antiglobalization agenda but an alternative and more equal globalization to fully integrate the South into global markets. As Julius Nyerere would argue in 1977 in a lecture he gave in the United States, it was "necessary for the community of nations to agree on deliberate actions to hasten industrialization in the developing nations."[92]

The objective, he added, was "that the share of Third World countries should be raised from its present 7 percent to 25 percent of world industrial production"—a task that would not "happen through what are called the natural forces of the market!"[93] Within that framework poverty was, as Joanne Meyerowitz has noted, "the consequence of a self-serving economic system created and sustained by the wealthier nations."[94] In that sense the central unit of poverty was "the state, not the individual."[95]

By the mid-1970s, however, this structural understanding of poverty, embedded in a wider critique of the global division of labor, would be slowly eclipsed by a more consensual, individual, and monetary understanding. Although the NIEO had captured the attention of the development community, it would be received with skepticism if not defiance within the US administration. Daniel Patrick Moynihan in particular, at the time US ambassador to India, did not hesitate to depict the movement as wielding a "threatening" redistributive agenda, endangering US interests. His plea to reject such plans and defend, as Meyerowitz noted, "the virtues of market economies, liberal trade policy, and multinational corporations" did not go unheard. The limits of the state-centered policies of the 1950s and 1960s would soon, as happened with the US War on Poverty, fuel demands for a more direct and market-friendly strategy toward poverty. It would mark a turn to poverty alleviation that, far from articulating the questions addressed by Prebisch and his generation, would, as development scholar Andrew Martin Fischer noted, displace "classical debates regarding the creation and division of wealth within and across societies."[96] By the mid-1970s, what was then called the "trade union of the poor" would fail, as Meyerowitz noted, to "restructure the international economy or recalibrate the balance of international power."[97] Instead, a narrower understanding of poverty alleviation and basic needs would be promoted, brushing aside the problem of global inequality and the division of labor. The new agenda prompted by the World Bank and international institutions implied a wholesale redefinition of what development itself meant.

From Industrialization to Poverty Alleviation

In early January 1976 American radical Michael Harrington arrived in India after a twenty-five-hour flight by way of Frankfurt, Istanbul, and Karachi. The trip was one of many he took from 1972 to 1977, taking him to Mexico, Guatemala, Kenya, and Tanzania. Boosted by the immense success of *The Other America*, he decided to travel to the Third World to understand and document poverty outside the affluent United States. He wanted to "speak to the American heart" about how "the vast majority" lived. When he arrived in New Delhi, he was overtaken by doubts about the ambitious scope of the project. Writing about countries he barely knew was a dangerous exercise, and he risked being simply another "tourist of misery."[98] "It seemed preposterous," he wrote, "to think that the meager gleanings of my daily brushes with this massive, convoluted reality could have any worth at all." A solution came from an unlikely source. Harrington had packed a copy of Hegel's *Phenomenology of Spirit*. Unable to sleep, he began rereading the voluminous masterpiece. It was a revelation. Phenomenology, Harrington realized, was about giving an account not of "the essence of reality," "but of how that reality appears to us." This gave him the idea to write the book by simply describing his travels and encounters, grasping the reality as it appeared to him, a "phenomenologi-cal report" on global poverty. In other words, describing his experience of poverty through the "simplest levels of perception," as a "very mundane member of the Western middle class." *The Vast Majority: A Journey to the World's Poor* was finally published in 1977 as Jimmy Carter was taking office as the thirty-ninth president of the United States after a campaign that had made human rights a central component of US foreign policy. By then poverty had slowly emerged as a problem in a distinct register of morality and compassion, anticipating the humanitarian turn of the mid-1980s with its rock stars and charity concerts.

The book itself reflected the decade's humanitarian ambience, calling for "the abolition of absolute poverty throughout the globe."[99] In the eyes of Harrington that absolute poverty was what tied together, beyond obvi-ous differences, the leprous children in the slums of Bombay, the informal workers in the streets of Nairobi, and the poor *campesinos* looking for work in Mexico City. It was a poverty that was "obvious, insistent, [and] overwhelming," he wrote, contrary to poverty in America, where "it takes an act of the imagination and will to see poverty."[100] But this vision of a planet mostly characterized by deprivation wasn't just something Har-rington experienced through Hegelian insights. The definition by which he characterized 54 percent of mankind as poor was defined as US$200 per year GNP per capita. This kind of abstract definition, allowing global comparisons, had become increasingly popular during the postwar pe-riod.[101] Based on the pioneering work of Simon Kuznets in the United States, new methods of counting and comparing income made it possible to build what historian Daniel Speich called "global abstractions," allow-ing researchers to compare what had before been seen as completely dis-similar situations. Notions like GDP per capita or, later, arbitrary poverty lines such as those created by the World Bank in the early 1970s,[102] al-lowed experts and policy makers to structure the planet on an income scale. A clear line could then be drawn between the rich and the poor and make it easier to formulate abstract strategies of development. The rapid spread of such indicators would permit a "sensational new view of the world as a place of enormous poverty."[103] But, as Speich noted, there was a "high price" to pay for generalizing the use of such abstractions, rapidly reducing "the complexity of the human world" and replacing "the manifold economic relationships within it with simple dichotomies."[104] In his book, Harrington still navigated between the radical calls of the NIEO, utopian ideas of a "world government," and an emerging, more pragmatic approach focused on guaranteeing basic needs, less concerned about modernization or industrialization.

However, a meeting with Robert McNamara at the World Bank led Harrington to focus more closely on absolute poverty. Indeed, if poverty lines were not new, the notion of an absolute global threshold was.[105] It was largely promoted by McNamara, since it provided a useful tool to measure poverty globally—as opposed to relative measures—and to monitor progress. Moreover, the idea of a global floor did not imply "alleviating relative inequality"[106] or instituting strong redistributive programs against inequality; it tackled only the most basic needs. As Rob Konkel has noted, "absolute poverty could be measured, quantified, and potentially eliminated, whereas the concept of relative poverty carried politically charged connotations of income distribution and inequality."[107] Harrington had met McNamara in his twelfth-floor office in Washington, DC, which displayed a giant globe beside the desk. Harrington discovered a man motivated by what he saw as a "sense of moral urgency" and "genuinely moved by the suffering of children."[108] The former secretary of defense explained "with a particular passion" what poverty does to children, "how a lack of food may well stunt the brain of a fetus or an infant." The World Bank itself had used such indicators to categorize stages of development since the late 1940s. But it was McNamara above all who, after becoming president of the bank in April 1968, shifted the focus to alleviating poverty, moving away from the growth-centered modernization projects of the earlier postwar period.[109]

After the Vietnam War debacle, McNamara had put all his efforts into turning the World Bank into more than just a bank and expanding its purpose.[110] In the decades before his presidency, the bank was indeed a conservative institution, lending essentially to safe countries for bankable infrastructure investments such as transportation, telecommunications, and power. He had notably been troubled that the bank had refused loans to most countries in Africa for fear of the risk it might incur.[111] It seemed then to him that its distinctive value compared with other banks was not clearly established. Moreover, the bank's aim generally was narrowly defined in terms of economic and productivity growth, which did not include projects in education or health care and sidelined poverty alleviation.[112] After McNamara left the Department of Defense, probably because he doubted the United States could win the Vietnam War, his appointment to the bank would radically reorient the institution's agenda toward a growing interest in poverty alleviation within the field of devel-

opment. In a matter of years, he would gain a reputation as an "antipoverty crusader" and the bank would be seen as one of the most "powerful
force[s] in development."[113] Of particular importance in this shift was the
speech McNamara made in Nairobi only a couple of years before Harrington made his trip. In his speech McNamara emphasized the importance of tackling absolute poverty around the world, with its devastating
effects. It meant, he argued, "a condition of life so limited as to prevent
realization of the potential of the genes with which one is born; a condition of life so degrading as to insult human dignity."[114] In his distinctively
moral tone, and by depicting the poor as victims, he reduced the political
character of such an enterprise, allowing the bank to portray poverty "as
a naturalistic state of affairs, which simply happened to affect some countries and populations more than others."[115]

This framework was part of a broader rejection of and disillusion with
theories of development centered on modernization and industrialization.
As Martha Finnemore has noted, before the McNamara presidency, to the
bank "poverty alleviation was not an end to itself but a happy by product of expanded production and efficient industrialization."[116] One of the
fiercest critics of the vision proved to be Mahbub ul Haq, a Pakistani economist trained at Cambridge and Yale who had developed a strong re-
buttal of the development approaches that dominated the postwar period. Having himself worked as chief economist for the Pakistani Planning
Commission, as Patrick Sharma noted, he "had seen how development
approaches that prioritized industrialization failed to result in widespread
improvements in living standards, even though they led to economic
growth."[117] The problem with development planners, he wrote, was "their
curious love for direct economic controls." "It is too readily assumed," he
added, "that development planning means encouragement of [the] public sector and imposition of a variety of bureaucratic controls to regulate
economic activity, particularly in the private sector."[118] When Pakistan decided to abandon the policy and to liberalize the economy (ending import
and price controls), it seemed clear to Haq "that the replacement of direct
controls by appropriate price signals and incentives"[119] was a key factor
in the following economic success of the country. While he mostly agreed
with the market-driven reforms the country implemented, he nonetheless
remarked that the growth generated did not trickle down. "The free play
of market mechanism[s]," he noted, "naturally favored the richer regions
as well as the richer income groups within these regions."[120] While Pakistan had undergone impressive economic growth, by the late 1960s Haq

began to express doubts about the way those policies favored "a handful of industrial family groups" and barely reduced poverty. It became clear to him that while the old model of development was outdated, the more market-friendly model could not allocate the "gains from development" "more equitably."[121] Planners had to learn how to use the "powerful force" of the "market mechanism" "to serve their national objectives."

By the time he became director of the Policy Planning Department at the World Bank, Haq had become convinced that the very notion of modernization was now "in serious trouble." "After two decades of development," he wrote in 1973, "the achievements are quite meagre."[122] The assumption that "poverty can be taken care of through high growth rates, which will eventually filter down to the masses" appeared to be obviously mistaken and, for Haq, "proved bankrupt."[123] This failure had also, by the late 1960s, become patent in India, where Mahalanobis himself had acknowledged that his expert-driven industrialization model led to very uneven economic gains.[124] By the early 1970s his vision had "lost much of the glamorous sheen that had surrounded it a decade earlier."[125] Planning, Mahalanobis would conclude, "had delivered growth but not greater economic equity."[126] In light of these partial failures, rather than assuming that poverty could be attacked "indirectly through the growth rates filtering down to the masses," Haq pleaded for a new policy that had to be based "on the premise that poverty must be attacked directly" and must immediately set "a basis of minimum human needs."[127] "The problem of development," he concluded, "must be redefined as a selective attack on the worst forms of poverty." Within that framework, Haq began to develop a "need-oriented strategy" that would redefine development goals "in terms of progressive reduction and eventual elimination of malnutrition, disease, illiteracy, squalor, unemployment, and inequalities." Although the market was a powerful engine for growth, it was clear that the price system was itself unable to "produce the kind of essential consumption goods which are required for such a strategy" "if the poor do not have the purchasing power to influence market decisions." As an alternative, Haq envisioned a strategy relying on "fixing national consumption and production targets on the basis of minimum human needs."[128] For him, this of course implied a clear expansion of public services (in education, access to water, health care, electricity, etc.) and of general purchasing power for the poor. And while he rejected too strict economic controls and an inward-looking strategy for development, when it came to basic needs Haq still strongly relied on the expansion of the state.

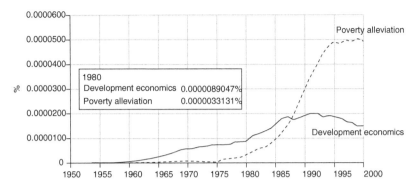

FIGURE 5.3. N-gram for "development economics" and "poverty alleviation," 1950–2000. *Source*: Google Ngram Viewer.

This turn to needs, however, was always about more than "poverty-focused" development. In fact, by the mid-1970s the whole framework of development was collapsing. "It was no longer a 1940s attempt to build a welfare state for citizens," Samuel Moyn noted, "but a new version of humanitarian concern now directed at the global poor, suddenly discovered as an aggregate entity."[129] A new subject became the launching pad for a larger shift from competing theories of economic development and modernization to a narrower economic focus on poverty alleviation that would culminate in the 2000s with the Millennium Development Goals.[130]

Antipoverty activists indeed generally emphasized inequality *within* each country rather than between North and South, implicitly sidelining broader considerations about the inequalities generated by free trade. Within the supporters of the NIEO, as Joanne Meyerowitz has noted, "basic needs seemed to serve as a substitute for the NIEO rather than a complement to it," a way to "avoid the issue of the global economic order and bypass postcolonial governments with programs and priorities devised in Washington."[131] Ajit Singh, an Indian-born Cambridge development economist who became a close economic adviser to Julius Nyerere in Tanzania, noted quite early how the basic needs approach could "discourage industrial development."[132] If in theory there was no conflict between the basic needs approach and the NIEO agenda, Singh nonetheless noted that "the former is concerned with national priorities and the problems of poverty and income distribution within countries, and the latter relates to the structure of the world economy and the distribution of resources between nations."[133] "It is undeniable," he added in 1979, "that the main

documents concerned with the [basic needs] strategy do not adequately
emphasize the positive, let alone the leading, role of industry in bringing
about a long-term structural transformation of the economy."[134] In fact, he
argued, for countries in the South it was clear that such an agenda was designed to "hamper their industrialization" and was not motivated mainly
by "altruistic theories."[135] Unless the basic needs approach was "integral
to an overall development plan of industrialization and structural change
in a country's economy," he concluded, it will be "unlikely to succeed even
[on its] own terms."[136]

This association, however, was never realized. If the World Bank and
McNamara did not reject out of hand the ideals of the NIEO, the poverty and needs discourse would slowly open the path for the promotion of
market-based reforms. Poverty would slowly be insulated from industrial
policy and the conditions of international trade. As Haq himself noted,
the bank wanted to "make poverty 'acceptable to the bankers.'" As Robert L. Ayres has argued, "the emphasis under McNamara was on improving the absolute incomes of the poor, not [on] alleviating relative inequality." Within that framework, he added, "the preference was for market
over governmental mechanisms."[137] As Rob Konkel noted, the World Bank
was always "reliant on the elite classes in the Bank's client countries making some voluntary self-sacrificial concessions to the poor, not on an interventionist redistributive scheme."[138]

More important, the emphasis put on internal factors apart from the
structure of international trade would strongly intensify over the coming
decade with the creation of structural adjustment loans (SAL) in 1979. The
bank would issue loans on condition that developing countries implement
specific prescribed reforms. As the Southern debt crisis was mounting in
the developing world, the SAL became a central component of a global
turn to neoliberalism in the Western development community. The whole
framework of those prescriptions implicitly set aside the international
trade imbalances to focus on internal factors. The Berg report, compiled by
the African Strategy Review Group headed by Elliot Berg and published
by the bank the year McNamara left the presidency, had definitively moved
the bank away from any kind of global and state-centered solution. Zero-
ing in on Africa's economic predicament, it focused on "domestic policy
inadequacies" and advocated a serious turnaround from previous development strategies. "To speed up development," the report stated, "the new
governments expanded the public sector." But "it is now widely evident,"
it added, "that the public sector is overextended, given the present scar-

cities of financial resources, skilled manpower, and organizational capacity."[139] To create a suitable environment for growth, it was now necessary to "enlarge" "the scope of private sector activity," to suspend price controls and cut public spending, to have "more open and competitive marketing systems," and to focus on "agriculture and exports" rather than industrial development. This strategy, as Patrick Sharma argued, marked a sharp break with the past debates and was seen by some inside the organization as a final rejection of "state-led development strategies."[140] By 1981, with the nomination of free-trade advocate Anne Krueger as the World Bank's chief economist, the institutions took a more definitive turn to macroeconomic discipline and market-based solutions. Change would soon be limited to, as Adom Getachew noted, "reform and disciplining of indebted nations" rather than "transformations in the developed economies designed to open markets in the global north to the developing world."[141]

The poverty-alleviation framework hardly disappeared, however. Indeed, McNamara started a more global shift toward monetized definitions of poverty that would culminate in 1990 with the "dollar-a-day" standard. This abstract vision of poverty would more or less cast aside the "causal processes that create poverty"[142] to focus only on the level of the floor. What Rob Konkel called the "monetization of poverty" would soon narrow its definition "to a person's ability to consume and to participate in a market economy."[143] It allowed a "very limited view of what poverty is or how it is generated" that somehow abstracts it "from all the basic economic processes and systemic features that determine poverty."[144] Cash would slowly appear, along with the market liberalization of the 1980s, as an attractive alternative to both state-led industrialization and public services expansion for basic needs. And it was with the disastrous effects of the structural adjustment policies of the late 1980s—especially in Latin America—that the "cash transfer revolution" took hold. It was with the demise of both state-led strategies and orthodox structural adjustment, as Erik S. Reinert, Jayati Ghosh, and Rainer Kattel have pointed out, that poverty alleviation would triumph to ameliorate "the conditions of those defined as poor, rather than transforming the economies in which they lived."[145]

Development without Development

One of the earliest adopters of a cash-transfer strategy in the late 1990s was Mexico. A country that had been rather successful in implementing the import substitution industrialization model would brutally reform its economy to conform to market signals. In August 1982, after decades of following an ISI policy, Mexico was on the brink of bankruptcy. On August 20 its finance minister, Jesús Silva-Herzog Flores, met his creditors at the Federal Reserve Bank in New York. It was a Friday, the Bank of Mexico had only $158 million in reserve, and on Monday a payment of more than $400 million was due. Facing imminent default, the minister addressed the creditors with an old Mexican saying; "Debo, no niego; pago, no tengo."[146] The news stunned the international community, and other Latin American countries such as Brazil and Argentina rapidly faced similar problems. The announcement marked the beginning of one of the worst and longest economic downturns on the continent since the Great Depression. For decades Mexico had been able to sustain growth rates above 6 percent a year, and of almost 10 percent in the late 1970s after the discovery of new oil fields, increasing the country's production and making new loans possible. By 1979, however, with the fall of oil prices and the rise of American interest rates decided by Paul Volcker, Mexico's debt rapidly became unsustainable. Considering the strong exposure of American banks, the crisis immediately took an international turn. At that time loans to Mexico alone accounted for 44 percent of the nine largest US banks' capital and one-third of their annual net profits.[147] To stop the crisis and avoid its spread, the International Monetary Fund and the US Treasury Department agreed to grant the Mexican government currency loans and accepted a restructuring of its debt on condition that the country implement radical structural adjustment measures to reform its economy.[148] From that perspective it was more than a mere economic crisis; it marked the collapse of the import substitution model that had guided the economic policies of many Latin American countries during the postwar period.[149]

In Mexico, the presidency of Miguel de la Madrid (1982–88) saw structural adjustment programs imposed by the IMF, the World Bank, and Washington, DC, and a dramatic turn toward economic orthodoxy. Although he was a member of the Institutional Revolutionary Party (PRI) that had ruled the country continuously since 1929, De la Madrid was more of a Harvard-trained technocrat, willing to place satisfying international investors above domestic concerns. The medicine was harsh, and it radically reoriented the economic framework of the country to rely more on market mechanisms and price signals. It implied notably drastic cuts in public spending, wage moderation, privatizing public assets, a credit crunch, dismantling price controls and, by the early 1990s, liberal-

izing trade. The result proved devastating. Although international investors made substantial gains during the crisis, per capita income fell, real
wages collapsed by more than 40 percent, the labor share of income dramatically declined, and in 1994 poverty skyrocketed from 23.5 percent to
38.9 percent.[150] By the early 1990s the GDP had hardly recovered its pre-
1982 levels, and it would sharply contract again in 1995 during the "tequila
crisis" that was the direct result of the wild 1989 privatization and liberalization of the whole banking system. It led to another dramatic wave
of malnutrition and to a sharp decline in school enrollment, which would
never recover.

The development community soon referred to this period as the "lost
decade," forcing many countries to partially rethink the neoliberal consensus.[151] In Mexico, by the mid-1990s the newly elected government of
Ernesto Zedillo chose to expand the safety net through direct cash transfers to the poor. This idea was highly unusual at that time, since before the
2000s the conventional wisdom among mainstream development agencies
and policy makers was that, as Martin Ravallion has pointed out, "income
transfers to the poor, and safety net policies more generally, are at best a
short-term palliative and at worst a waste of money."[152] During the lost
decade, a strong trade-off between redistribution and economic growth
became default. Mexico's program Progresa, launched in 1997 and granting payments to more than 300,000 families, slowly changed this view. The
reform, mostly designed by Mexican economist Santiago Levy, was meant
to replace old policies of price controls, in-kind transfers, and food subsidies with direct cash transfers giving, as Levy put it, "beneficiary families complete freedom in their spending decisions."[153] A decade after its
creation, the program covered a third of the country's households and
became by far the country's biggest antipoverty program. The transfers,
however, differed slightly from Western family allowances in that they were
conditional on recipients' specific behavior patterns, such as children's
school attendance, visits to health clinics, or labor market participation.
The initiative soon became an example for many countries that underwent a similar shift during that period. Indeed, by the early 1990s nearly
all Latin American countries and more than thirty sub-Saharan countries
had undergone harsh market-oriented reforms. Among those programs
there was, of course, Brazil's Bolsa Família, which had existed locally since
1995 but became a nationwide program under Luiz Inácio Lula da Silva's
government in 2003, constituting what is arguably the largest cash transfer
program in the developing world.

India, the other main country that had opted for a strong import substitution model by the mid-1950s, followed a similar curve by the late 1980s. The slowing growth rate in manufacturing, the investment depression, and national manufacturers' inability to properly modernize soon accelerated the bankruptcy in industries such as textiles. The rising gap in productivity, aggravated by the difficulty of buying technology abroad, also made the Indian economy insufficiently competitive on the global scale. By the late 1980s and early 1990s, growing fiscal and trade deficits turned into a crushing burden. By 1992, while the future Indian prime minister Manmohan Singh was minister of finance, India was heading toward a structural adjustment program. Closely monitored by the IMF, the country slowly reduced tariffs, liberalized exchange rates and industrial regulations, and rolled back state investment. Subsides were cut, the labor market and the banking system were deregulated, and state companies were privatized. In a year or two the Nehruvian model was definitively dismantled.[154] Although, as Amartya Sen has pointed out, the market reforms of the 1990s did lead to more efficiency in the productive sphere and achieved record high growth rates, they completely failed to fulfill the basic needs of most Indians. Whether in education, food security, or health care, the adjustment of the 1990s did not bring the expected "redistribution through growth."[155] This turn would also boost basic income advocates in India. In 2009 Standing would again play a crucial role in launching an important pilot program, with the Self-Employed Women's Association (SEWA) in Madhya Pradesh, supported by the United Nations Development Program. The experiment, conducted in one of India's most backward regions and conceived as a randomized controlled trial (RCT), lasted two years and involved six thousand people who were given from 150 to 300 rupees a month.[156] Part of the rising popularity of cash transfers in India, however, must be understood in the particular context of heated political debates about the efficiency of well-established programs of food subsidy like the Public Distribution System (PDS) or of public works like the National Rural Employment Guarantee Act (NREGA). The PDS, perhaps the largest program of economic support in India, gave households access to subsided commodities according to their ration cards. And the NREGA, a piece of legislation aimed at effectively instituting a "right to work," guarantees one hundred days of employment to any households that volunteer for public works. Since the late 2000s, about fifty million Indians every year have taken part in this massive expansion of public works.[157]

As an alternative to those programs, an increasing number of scholars and political leaders began to advocate for the reliability and market efficiency of direct transfers over heavy-handed and bureaucratic state programs.[158] By 2013, Narendra Modi's government began to effectively replace price subsidies, especially in fertilizer and gasoline, by direct cash transfers as a broader attempt to reduce the state bureaucracy. Over the next couple of years, experiments in replacing the popular food subsidies altogether began in several places in the country, without having yet achieved a complete transition. This shift was patent when Rahul Gandhi, the Indian National Congress candidate for the 2019 national election, included a guaranteed income of 6,000 rupees a month in his electoral platform to mount a "final assault on poverty."[159]

More than any other region, it was in however in southern Africa that Armando Barrientos and David Hulme's "quiet revolution" came out in full force.[160] South Africa and Namibia had of course, through a slightly different policy path, substantially accelerated their transfer machine during the 2000s. Part of the appeal of a guaranteed income came from the failure of the microexperiments led by the development establishment in the early 2000s to achieve the Millennium Development Goals. Based on the Human Development framework, the United Nations became more sensitive to actual improvements in the lives of the poor, but without challenging either the market model or liberalization and global trade.[161] Development offered a way to increase individuals' production capacities rather than to reframe the economic structure within which they operated: an approach shifting development theories away from the highly formalized models of the postwar era.[162] Fueled by the rise of randomized controlled trials in the field of development, the proliferation of these new microsolutions often conducted by nongovernmental organizations or philanthropic foundations (microcredit, small investments in women, education experiments, training, etc.) was thought of as an alternative to state-led macrointerventions. The demise of the postwar macroeconomic perspective opened the space to small decentralized and targeted investments that were supposed to enhance poor people's production capacity.

In countries such as Kenya, Tanzania, Uganda, and Ethiopia, the UN Millennium Villages Project, directed by Jeffrey Sachs through his Columbia Earth Institute, had also shifted the analysis of poverty from the structural characteristics of the world economy to deficiencies of the economic environment in which individuals evolve. After becoming the leading ideologue of shock therapy in the early 1990s, Sachs underwent a conversion. Instead, he began to champion international poverty relief along with agencies such as the World Bank and the United Nations. His conversion, however, was not a rejection of the structural adjustment framework, but rather a slight complement. Indeed, Sachs rejected the "debilitating" experiments of state-led industrialization and the socialist tone of postcolonial leaders. The problem for him was not free market or international trade but rather, as Japhy Wilson noted, the lack of incorporation within it. Africa in particular would be framed as a space "of exception," a global zone whose "developmental failures" "were due not to its subordinate incorporation into global capitalism, but to its exclusion from globalization."[163] From that perspective Sachs was able to safeguard most of the tenets of the structural adjustment framework (openness to trade, labor market liberalization, privatizing public companies, low taxation on the private sector, etc.) while at the same time promoting measures targeted on "the poorest of the poor." "Africa is as hungry as can be," he wrote, "because you have hundreds of millions of impoverished people who are too poor to be part of any market."[164] To implement his views, in 2005 he set up a series of pilot projects in West Africa that sought, essentially, to enhance farmers' productivity, children's school attendance, and health care. Focused on local infrastructure and community-based investments at fourteen sites across ten sub-Saharan countries, the model sought to reinvent development in an age of declining state capacity. With the right investments in human capital, basic needs, and small farmers, the idea was that it would be possible to transform all villagers into effective entrepreneurs able to lift their communities out of poverty. The aim was to metamorphose "sub-subsistence farmers [into] small-scale entrepreneurs."[165] Development, as Ha-Joon Chang noted, here came to mean "something quite different from what it used to mean." Poverty alleviation and basic needs would, in a sense, he adds, promote "development without development," a vision of development where individual betterment is disconnected from the transformation of the "existing productive structure."[166]

The patent failure of Sachs's Millennium Villages, however, offered the advocates of basic income and opponents of any kind of social planner (either state socialist or Washington technocrat) much-needed momentum for their own agenda. Indeed, as Sachs himself would acknowledge, his ten-year, $120 million experiment produced meager results. His unreliable data and poorly planned methodology were not much help in salvaging his achievements.[167] Sachs, wrote development economist William Easterly, created "an island of success in a sea of failure."[168] While it seemed to have a positive impact on maternal health care and agricultural output, it had inconclusive results on nutrition and education and, perhaps more important, "no discernible impact" on consumption-based poverty.[169] This result was particularly questionable because Sachs did not hesitate to announce, numerous times, that the problem of poverty could "easily" be solved by 2025. "This village," he said confidently on an MTV show called *The Diary of Angelina Jolie and Dr. Jeffrey Sachs in Africa*, is "going to end extreme poverty." Posing alongside rock stars such as Bono, his repeated promise to make "poverty history" ended in a public disaster.

The failure of Sachs's program strengthened distrust of these top-down approaches even among the staunchest proselytizers of structural adjustment. For instance, New York University professor William Easterly — former World Bank official and poverty expert — began to champion a "bottom-up" approach to alleviating poverty.[170] A keen reader of Friedrich Hayek trained at MIT, by the early 2000s Easterly began to move away from the humanitarian paradigm. He also repented his harsh emphasis on structural adjustment of the 1990s. At the World Bank, Easterly had begun reporting on Russian attempts at shock therapy and surveying Latin American efforts. For "economists like me," he confessed, it "took . . . a decade of failure to convince us that top-down imposition of markets did not work." "I believed in shock therapy," he said, even if he had "the most superficial knowledge of Russian institutions and history."[171] Yet top-down marketization was bound to fail in a country that lacked the right cultural hardware such as property rights and contract law. The same mistake was repeated by World Bank officials in Africa, where desperate attempts at development aid ricocheted off local brokerage and power networks. A "white man's burden" still stalked Western approaches to global poverty. This burden was then compounded with a utopian emphasis on planning, a hangover from earlier commitments to modernization theory and Marxism alike. "Social interplay," Easterly claimed in 2006, is "so complex that a top-down reform that tried to change all the rules at once could make things worse rather than better."[172] Thinkers like Hayek and Edmund Burke, he claimed, had long since seen the dangers of haughty social engineering. Countries undergoing a market revolution needed space and time to experiment — something cash transfers did elegantly, bypassing local power brokers and leaving purchasing power in the hands of residents. The "tyranny of experts" that had led to Latin America's and Africa's "lost decades" in the 1980s and 1990s, was nearing its end.[173]

Cash transfers offered a final alternative after the top-down big push and structural adjustment—a "market populism" that would commodify from *below* rather than from above. In the 2010s, the fate of Easterly's policy could only be propitious.[174] As the authors of *Just Give Money to the Poor* argued in their seminal volume, if "the fall of the Berlin wall marked the end of an era of state-dominated economic development," then "the successor vision of global development led by international corporations and banks lasted only 15 years before it, too, was shown to be a failure."[175] By contrast, a guaranteed income would finally get rid of any notion of planning, of conscious direction in development. On the ashes of these past frameworks, Barrientos added, "cash transfers recognize the right of each individual to an adequate standard of living" and at the same time "provide the resources for people, individually and collectively, to participate in the economy."[176] It has, then, the advantage of giving the money "directly to those who have the least of it" but also, from a more Hayekian outlook, to those "who know how to make the best use of it."[177] Cash transfers therefore were not a type of charity; rather, they were decentralized "investments that enable poor people to take control of their own development and end their own poverty."[178] From a vision of development aimed at industrializing and bringing people into formal jobs, the Global South transitioned toward a model relying on informal jobs and decentralized investments.

While before the early 2000s almost no mainstream development policy circles advocated giving cash directly to the poor, the positive effects of this "cash transfer revolution" opened the way for new experiments and debates. Facing the failures of the polices pursued during the 1980s, international institutions became more open to such policies and recommended combining "conventional pro-market adjustment policies with social programs."[179] From that perspective the rise of cash transfers, as Richard Ballard notes, "does not signal mainstream development's abandonment of neoliberalism for welfarism." Rather than aiming at "decommodify people," cash allowed "support to become demand-driven rather than supply-driven."[180] As Rob Konkel noted, by the 2000s the World Bank itself would bridge "the emphasis on market liberalization of the 1980s and the war on poverty of the 1970s" by promoting "liberalization reforms strategically while supporting increased social funding to address poverty directly."[181] Therefore, though most international institutions would modify their narrative concerning poverty, they never overtly challenged the market framework. The agenda, as Frances Stewart has noted, became to realize the human development goals "by growth-oriented market development, but with much more attention to income distribution and poverty."[182]

By 2009 the World Bank estimated that more than 120 programs had been implemented on the continent.[183] In 2011 the Social Protection Floor Initiative, convened by the ILO in collaboration with the WHO and the UN under the direction of Chile's former president, Michelle Bachelet, put the emphasis on "basic income security" and made the case for universalism by extending social security systems and transfers around the world.[184] By 2016, more than sixty countries in the developing world had state-led cash transfers programs.[185] "Social justice was globalized and minimized," as Samuel Moyn argued, favoring the establishment of a floor below which "no one is allowed to sink," yet in strong opposition to the original dreams of development put forward by postcolonial leaders.

This shift also sparked an unprecedented interest in cash-based solutions within the development community, to the point that in June 2017 Philip Alston, special rapporteur on extreme poverty and human rights at the United Nations, presented a report in Geneva on basic income as a solution for eradicating global poverty. "In the world of economics and even in development policy," he argued, "one of the most vibrant debates centers around proposals to replace or supplement existing social protection systems with a universal basic income." "Rather than messy in-kind support," Alston noted, the idea promised "minimal bureaucracy and low administrative costs."[186] Moreover, the report stated, the traditional focus on "respect for labour rights" and on reducing "to the fullest extent possible the number of workers outside the formal economy" seemed increasingly out of reach in light of a globalized division of labor. In a world where "forms of employment are ever more precarious; global supply chains and outsourcing are making traditional forms of labour market regulation increasingly less relevant"; and "vast swathes of the existing workforce will be made redundant by increasing automation and robotization," new solutions for tackling economic insecurity must be explored. While this did not imply "that labour rights should be . . . abandoned," it still assumed that in the contemporary Global South, "traditional approaches might not have much traction in the face of the systematic weakening of labour market institutions."[187] Finally, in July 2020, at the annual Nelson Mandela Lecture, António Guterres, secretary-general of the United Nations, promoted "a new social contract for a new era," including "the possibility of a Universal Basic Income."[188]

*   *   *

In the introduction to his 2017 monograph *Give a Man a Fish*, American anthropologist James Ferguson recalled that, when criticizing development strategies, he often was asked, "Well, then, what should we do?" The answer came from one his colleagues, who once proposed, half-seriously, to simply throw "out of helicopters" the money usually spent on development so "the local people could harvest it."[189] Ferguson's Friedmanesque metaphor captured an understanding of development radically transfigured by the past fifty years. It's the very idea of directing investment—either through macroeconomic policy or through small-scale "experiments"—that was gradually cast aside in favor of the decentralized and autonomous decisions of the target population.

Not surprisingly, a newly antistatist form of development would also find its way back to the northern metropoles as tech giants like Google or Facebook were increasingly on the lookout for ways to think about welfare in a world mediated by apps. When Chris Hughes, cofounder of Facebook, and Michael Faye, cofounder of Google's GiveDirectly fund, traveled to Kenya as part of a delegation visiting Sachs's recently set up Millennium Village, Hughes was hardly convinced.[190] His visit made it clear that antipoverty campaigns that relied on strongly prescriptive notions of human flourishing were both inefficient and undesirable. As he looked at a school with no pencils, no soap, no paper, and "[in] general no signs of life"—"more like a movie set than a kids' dorm," "a Potemkin Village"—"something felt off." Sachs's promise of resource-driven development left Hughes "with more questions than answers."[191] The two clearly belonged to different generations, as Hughes recounted in a memoir:

> I loved the idea of nomads in the Somali desert exploring the world through their Google searches, but it seemed nearly unbelievable that an Internet built for the West would be of much day-to-day use to the people here, if it worked at all. . . . When Nina Munk (a friend) later visited the village, she discovered that the computers had never been connected to the Internet, and all of them were eventually stolen.[192]

Although driven by private donors, the Sachs approach still sought a mixture of in-kind and money transfers, mediated by local players. After reading up on the question, Hughes came to see Sachs's strategy as the hopeless leftovers of a more paternalist approach to welfare. Dictating needs and desires to the world's poor would never lead to emancipation. The village model instead represented "an approach to combating economic injustice and poverty that was about engineering progress from the top down, rather than respecting the agency and autonomy of the people you set out to empower."[193] Pluralism and democratic empowerment, however, were increasingly at odds with this need determination. Instead, "every culture and place present[s] unique and often hidden challenges, and a lot of money and energy can be wasted quickly."[194] Basic income was "confidently liberal and market-oriented," but it still required a "strong central government to guarantee the rights and freedoms of citizens."[195] Hughes also "marveled at the simplicity of the idea of giving cash directly," as he noted in a diary entry:

> Why was my default to trust an educated outsider or nonprofit executive with resources rather than the poor themselves? The radical, irreverent nature of the idea that the poor might know the best way to solve their own problems hit a nerve. It connected to my natural skepticism of people in power that my parents had inculcated in me from a young age and which had only grown with exposure to the professional nonprofit infrastructure. . . . What if the most effective way to help somebody might be to get all those experts' intent on over-engineering progress out of the way?[196]

Rather than taking orders from Washington experts, local communities could now receive cash directly on their phones: marketization from the bottom up. By August 2012, Hughes had joined the board of GiveDirectly while they were conducting numerous pilots in Kenya, Uganda, and Rwanda. Founded in 2008 by four Harvard and MIT graduates in economics, the small development start-up would soon drain money from powerful companies like Facebook and Google.[197] While Sachs's edifice was teetering, GiveDirectly was starting its experiment in 2009, by the close of the decade sending $1,000 each to more than twenty thousand randomly selected recipients in 197 villages across rural Kenya. The money, wired directly through mobile phones, was given with no strings attached. There was no need to vaccinate one's children or send them to school; no distribution of mosquito nets or directives on how to manage cattle. Instead, the program would "empower poor households to make their own consumption and investment decisions based on their individual needs and preferences."[198] Carefully monitored and evaluated by top economists from Nobel Prize winner Abhijit Banerjee to Alan Krueger,

FIGURE 5.4. Kenyan recipient of the GiveDirectly pilot. *Source*: givedirectly.org.

former chairman of President Obama's Council of Economic Advisers, GiveDirectly's missionary statement was widely praised.[199] With more than 90 percent of the funds effectively delivered to the participants, it realized the utopia first projected by the humanitarian turn of the 1980s, in which TV ads and rock concerts exhorted people to wire their money to destitute children ("We are the ones who make a brighter day," Michael Jackson sang in "We Are the World," "so let's start giving").

To critics, the Global South's antipoverty turn—or what Chang termed the "antidevelopmental" turn—also seemed premised on evasion of "the classical debates regarding the creation and division of wealth within and across societies, not [on] how this is related to social and economic structural transformations associated with modern capitalist development."[200] The world in which basic income thrived separated poverty as such "from the more uncomfortable questions about whether modern poverty in developing countries is fundamentally due to a lack of integration of poor people into local, national and global socio-economic systems, or whether it is due to the manner by which they have already been integrated."[201] Development as a state-led enterprise was soon dissolved in the vast impersonal ocean of aggregated consumer choices.

Inspired by such success stories, Hughes set up his own Economic Security Project, dedicated to research on guaranteed income in America and with an antimonopoly agenda.[202] From the start he cast his organization as serving a task that went beyond the former developing world. Although he first looked at the problem through an international lens, he immediately wondered, "Well, this works in Kenya; why can't it work here?"[203] By the end of the decade his organization had channeled more than $10 million in pilots, think thanks, conferences, studies, and direct relief to American cities. Presented enthusiastically as a way "to modernize and expand the Earned Income Tax Credit," Hughes's experiment in alleviating poverty reconnected the early attempts of the 1960s with the small-scale RCT experiments of the 2000s. This approach was hardly exclusive to the postdevelopmental South. Instead, a modernized version of Friedman's negative income tax—pegged at $500 a month for the bottom 40 percent of Americans—would let every US recipient "choose her or his own destiny." The expansion of the transfer nexus was, as Hughes argued at a Goldman Sachs talk, "the kind of government we should move in the direction of."[204] "We can be the generation," he added, "that eradicates poverty in the United States once and for all." While GiveDirectly was still an outlier when it launched its Kenyan pilot, along with Standing's experiments in Namibia and India the following decade would see a proliferation of transfer experiments all over the globe. The South's cash transfer revolution was now finding its way back to the Global North, fueled by a new "populist explosion."

Basic Income in the Technopopulist Age

We should explore ideas like universal basic income . . . from [the] conservative principles of smaller government, rather than progressive principles of a larger safety net. — Mark Zuckerberg, *World Economic Forum*, 2017

It is the periphery, not the metropolis, where the future will reveal itself. — Ian Thompson, *Independent*, 2003

On December 10, 2020, Twitter CEO Jack Dorsey announced a $15 million donation for a policy pilot across several American cities. About seven months earlier, economies crashed in the midst of a global COVID-19 pandemic, leaving behind a workforce desperate for funds. Public responses to the crisis had been haphazard at best—stuck in congressional gridlock, for instance, a meager $1,200 relief package had only recently found its way into Americans' bank accounts. In response, GiveDirectly, the philanthropic start-up that had sent millions to the Kenyan poor, began to expand its activity in the United States. "What people need now, more than ever," the organization declared, "is cash."[1] As one of the largest private cash transfer initiatives in US history, the organization swiftly began to deliver $1,000 relief checks to over 200,000 households. Together with Facebook founder Chris Hughes, Dorsey was determined to "close the wealth and income gap, level systemic race and gender inequalities, and create economic security for families," fulfilling "the old dream of Martin Luther King and the Civil Rights movement": a universal basic income.[2] After a twenty-year detour, cash transfers had made a spectacular comeback to the United States.

The uptake of the proposal in the 2010s was impressively ecumenical. Even a notoriously conservative World Economic Forum came around to the idea after the pandemic. As Guy Standing noted in a 2020 reflection for the organization, "The combination of rentier capitalism, a technological revolution and rampant globalization has created eight modern Giants— Inequality, Insecurity, Debt, Stress, Precarity, Automation, Extinction, and Neo-Fascist Populism."[3] The coronavirus joined these horsemen, as the terrifying "ninth Giant" and the "trigger that tips a fragile global system."[4] Through the back door basic income found its way in again, from Rio's favelas to think tanks in California's Palo Alto.

The California Welfare Ideology

Dorsey and Hughes were far from alone with their enthusiasm for cash-based solutions within the American tech sector. In the preceding decade, financiers and entrepreneurs from across the industry had steadily come out in favor of the UBI.[5] The proposal now united figures such as Tesla CEO Elon Musk, Virgin founder Richard Branson, Amazon founder Jeff Bezos, and Facebook chief Mark Zuckerberg, added to older proponents such as Philippe Van Parijs, Charles Murray, David Graeber, Greg Mankiw, Chris Hughes, John McDonnell, Yannis Varoufakis, Kathi Weeks, Jim O'Neill, Nick Srnicek, Anne Lowrey, and Andrew Yang.

It was difficult to connect such disparate figures. Set against a fuller historical backdrop, however, the cash transfers proposed left and right relied on developments that long preceded the boom in the 2010s: an increasing abstraction and privatizing of needs, the decentering of labor as a source of social identity, and the disorganizing civil society into a more atomized landscape structured by social media. California had always served as a natural homeland for this tendency. With its legacy of frontier boosterism and settler colonialism, the state was known for its populist activity in the late nineteenth century and for its early adoption of antitrust laws. It also counted some of the first experiments in direct democracy, with Progressive reformers introducing provisions for referenda in the early 1900s.[6] The 1960s and 1970s gave birth to an even more unpredictable variant of this plebiscitarianism. The Proposition 13 movement, for instance—in which suburban homeowners pushed for a state referendum to institute a constitutional limit on public spending—also drew on an older legacy of direct democracy.[7] Homeowners and counterculture activists found some room for cautious agreement here. Cybernetic radicals had long recognized the potential of the technologies spawned by the Cold War arms race, seeking to retool them to emancipatory ends—much the way leftists such as van Duijn, van Ojik and Vaneigem had sought to fight cyberneticians on their own terrain.[8] These "hippie modernisms" also began to see guaranteed income schemes as a natural policy for the emerging cybernetic welfare state.[9]

A tech literature streaming out from the Bay Area in the 1990s offered its own reworking of these modernist themes, from magazines such as *Wired* and *Forbes* to an early blog culture advocating effective altruism.[10] Management guru Peter Drucker and libertarian social scientist Charles Murray also inspired the state's informal basic income movements.[11] Murray drew on the antipoverty strategies Moynihan had first devised in the late 1960s, when concerns about the black family drove America's experiments with cash allowances. For Murray, the extension of Nixon's tax credits in the 1970s and 1980s offered a promising precedent for a wholesale transformation of the American welfare state.[12] Its setup would be simplified by tying benefits to stock options and handing out all benefits in money rather than by providing public services. "Since the American government [was going to] continue to spend a huge amount of money on income transfers," Murray claimed, it would be preferable to "take all of that money and give it back to the American people in cash grants."[13] Murray's book did attach strong conditions to his grant, hoping to revitalize a desiccated civic landscape: the handout would be conditional on membership in a voluntary body, which would pay out the grants and impose standards of behavior on recipients. Coupled with a broader program of tax cuts, Murray's transfer state could both solve labor market rigidity and remedy the crisis of the American breadwinner—black and white.[14] In the 2010s his proposal gained headway across the American tech sector, from the Cato Institute to a new Basic Income Lab in Stanford.[15]

By the early 2010s, Murray's concerns about family stability were already proving less important to a new American basic income scene. After the dot-com crash of 2001, companies such as Google, Facebook, and Twitter began to emerge as the vanguard of a newly "social" internet. Focusing on retail possibilities, these companies also came with a specific professional culture of short-term and casual work based in cities with rising rental costs. This platform economy could no longer presuppose the stable unit of the male breadwinner model. The automation apocalypse had also failed to materialize: rather than being displaced by robots, labor in the American service economy became ever more supervised and mediated by digital platforms, barely increasing its productivity. "Full automation," Hughes saw, mainly seemed to come for a dwindling layer of middle managers, with a new "despotism on demand" taking over the informal sector.[16]

This new economy need not be one of pointless drudgery, however. Just like labor, social interaction had become more informal and fleeting in the postindustrial era. In contrast to traditional newspapers, civic organizations, and parties, social media allowed for a more open and nonhierarchical engagement between citizens. Cash welfare was a natural complement to this new openness. Just as money only prescribed a set of simple parameters within which the recipients could operate, the algorithms of Facebook had no built-in assumptions about individual norms. Within this protocol, it allowed users to gather spontaneously, with lower exit costs than existing groups and associations.[17] The World Bank's turn to bottom-up marketizing already offered a useful parallel. For Facebook's Chris Hughes in particular, American history offered ample alternatives for "overengineering" approaches to welfare. "The United States already runs the biggest cash transfer program in the world," Hughes noted in his book, "giving tens of billions of dollars, no strings attached, to struggling poor families to help boost their incomes and stabilize their financial lives."[18] Citing Moynihan and Nixon as precedents, Hughes drew a straight line from the 1960s to the 2010s: just like such platforms as Facebook, Twitter, and Reddit, Nixon's Earned Income Tax Credit scheme relied on the idea that state-driven public services were inferior to putting money into the hands of wage earners. Online and offline, individuals could now determine their own needs and preferences.

Hughes's "quantitative easing for the people" also shared a family tree that could be traced to Friedman's 1930s. As Friedman made clear, the New Deal era had rightly realized that the era of laissez-faire had ended. The state had a clear duty to stabilize market economies. Yet Friedman was also specific about how this stabilizing could be carried out: forms of direct price control, public utility, or state managerialism remained taboo. Instead, economic action could be delegated chiefly to the central bank, whose technical expertise could fuel popular purchasing power through helicopter drops. An early "technopopulist" case for cash transfers was crystallizing here: central banks dropped cash directly to consumers in cyclical downturns, which the people could use to kick-start the growth engine.[19]

To Hughes and other populists, this vision held both at home and abroad. After his encounter with GiveDirectly in 2012, the Facebook shareholder increasingly became convinced that such framework was also the future for a modernized American welfare state. As Hughes wondered in 2019, "Not to say we do not need hospitals and schools. . . . on balance, however, I think we should be asking if we're going to invest you know a dollar in a hospital might it be better to provide that dollar in cash for people to be able to go and find the health resources that they need?" GiveDirectly also did not speak to an exclusively African problem. "If your concern as an individual donor is making life easier and more fulfilling for the poor," a journalist noted at the time, "GiveDirectly's model warrant[ed] close consideration."[20] To a tech sector increasingly drawn to philanthropy, Hughes's initiative also offered a convincing counter to the idea "that they can do more good with the money than a person would do for themselves."[21]

This skepticism among tech barons over a top-down solution was reinforced by the total failure of Mark Zuckerberg's $100 million experiment to revolutionize education in New Jersey. Launched in 2010 with an army of consultants, among them Cory Booker and Chris Christie, the paternalistic bent of the reform seemed disconnected, driven by an ideological bias for private solutions and charter schools.[22] The public relations disaster of an initiative supposed to become the blueprint for the entire educational system echoed Sachs's failure in Africa and engendered a more cautious attitude among tech philanthropists. By 2016 the start-up incubator Y Combinator, funder of companies such as AirBnb, Dropbox, and Twitch, decided to launch its own basic income pilot in Oakland.[23] Although the first pilot was quite modest, the experiment would be expanded in 2018 and again in 2020, after the pandemic drew in substantial funding from tech hubs.[24]

Soon renamed Open Research Lab and boosted by additional capital from Jack Dorsey's and Hughes's funds, the pilot consisted of an RCT randomly selecting one thousand recipients to receive $1,000 a month for three years.[25] The experimental framework was explicitly inspired by the sub-Saharan pilots led by GiveDirectly, exporting the hype of RCTs from the South to the North. Through his own organization, the Economic Security Project, Hughes would go on to fund in 2018 the Stockton Economic Empowerment Demonstration (SEED) project, a twenty-four-month experiment in the city of Stockton, California. The pilot consisted of sending a $500 check every month to 125 randomly selected residents of the city.[26] Its political philosophy was also sensitively different from the humanitarian mood of the 1990s. The "root cause of poverty," the leaders of the project claimed, was a "lack of cash." Providing "the dignity and agency that everyone deserves," a check could revolutionize welfare in America. As argued on Hughes's website, "instead of a patriarchal approach of dictating how, where and on what terms individuals can build their lives, cash offers the dignity and self-determination that recognizes a one-size-fits-all approach is antiquated and rooted in distrust."[27] With "unrestricted payments," the website added, "recipients are able to pull themselves out of poverty and create economic stability for themselves and their families."[28]

Party politics steadily began to follow suit. By 2020 the pilot would become the centerpiece of Andrew Yang's plea for a "freedom dividend" in his presidential campaign. Stockton mayor Michael Tubbs even founded his own organization, Mayors for Guaranteed Income, to boost the policy across the country. Backed by more than fifty mayors, Tubbs's coalition would launch and help pilots from New Jersey to Indiana to New York.[29] After the pandemic crash, Jack Dorsey would give an unprecedented amount to fund experiments and research for the proposal. In April 2020 he announced the creation a new philanthropic initiative, #startsmall, to give away about a third of his wealth, $1 billion, becoming probably the largest funder of basic income initiatives.[30] The fund was designed to promote girls' health and education through UBIs. To accelerate the shift toward cash transfers, Dorsey notably donated $18 million to Tubbs's mayors' coalition, $15 million to the Y Combinator experiment in Oakland, $10 million to Andrew Yang's foundation, $5 million to the One Family Foundation in Philadelphia, and $3.5 million to the Cash Transfer Lab at New York University, where Dorsey had been a graduate student.[31]

While they grew out of the digital enthusiasm of the 2010s, these initiatives also came with an older history. They relied on an armory of arguments built up by two generations of basic income activists and the expiration of older remedies for market dependency. Basic income here was both an index of retreat—the demise of an older social statism—and an accelerant of entrenchment. The proposal flourished in the wake of a double disorganization: the weakening of a dense union movement as a countervailing power and the dwindling of mass parties tied to a hinterland of civil society organizations. In its place came a new "technopopulist" politics, focusing on public relations and media outreach, in which community activists spoke for a silent constituency as "advocates without members." Unlike older interest groups, these would principally voice their welfare demands in the abstract: increased cash rather than specific resource allocation.[32] The movement's success stood as a sign of the times:

cash transfers were the social policy of a new "liquid" democracy.[33] West-erners "need[ed] to define a new social contract for our generation" and "to explore ideas such as the universal basic income," as Mark Zucker-berg proclaimed in 2017.[34] This implied redrawing the social contract in accordance with "the conservative principles of a restricted government, rather than progressive ideas of an expanded social safety net."[35] For left-populists, basic income offered relief to a growing "precariat" beyond the grasp of classical insurance models, at home with new digital media and less taken with the industrial work ethic. In the 2000s, the proposal settled as the outer limit of a new welfare world in North and South—not just the "capitalist road to communism" as Philippe Van Parijs had presaged in the 1980s or the new development economics of the 2000s, but the "utopia for realists" who had altogether given up faith in transformative politics.[36]

Needs in the Technopopulist Era

Behind the successes of a new basic income stood the slow splintering and decomposition of the developmental coalitions that had undergirded older planning states. The slow death of developmentalist democracy in the Global South and North proved one of the strongest drives of the cashification of welfare through the 1990s and 2000s.[37] As citizens moved out of the civil society organizations and states increasingly stepped down from their interventionist role, politicians turned to public relations experts to win office. Poverty was definitively conceptualized as a simple lack of money, not as inadequate access to services. The "populist explosion" after 2008 both consolidated and accelerated this process of abstraction.[38] A curious alliance formed between technocrats and populists—both opponents of an older party democracy—over their shared preference for cash transfers. Both were conventionally conceived as opposites. Whereas populism celebrates the wisdom of the people, technocrats pleaded for expertise and sought to insulate policymaking from partisan interference. Whereas populists insist on the sovereignty of an indivisible people, technocrats sought to insulate expertise from popular power. Yet technocracy and populism shared an unexpected overlap. These two genres of politics both arose out of the decomposition of party democracy in the preceding thirty years, with declining membership rates, increased volatility, and falling voter participation as the most acute symptoms. Populism and technocracy steadily began to appear as the ideologies of this increasingly "disorganized" democracy.[39] Rather than being starkly opposed, technocracy and populism seemed to share an essential complementarity in their rejection of political mediation. Both also spoke to a refusal to filter collective wills through intermediary bodies; "populist and technocratic forms of discourse" could here even be "considered as two sides of the same coin."[40]

The economic drivers of the shift were evident. In a society with fewer permanent industrial jobs, more precarious work, and higher rates of self-employment, a corporatist welfare state built on trade unions and insurance funds seemed more and more obsolete. Instead, direct cash payments could furnish security for the new platform "precariat," no longer embedded in the political parties, development coalitions, or family units presupposed by an older welfarist tradition.[41] These changes epitomized a unique "technopopulist" front for basic income. For instance, in her memoir of the 2016 presidential contest, *What Happened*, Hillary Clinton recounted the way the proposal of a universal basic income "fascinated" her as she looked forward to an "Alaska for America" plan.[42] Inspired by the self-described "entrepreneur" Peter Barnes, whose best seller *With Liberty and Dividends for All* argued for "everyone-gets-a-share capitalism," Clinton almost included the proposal in her bid for the presidency. Before her, right-wing figures such as Pim Fortuyn began to argue for Friedman's negative income tax as a "revolt of the workers," letting go of "criticisms of the ethos of achievement" and his "careful sympathy of the basic income."[43] In the same period, the "antiparty" Five Star movement, Pirate movements, or Spain's Podemos pioneered a populist retake of the proposal.[44] Technocracy and populism here neatly joined hands: alleviating poverty need not imply a top-down approach to needs or crowd the market out of social life.

More than a vision of representation, however, in the 2010s this "technopopulism" also began to cohere around a distinct vision of social policy. As Chris Bickerton and Carlo Invernizzi have noted, technocrats and populists overlapped in their opposition to the transactional politics of the postwar period, leaving intermediate bodies out of government. In laggard fashion, the crisis had begun to span a new basic income movement: in the programs of presidential candidates, the policy briefs of British shadow prime ministers, tracts by accelerationist philosophers, and manifestos of new humanitarians and welfare reformers.[45]

The cashified welfare states of the 1990s and 2000s were also built on a distinctly new civil society. This society seemed increasingly unable to articulate concrete needs and had to consider its welfare requirements in the abstract. The link between politicians and the public also shifted: instead of attending to an organized civil society, they began to project "opinions" onto an atomized public. This revolution also implied a drastically different view of human needs. Rather than being seen as constituted through a democratic process and transactional politics, needs could simply be revealed as consumer choices or in our new virtual ecosystems. In the Zuckerberg welfare state, citizens would be able to receive monetary "dividends" directly on their phones by Apple Pay, Twitter, Facebook, or Weibo (like the Chinese beggars using a QR code to receive money directly on their smartphones), and the digitizing of our public sphere would be complete. Platforms were becoming the ideal vehicle for the technopopulist "welfare state 2.0," moving beyond the twentieth century's thickly mediated relationship between traditional media and institutions—including parties—and allowing for a less vertical and more direct interaction with their consumers.

The increasing popularity of Alaska's dividend model remains one of the best illustrations of this shifting conception of welfare—from a concrete notion of poverty as a lack of access to socially constituted needs (housing, employment, education, health care) to an abstract definition of poverty as a lack of money. The Alaska Permanent Fund (APF) itself was created in 1976 after an amendment to the state constitution. The initial impulse was for the government to invest a share of the revenue into an alternative source of revenue for the time when the state's oil fields would be depleted. Within such an initial framework, it seemed clear that the state had to invest the money in strategic sectors to prepare for an energetic transition. While this strategy never really materialized, by 1982 the Permanent Fund Dividend (PFD), was created and what was meant as a state fund became a source of individual dividends.[46] Rather than serving as a source of income for the state and government programs, the fund became a cash transfer program for the direct benefit of residents. This shift put the state in an increasingly difficult budgetary situation, since Alaska has no income tax or sales tax. In September 1999 the state even submitted to the ballot box an advisory question to decide whether it could use a portion of the Alaska Permanent Fund to fund government programs. In a significant vote, the proposal was decisively rejected, with 83.25 percent voting no. This clear rejection of public goods in favor of direct transfers would become even more salient in the following decades. When in July 2019 the governor of Alaska announced drastic cutbacks to the state's public university system, he implicitly chose between two visions of social policy. As part of a general austerity drive, half of state expenditure was to be scrapped, with buildings sold off and staff fired. The justification for the cuts was specific: Alaska wanted to maintain its citizen dividend and could not do so in a falling oil market.[47] Alaskan conservatives defended their grant with a variant of Hughes's argument: Who needed a public university if every book had become available on Amazon?

The Alaskan debate also hinted at one of the oldest questions in the basic income debate ever since its inception in the 1930s. What was the right balance between individual and collective consumption? And where and how should the state draw this line? Before the 1930s, grant thinkers made firm commitments to collective notions of freedom a precondition for their grants. In the same decade, economist John Kenneth Galbraith coined the notion of a "social balance" to denote the question of where to draw the line between public and private goods. Himself trained in agricultural economics, he was used to thinking in concrete units—horses, bales of hay, tractors. These models themselves suppressed genres of economic reasoning in abstract money sums.[48] As Galbraith noted about Pigouvian externality theory, the "final problem of the productive society is what it produces," manifested "in an implacable tendency to provide an opulent supply of some things and a niggardly yield of others."[49] This "disparity between our flow of private and public goods and services" also could be "no matter of subjective judgment."[50] Instead, whether to provide "private automobiles or public bus services" was a matter of democratic deliberation, not consumer wants.

Interwar discussions in welfare economics repeatedly pitted these individualist and collectivist visions against each other.[51] As Maurice Dobb observed in 1940, socialist policy would allow for a "large sector of . . . 'communal consumption,' where things are supplied free (or at nominal prices) by the state."[52] In his view it was "possible that such a system would in time, by the gradual extension of communal at the expense of individual consumption, evolve into a condition of complete communism."[53] In the first socialist calculation debates of the 1920s, Austrian thinkers such as Otto Neurath, Friedrich Hayek, Gottfried Haberler, and Ludwig von Mises already faced off on these questions of coordination and in-kind investment. In this setting, socialists like Neurath could be confident that all goods could eventually fall into the public category.[54] Neurath's plea never was a purely intellectual one. In a world of welfare-warfare states, mass parties, price controls, and public control were a desideratum across society. The United States always had the weakest of these "countervailing powers": by the late 1940s, American business was organizing against Taft-Hartley and removed price controls, pushing out the option of a "social Keynesianism" that was becoming feasible in the United Kingdom and Sweden. By the mid-1960s these currents provided enough momentum for a powerful cash transfer movement in Europe and the United States. In the Global North it birthed and stimulated "welfare without the welfare state"; in the South it entrenched "development without development."

After the Century of Laboring Man

The abstraction of needs implicit in the transfer paradigm also translated into an increasing abstraction of *labor* itself. As a sphere of human life, it was increasingly unmoored from humanist visions of flourishing or public service. Basic income shows how actors on both the left and the right found a welcome pivot in the market after "the end of the century of the laboring man."[55] Inspired by the antiauthoritarian potential of cybernetics, neoleftists began not just to think of basic income as a tool to deconstruct social policy but to rethink socialism beyond the worker and the social itself. Stuck in prison in 1997 after his red years, Antonio Negri declared that "flexibility and mobility of [the] labor force . . . were irreversible."[56] The development was hardly exclusive to the far left: Vladimir Putin's 2005 l'goty welfare reforms, for instance, equally tore up a tapestry of in-kind benefits modeled on the Soviet "laboring man" and further facilitated the country's transition to a liberal market economy.[57]

A rift with earlier, twentieth-century welfare revolutions also proved a constant in these cases. As Mark Mazower noted, during the 1970s inflation and capitalist crisis work itself "was assuming a different significance in people's lives."[58] While both communists and fascists had granted a central place to work as "redemption from uselessness and entry-ticket to the community," the 1970s saw an intense and long-standing decoupling of work and income.[59] Mass unemployment reemerged, although often in the guise of underemployment, and remained a "major social problem despite economic recovery and the creation of jobs in the service sector."[60] "Unimaginable to most people twenty years earlier," this rise was now "accompanied by very little serious unrest."[61] Citizens had "come to accept high levels of poverty and inequality," even while their "social contract was in crisis."[62] As the British critic N. P. Barry noted in 1992, neoliberalism was correct in its dichotomy between "freedom and coercion" and rightly recognized the "intrinsically coercive character of the welfare state" and its "form of social control."[63] In the early 1980s postworkerists could still organize their own anti–May Day events, hoping that the labor movement would let go of its "cult of labor" and regain revolutionary élan. As sociologist Ulrich Beck noted in a 1999 lecture at the London School of Economics, the end of "the zombie category of 'full employment' . . . need not be a catastrophe," instead allowing "every person to become a member of a cosmopolitan civil society" by "decoupling . . . income entitlements from paid work and from the labour market."[64]

Beck and Gorz could hardly anticipate a world in which asset appreciation, financialization, and decades-long wage stagnation would radically marginalize labor as a source of identity. In a 2015 poll conducted by the British agency YouGov, for instance, a staggering 37 percent said their jobs didn't "make a meaningful contribution to the world" and consequently were pointless, versus an astonishing 87 percent of people with "work fatigue."[65] Structurally, notions of "employment" were still at the center of capitalist economies, of course. According to the International Labour Organization, the global labor force grew by 25 percent from 2000 to 2019, of which 53 percent were wage or salary earners and 34 percent were considered "own account" workers.[66] Yet in an epoch when capitalism had eliminated all other social markers except work, opportunities for work itself were increasingly scarce, with growth stagnant and most labor gains in the past ten years in a low-paying service sector — "the paradox of a society full of workers with no work."[67] Deindustrialization spurred the weakening of organizations that politicized and constituted needs. Many leftists turned to basic income as a substitute for forlorn utopias. While Erik Olin Wright could still criticize Van Parijs and van der Veen's "capitalist road to communism" in 1986, by the 2000s he was embracing the proposal as a "real utopia" for a partially decommodified labor market.[68] As André Gorz concluded in 1994, "If [socialism] means fighting for the emancipation of the workers, then socialists are merely the elitist ideological spokespersons for those 15 per cent who still define themselves chiefly by their work" — the supposedly dwindling minority "who feel they are workers first and foremost."[69]

*　*　*

In his psychohistory of nineteenth-century Paris, German cultural critic Siegfried Kracauer described the oeuvre of composer Jacques Offenbach both as "the most representative expression of [an] era" and as "exerting a transformational energy" on it. In Kracauer's view, ideas could both "mirror their epoch and help to explode it."[70] The same can be said for the story of basic income; through its prism, historians observe evolving conceptions of economic justice, social rights, the state, markets, and political organization *tout court*, but also transformative visions. Above all, however, basic income has important consequences for how we think about the rise of neoliberalism at the close of the twentieth century. Although the core of the idea of basic income was established by thinkers of neoclassical bent, its appeal was never exclusive to that tradition. This urges a reconsideration of a now powerfully prevalent schools-based approach to the neoliberal turn, which has sought to track the late-century market revolution back to a series of thought collectives. Instead of focusing on a monocausal neoliberalism, it sees the global rise of cash transfers as hinting at a deeper and messier market turn that ran through many traditions and currents in the late twentieth century. This late-century "market turn" united both left and right in an increasingly inescapable embrace of the decentralized operations of the price mechanism.[71] In this techno-populist compound, "traditional forms of state control were replaced by more complex regulatory frameworks," and "expertise rather than political judgement was likely to prove valuable and effective."[72]

Across these contexts, basic income seemed less of a neoliberal plot to commercialize the welfare state or a libertarian ploy to rip up corporatist labor standards. Nor was it an incremental anarchist tool to move the left beyond an antiquated work ethic. More critically, scholars such as Daniel Rodgers, Reuel Schiller, and Gary Gerstle trace a "market-friendly" left visible in the UBI as specifically left wing. It was not simply an import or a colonization from the neoliberal camp, even though promiscuous interaction was always possible, as Van Parijs and Standing exemplified in the 1980s. Such an embrace of market politics on the left can be traced back to the market socialisms of the 1930s and 1940s, when writers such as Abba Lerner, Oscar Lange, and James Meade already constructed visions that recuperated rather than abjured the price system. Yet this left-wing turn to the market also had causes that go beyond this older tradition: the weight of the '68 moment, for instance, when theories of cybernetics and self-organization helped a new left free itself from certain statist orthodoxies, was even more cardinal in powering the UBI wave. A rich literature on Albert Hirschman's "exit fantasies" has been written in the past ten years, mainly for the right. Yet the story of basic income shows us the rise of a particular "exit" or "exodus fantasy" *on the left.*

The story of basic income thereby adds an important piece to the current literature on social policy. The first can be traced to the work of Paul Pierson. Since 1994, scholars have heeded Pierson's critique of the idea that the welfare state declined in the age of neoliberalism, when it was clear that public expenditure and even participation in many programs were still rising. In Pierson's view, "the welfare state's political position does not seem to have been seriously eroded by the decline of its key traditional constituency, organized labor."[73] Instead, "the maturation of social programs has produced a new network of organized interests," from NGOs to welfare rights bureaucracies, that pushed for streamlining social services throughout the deflationary 1990s and the 2000s.[74] The story of basic income both contests and supports this hypothesis. The welfare state is still here, yet its classical form has been thoroughly transformed in the postindustrial era: commercial and market-friendly, but deeply averse to decommodification. The story of basic income tells a history not of quantitative decline for welfarism, but rather of qualitative change, from in-kind redistribution to monetary transfers. Yet this basic income story also decenters the neoliberal heuristic in favor of a more general market turn, pointing to the more "enduring features of capitalism" that have inflected the new welfare turn.[75] This was a turn that also was indigenously left wing and centrist, not just an emanation from the neoliberal right. Second, the UBI story also extends an existing thesis of the "politics of exit," or the disorganization of mass politics into the realm of policy—visible in the rise of a new form of technopopulist welfare and the increasing abstraction of needs it relied on. Here a new state arose that "did not order . . . negotiate, persuade, and advise."[76] This was also a state "less suspicious of markets" that "encourage[d] (and sometimes require[d]) individuals to enter these markets," promoting "regulatory goals with minimal impact on individual autonomy."[77]

Behind the rise of the basic income thus stood a deeper shift in modern political culture. More than a system of economic organization, markets now seemed to become an indispensable anthropological tool for thinkers on both left and right. As French philosopher Marcel Gauchet noted in 1998, the late-century revival of the idea of "the market" had "very little to do . . . with considerations of economic efficiency."[78] Rather, it followed "a reconsideration of the political status of the actor" itself. "How can we imagine the form of relations that can be established between agents who are all independent of each other," Gauchet wondered, "and all entitled to pursue the maximization of their advantages as they see fit, in the absence of an imperative composition in the name of the interest of all?"[79] "Once institutions have been delegitimized and bypassed on the grounds that they disregard singularities," humans could "only move towards a coexistence of private singularities, arbitrated by rules that are again impersonal. . . . a self-regulated coexistence of singular offers and demands."[80] As a policy the basic income thus presupposed a new anthropology: no longer that of the *animal laborans* in a community of citizens, but that of the "sovereign consumer" inscribed into a network of users.[81] This new model of "market sovereignty," as Eric Hobsbawm saw in 2001, now appeared to offer "an alternative to any kind of politics" as such.[82]

Together with this "reconfiguration" of the actor, the move to cash transfers also implied a radical reconfiguration of the state. Rather than being a public power that could participate in and order the economic game, the state now had to supervise or arbitrate between individuals—as a referee that would not interfere in the game. Marcel Gauchet's "market model" brought forth a new "manifestation of the authority of that State," now merely the "instrument of a civil society in a state of perfect self-sufficiency."[83] For the French philosopher this notion of self-sufficiency "was as old as the idea of the market itself."[84] It had driven the first pleas for "commercial society" in the eighteenth century, equally inflecting later debates on development.[85] Yet in the late twentieth century this market now "fulfilled a function that it did not have before"—the "old idea becoming what it potentially was, perhaps always has been, but had never been in practice: a model far beyond the economy, for all actions in all sectors of social life."[86] In Gauchet's view:

> Once the absolute independence of individual actors is consecrated, the coordination of the whole necessarily takes the form of a market . . . a more or less automatic arbitration between the initiatives, offers, and demands of the various actors involved. In themselves these ideas are nothing new. What *is* new is the extent of their application: they are beginning to shape social life from top to bottom.[87]

As Gauchet insists, the story of basic income will never be the exclusive province of policy makers, economists, politicians, social scientists, or activists; it is only partially covered by terms such as neoliberalism, neoclassicism, automation, or deindustrialization. Instead, it hints at a more profound break at the heart of modern political culture: the occurrence of a "second capitalist revolution" somewhere in the second half of the twentieth century, when humanity undertook its second move from markets to market societies.[88] After "the end of labour, the end of production, and the end of political economy," money had now "found its proper place . . . an orbit which rises and sets like some artificial sun."[89] Through the prism of basic income, we receive just a fascinating glimpse of this orbital movement.

Acknowledgments

This book began as a friendship, when two Belgian émigrés met in Cambridge in January 2017. Like any form of work, its completion proved to be a social process: this book would never have seen the light of day without a close circle of interlocutors. First, Pedro Ramos Pinto and Peter Sloman supported our project from the very start. Their advice, and more specifically a conference on the history of basic income they co-organized at Cambridge in January 2019, proved indispensable in encouraging us to actually write the book. We also thank Samuel Moyn, Corey Robin, Niklas Olsen, Alex Gourevitch, and Daniel Steinmetz-Jenkins for help and enthusiasm during the project's embryonic stages. This also holds for veterans of the basic income movement such as Philippe Van Parijs, Walter Van Trier, and Guy Standing, who generously shared details about the early years. We'd also like to express all our gratitude to our editors, Darrin McMahon and Chad Zimmerman, who have been there throughout the whole writing process, and to Alice Bennett for her incredible work on the manuscript. We both also thank the Wiener-Anspach Foundation, which gave us the material support to finish this book. Finally, we are grateful to those who took time to read, comment on, and discuss our early drafts. Their organization of conferences, workshops, and reading groups formed an essential part of our writing and thinking. In particular we thank Jean-Luc De Meulemeester, Jennifer Burns, Jean-Baptiste Fleury, Cléo Chassonnery-Zaïgouche, Maxime Desmarais-Tremblay, David

Grewal, Giacomo Gabbuti, Carolina Alves, Mateo Alaluf, Frédéric Panier, Vanessa De Greef, Daniel Dumont, Camille Coletta, Pierre-Étienne Vandamme, Marc-Antoine Sabaté, Angus Burgin, Jayati Ghosh, David Priestland, Simon Szreter, Alyssa Battistoni, Gautham Shiralagi, Rudi Laermans, Arthur Borriello, Télémaque Masson-Récipon, Noam Maggor, Erez Maggor, Roni Hirsch, Alice O'Connor, Jan Overwijk, William Shoki, Esteban Van Volcem, Alex Wood, Daniela Gabor, Merijn Oudenampsen, Axel Jansen, Ed Quish, Adam Lebovitz, Dominik Leusder, Seth Ackerman, Jens van 't Klooster, Benjamin Braun, Max Krahé, Aaron Benanav, Isabella Weber (and the entire Brussels reading group), Adolph Reed, Cedric Johnson, Todd Cronan, John-Baptist Oduor, Caitlin Doherty, Grey Anderson, and Dustin Guastella. Without them there would be no book at all.

Notes

Introduction

1. Colm Quinn, "Will the White House Send Cash to All Americans?," *Foreign Policy* (March 18, 2020). See also Adam Tooze, *Shutdown: How Covid Shook the World's Economy* (London: Penguin, 2021); Toby Green, *The Covid Consensus: The New Politics of Global Inequality* (London: Oxford University Press, 2021); Paulo Gerbaudo, *The Great Recoil* (London: Verso Books, 2021).

2. Eileen Sullivan, "5 Takeaways from the Coronavirus Economic Relief Package," *New York Times*, March 25, 2020; Susan Watkins, "Paradigm Shifts," *New Left Review* 128 (March-April 2021): 5–22; Robert Brenner, "Escalating Plunder," *New Left Review* 123 (May-June 2020): 5–22. Although bookended by the Treasury Department, the amount itself was disbursed by the Internal Revenue Service, which used the United States' existing tax rolls to deposit the funds. This generated risk for American citizens with no direct tax returns, whose direct deposit information was not available to the IRS—a problem examined in Sidhya Balakrishnan, Sara Constantino, and Stephen Nuñez, "Building a Helicopter: Pathways for Targeting and Distributing a US Guaranteed Income," *Jain Family Institute*, July 2020, 1–18.

3. See Philippe Van Parijs, "Five Questions to Philosopher Philippe Van Parijs on Basic Income and the Coronavirus," *Brussels Times*, April 2, 2020; https://www.brusselstimes.com/news/magazine/104273/five-questions-to-philosopher-philippe-van-parijs-on-basic-income-and-the-coronavirus/; Philippe Van Parijs, "Why Surfers Should Be Fed: The Liberal Case for an Unconditional Basic Income," *Philosophy and Public Affairs* 20, no. 2 (Spring 1991): 101–31.

4. Van Parijs, "Five Questions."

5. Van Parijs, "Five Questions."

6. Van Parijs, "Five Questions."

7. Van Parijs, "Five Questions."

8. Howard Reed and Stewart Lansley, *Universal Basic Income: An Idea Whose Time Has Come* (London: Compass, 2016); Andrew Yang, *The War on Normal People: The Truth about America's Disappearing Jobs and Why Universal Basic Income*

Is Our Future (New York: Hachette, 2018); Andy Stern, *Raising the Floor: How a Universal Basic Income Can Renew Our Economy and Rebuild the American Dream* (New York: Hachette, 2016); David Frayne, *The Refusal of Work: The Theory and Practice of Resistance to Work* (New York: Zed Books, 2015); Nick Srnicek, *Platform Capitalism* (London: Polity, 2017); Peter Frase, *Four Futures: Life after Capitalism* (New York: Verso Books, 2016).

9. Philippe Van Parijs and Yannick Vanderborght, *Basic Income: A Sane Proposal for a Free Society* (Cambridge, MA: Harvard University Press, 2017); Rutger Bregman, *Utopia for Realists* (New York: Penguin, 2017).

10. Quentin Skinner, *The Foundations of Modern Political Thought*, vol. 2 (Cambridge: Cambridge University Press, 1978), 3–53; Ludwig Wittgenstein, *Blue and Brown Books* (London: Blackwell, 1958), 17–20.

11. Fredric Jameson, *The Political Unconscious: Narrative as a Socially Symbolic Act* (Ithaca, NY: Cornell University Press, 2015); Peter Berger, *The Sacred Canopy: The Social Reality of Religion* (London: Faber and Faber, 1969), 45. As Dylan Riley notes, such a critical-theoretical history primarily concerns itself with "an elucidation of the conditions of possibility for something to exist, and more specifically, an explanation of the conditions under which certain claims, or even whole styles of reasoning, are valid." See Dylan Riley, *Microverses: Observations from a Shattered Present* (London, New York: Verso Books, 2022), xiii.

12. Friedrich Hayek, *The Road to Serfdom: Text and Documents; The Definitive Edition* (New York: Routledge, 2008), 125.

13. Hayek, *Road to Serfdom*, 89.

14. Mathew Forstater, "From Civil Rights to Economic Security: Bayard Rustin and the African-American Struggle for Full Employment, 1945–1978," *International Journal of Political Economy* 36, no. 3 (Fall 2007): 63–74; David Stein, "Containing Keynesianism in an Age of Civil Rights: Jim Crow Monetary Policy and the Struggle for Guaranteed Jobs, 1956–1979," in *Beyond the New Deal Order: U.S. Politics from the Great Depression to the Great Recession*, ed. Gary Gerstle, Nelson Lichtenstein, and Alice O'Connor (Philadelphia: University of Pennsylvania Press, 2019), 124–42; Samir Sonti, "The Price of Prosperity: Inflation and the Limits of the New Deal Order" (PhD diss., University of California, Santa Barbara, 2017).

15. Friedrich Hayek, *Law, Legislation and Liberty*, vol. 3, *The Political Order of a Free People* (Chicago: University of Chicago Press, 1979), 55.

16. Arthur Kemp, "Welfare without the Welfare State," *Il Politico* 31, no. 4 (Dicembre 1966): 716.

17. Kemp, "Welfare without the Welfare State," 716.

18. Kemp, "Welfare without the Welfare State," 719. For Hayek's phrase, see Hayek, *Road to Serfdom*, 44.

19. Kemp, "Welfare without the Welfare State," 719.

20. Kemp, "Welfare without the Welfare State," 721.

21. Kemp, "Welfare without the Welfare State," 726.

22. Kemp, "Welfare without the Welfare State," 716.

23. Kemp, "Welfare without the Welfare State," 722.

24. Kemp, "Welfare without the Welfare State," 727f.

25. Hyman Minsky, "Effects of Shifts of Aggregate Demand upon Income Distribution," *American Journal of Agricultural Economics* 50, no. 2 (May 1968): 330. See also Hyman Minsky, *Ending Poverty: Jobs, Not Welfare* (London: Levy Economics Institute, 2013).

26. Minsky, "Effects of Shifts of Aggregate Demand," 330.

27. Nelson Lichtenstein, "From Corporatism to Collective Bargaining: Organized Labor and the Eclipse of Social Democracy in the Postwar Era," in Lichtenstein, *A Contest of Ideas: Capital, Politics, and Labor* (Urbana: University of Illinois Press, 2013), 79–99.

28. Nelson Lichtenstein, "Review of Mike Davis, 'Prisoners of the American Dream: Politics and Economy in the History of the U.S. Working Class'"; Kim Moody, "An Injury to All: The Decline of American Trade Unionism," *International Labor and Working-Class History* 36 (December 2008): 118.

29. Steve Meyer, "An Economic 'Frankenstein': UAW Workers' Responses to Automation at the Ford Brook Park Plant in the 1950s," *Michigan Historical Review* 28, no. 1 (Spring 2002): 69. See also Andrew V. Sanchez, "American Cybernation: Technological Upheaval and Guaranteed Income Advocacy in the 1960s United States," in *Universal Basic Income in Historical Perspective*, ed. Peter Sloman, Daniel Zamora Vargas, and Pedro Ramos Pinto (London: Palgrave, 2021), 67–88.

30. William J. Baumol and Alan S. Blinder, eds., *Economics—Principles and Policy* (New York: Harcourt Brace Jovanovich, 1982), 810.

31. For an overview, see Johan Christensen, *The Power of Economists within the State* (Stanford, CA: Stanford University Press, 2017); Lynn Turgeon, *Bastard Keynesianism: The Evolution of Economic Thinking and Policymaking since World War II* (New York: Greenwood, 1999); Steve Fraser and Gary Gerstle, eds., *The Rise and Fall of the New Deal Order, 1930–1980* (Princeton, NJ: Princeton University Press, 2020); Aaron Major, *Architects of Austerity: International Finance and the Politics of Growth* (Stanford, CA: Stanford University Press, 2014); Johanna Bockman, *Markets in the Name of Socialism: The Left-Wing Origins of Neoliberalism* (Stanford, CA: Stanford University Press, 2011); Stephanie L. Mudge, *Leftism Reinvented: Western Parties from Socialism to Neoliberalism* (Cambridge, MA: Harvard University Press, 2018); Timothy Shenk, "Inventing the American Economy" (PhD diss., Columbia University, 2016).

32. Mark Mazower, *Dark Continent: Europe's Twentieth Century* (New York: Knopf, 1998), 340; Goran Therborn, *European Modernity and Beyond: The Trajectory of European Societies, 1945–2000* (London: Verso, 1995).

33. Stuart Hall, *Selected Political Writings: The Great Moving Right Show and Other Essays* (Durham, NC: Duke University Press, 2017), 389–92; Stuart Hall, "The Neoliberal Revolution," *Cultural Studies*, 25, no. 6 (2011): 705–28; Melinda Cooper, "Workfare, Familyfare, Godfare: Transforming Contingency into Necessity,"

South Atlantic Quarterly 111, no. 4 (Fall 2012): 640–57; Jamie Peck and Nikolas Theodore, "'Work First': Workfare and the Regulation of Contingent Labour Markets," *Cambridge Journal of Economics* 24, no. 1 (2000): 119–38.

34. Sloman, "Basic Income," 20.

35. Reuel Schiller, "Regulation and the Collapse of the New Deal Order, or How I Learned to Stop Worrying and Love the Market," in *Beyond the New Deal Order: U.S. Politics from the Great Depression to the Great Recession*, ed. Gary Gerstle, Nelson Lichtenstein, and Alice O'Connor (Philadelphia: University of Pennsylvania Press, 2019), 185.

36. Dylan Riley, "Bernstein's Heirs," *New Left Review* 76 (July-August 2012): 150.

37. See Richard Barbrook and Andy Cameron, "The Californian Ideology," *Science as Culture* 6, no. 1 (1996): 44–72; Evgeny Morozov, *To Save Everything: Click Here* (London: Penguin, 2013); Ash Amin, *Post-Fordism* (London: Wiley, 2011); Gavin Mueller, "Digital Proudhonism," *boundary 2* (July 2018): 1–22.

38. James Ferguson, *Give a Man a Fish: Reflections on the New Politics of Distribution* (Durham, NC: Duke University Press, 2015), passim.

39. Ellen Meiksins Wood, "A Social History of Political Thought," in Wood, *Liberty and Property: A Social History of Western Political Thought from the Renaissance to Enlightenment* (London: Verso Books, 2012), 27; "Why It Matters," *London Review of Books* 30, no. 18 (September 25, 2008); Neal Wood, *Reflections on Political Theory: A Voice of Reason from the Past* (New York: Springer, 2001), 103–5. As Neal Wood notes, "although the Cambridge School has made an unquestionable advance in methodological sophistication and historical rigour," its focus is "almost exclusively upon the relationship among linguistic formulations" and sometimes neglects "social, political, and economic referents in the world of human existence" (103). See also Andrew Sartori, "Bengali 'Culture' as a Historical Problem," in Sartori, *Bengal in Global Concept History: Culturalism in the Age of Capital* (Chicago: University of Chicago Press, 2008), 1–24.

40. Samuel Moyn, "Imaginary Intellectual History," in *Rethinking Modern European Intellectual History*, ed. Darrin M. McMahon and Samuel Moyn (New York: Oxford University Press, 2014), 126. See also Andrew Sartori, "Global Intellectual History and the History of Political Economy," in *Global Intellectual History*, ed. Samuel Moyn and Andrew Sartori (New York: Columbia University Press, 2013), 110–33; Mark Goldie, "The Context of *The Foundations*," in *Rethinking the Foundations of Modern Political Thought*, ed. Annabel Brett and James Tully (Cambridge: Cambridge University Press, 2006), 9; Martin B. Carstensen and Vivien A. Schmidt, "Power through, over and in Ideas: Conceptualizing Ideational Power in Discursive Institutionalism," *Journal of European Public Policy* 23, no. 3 (2016): 318–37.

41. Christopher Hill, *Intellectual Origins of the English Revolution* (Oxford: Oxford University Press, 1965), 3. For this vision of intellectual history on the intersection of "fact" and "value, see also Daniel Rodgers, *The Work Ethic in Industrial America, 1850–1920* (Chicago: University of Chicago Press 1979), xii.

42. Our emphasis. See Angus Burgin, "The Reinvention of Entrepreneurship," in *American Labyrinth: Intellectual History for Complicated Times*, ed. Raymond Haberski Jr. and Andrew Hartman (Ithaca, NY: Cornell University Press, 2018), 165.

43. See Charles Maier, "The Politics of Productivity: Foundations of American International Economic Policy after World War II," *International Organization* 31, no. 4 (1977): 607; Brett Christophers, *Rentier Capitalism* (London: Verso, 2020).

Chapter One

1. The episode is recounted in Delbert Burkett, ed., *The Blackwell Companion to Jesus* (London: John Wiley, 2011), and in Christopher Douglas, *If God Meant to Interfere: American Literature and the Rise of the Christian Right* (Ithaca, NY: Cornell University Press, 2016), 252–54. Plantard's genealogical claims and his membership in the "Priory of Sion" were later popularized in *The Holy Blood and the Holy Grail: The Secret History of Christ and the Shocking Legacy of the Grail*, by Michael Baigent, Richard Leigh, and Henry Lincoln (London: Jonathan Cape, 1982), used by Dan Brown in writing *The Da Vinci Code* (New York: Doubleday, 2003); see Simon Hoggarth, "Da Vinci Court Wrangle Is Hilarious Fun," *Guardian* (March 4, 2006), 18.

2. For the classic account, see Eric Hobsbawm and Terence Ranger, eds., *The Invention of Tradition* (London: Cambridge University Press, 1983), 1–14. See also Stephen Prickett, *Modernity and the Reinvention of Tradition: Backing into the Future* (Cambridge: Cambridge University Press, 2009).

3. Jurgen De Wispelaere and Lindsay James Stirton, "The Many Faces of Universal Basic Income," *Political Quarterly* 75, no. 3 (July 2004): 266–74; James Ferguson, *Give a Man a Fish: Reflections on the New Politics of Distribution* (Durham, NC: Duke University Press, 2015), 52–57. For examples, see Guy Standing, *Basic Income: And How We Can Make It Happen* (London: Pelican, 2017), chap. 1; Guy Standing, *Battling Eight Giants: Basic Income Now* (London: Bloomsbury Publishing, 2020); Guy Standing, *The Corruption of Capitalism: Why Rentiers Thrive and Work Does Not Pay* (London: Biteback, 2016); Guy Standing, *Beyond the New Paternalism: Basic Security as Equality* (London: Verso Books, 2002), 203–4; Malcolm Torry, ed., *The Palgrave International Handbook of Basic Income* (New York: Springer, 2019).

4. For more popular examples, see Douglas Carswell, *Progress vs. Parasites: A Brief History of the Conflict That's Shaped Our World* (London: Head of Zeus, 2013), 12–13; Rutger Bregman, *Utopia for Realists: And How We Can Get There* (London: Bloomsbury, 2017), 133; Steven Pinker, *Enlightenment Now: The Case for Reason, Science, Humanism, and Progress* (London: Penguin, 2018), 119; Karl Widerquist, ed., *Exploring the Basic Income Guarantee* (London: Palgrave Macmillan, 2021).

5. Bregman, *Utopia for Realists*, 133.

6. Standing, *Basic Income*, 17.

7. Walter Van Trier, *Every One a King: An Investigation into the Meaning and Significance of the Debate on Basic Incomes, with Special Reference to Three Episodes from the British Inter-war Experience* (Leuven: Departement sociologie, 1995). See also the excellent Walter Van Trier, "James Meade's 'Social Dividend' to 'State Bonus': An Intriguing Chapter in the History of a Concept," *Association Œconomia* 8, no. 4 (2018): 439–74; Walter Van Trier, "Basic Income: Pedigree and Problems," in *Real Libertarianism Assessed: Political Theory after Van Parijs*, ed. John Cunliffe, Guido Erreygers, and Walter Van Trier (London: Springer, 2003), 15–28; Walter Van Trier, "A. R. Orage and the Reception of Douglas's Social Credit Theory," in *Language, Communication and the Economy*, ed. Guido Erreygers and Geert Jacobs (Amsterdam: John Benjamins, 2005), 199–229.

8. Peter Sloman, *Transfer State: The Idea of Guaranteed Income and the Politics of Basic Income in Britain* (London: Oxford University Press, 2019); Anton Jäger and Daniel Zamora, "Free Money for Surfers: A Genealogy of the Idea of Universal Basic Income," *Los Angeles Review of Books* (April 17, 2020); Peter Sloman, "Universal Basic Income in British Politics, 1918–2018: From a 'Vagabond's Wage' to a Global Debate," *Journal of Social Policy* 47, no. 3 (July 2018): 625–42; "'The Jehovah's Witnesses of Social Policy'? The Basic Income Research Group and the Politics of Work in the Long 80s," unpublished paper presented at the Modern British History Research Seminar, University of Cambridge (May 2018), 1–28.

9. Cited in Marci Shore, "Can We *See* Ideas?," in *Rethinking Modern European Intellectual History*, ed. Darrin M. McMahon and Samuel Moyn (London: Oxford University Press, 2011), 207.

10. Politically, such claims are understandable from an activist's vantage point, much as Plantard needed a consistent family tree. Scientifically, however, they come painfully close to Karl Popper's naming Plato a "totalitarian" or Umberto Eco's portrait of Pericles as "the first populist." See Karl Popper, *The Open Society and Its Enemies* (Princeton, NJ: Princeton University Press, 2013), 1–112; Umberto Eco, "Pericle il populista," *La Repubblica* (January 14, 2012). Such skepticism need not imply that our current basic income has *no* historical precedents. Thinkers across history have always concerned themselves with issues of distribution and minimal provision. All in all, our UBI appears to be exactly that: *ours*.

11. Moses Finley, *Ancient Slavery and Modern Ideology* (New York: Markus Wiener, 1998), 85.

12. J. M. Dunn, "The Identity of the History of Ideas," *Philosophy* 43 (1968): 85–104.

13. Philippe Van Parijs and Yannick Vanderborght, *Basic Income: A Sane Proposal for a Free Society* (Cambridge, MA: Harvard University Press, 2017), 12–21.

14. See John Cunliffe and Guido Erreygers, Preface, in *Origins of Universal Grants: An Anthology of Historical Writings on Basic Capital and Basic Income,*

ed. J. Cunliffe and G. Erreygers (New York: Springer, 2004), x-1; Standing, *Basic Income*, chap. 2; Ingrid Robeyns, "Care, Gender and Property-Owning Democracy," in *Property-Owning Democracy: Rawls and Beyond*, ed. Martin O'Neill and Thad Williamson (London: John Wiley, 2012); Carole Pateman, "Freedom and Democratization: Why Basic Income Is to Be Preferred to Basic Capital," in *The Ethics of Stakeholding*, ed. K. Dowding (London: Palgrave, 2002), 130–48. for explorations of this difference.

15. For classical statements, see Quentin Skinner, *Visions of Politics*, vol. 1, *On Method* (Cambridge: Cambridge University Press, 2002); Reinhart Koselleck, *Futures Past: On the Semantics of Historical Time* (New York: Columbia University Press, 2004); Terrence Ball and James Farr, eds., *Political Innovation and Conceptual Change* (Cambridge: Cambridge University Press, 1989); Quentin Skinner, *Reason and Rhetoric in the Philosophy of Thomas Hobbes* (Cambridge: Cambridge University Press, 1996); Quentin Skinner, "The Empirical Theorists of Democracy and Their Critics: A Plague on Both Their Houses," *Political Theory* 3 (1973): 287–306.

16. See Mark Bevir, "What Is Radical Historicism?," *Philosophy of the Social Sciences* 45 (March 2014): 258–65; Mark Bevir, *The Logic of the History of Ideas* (Cambridge: Cambridge University Press, 2004).

17. For a similar classification, see Philippe Van Parijs, Bruce Ackerman, and Anne Allstot, *Redesigning Distribution: Basic Income and Stakeholder Grants as Alternative Cornerstones for a More Egalitarian Capitalism* (London: Verso Books, 2006), 14–25; Stuart Gordon White, *The Civic Minimum: On the Rights and Obligations of Economic Citizenship* (London: Oxford University Press, 2003); Ugi Gentili et al., *Exploring Universal Basic Income: A Guide to Navigating Concepts, Evidence, and Practices* (Washington, DC: World Bank Publications, 2005).

18. Bertrard de Jouvenel was the first to divide this strand of thought into "agrarianism" and "redistributionism." See Bertrand de Jouvenel, *The Ethics of Redistribution* (Cambridge: Cambridge University Press, 2010), 8–9. This distinction between cash-based and asset-based distribution also plays a paramount role in later welfare discussions; see Will Paxton et al., *The Citizen's Stake: Exploring the Future of Universal Asset Policies* (London: Policy Press, 2006).

19. Drew McCoy, *The Elusive Republic: Political Economy in Jeffersonian America* (Chapel Hill: University of North Carolina Press, 1980); Sean Wilentz, *Chants Democratic: New York City and the Rise of the American Working Class, 1788–1850* (New York: Oxford University Press, 1986). For larger republican languages, see Michael Sonenscher, *Before the Deluge: Public Debt, Inequality, and the Intellectual Origins of the French Revolution* (Princeton, NJ: Princeton University Press, 2009), 249–60; Béla Kapossy, Isaac Nakhimovsky, and Richard Whatmore, eds., *Commerce and Peace in the Enlightenment* (Cambridge: Cambridge University Press, 2017); Béla Kapossy, "Neo-Roman Republicanism and Commercial Society: The Example in Eighteenth-Century Berne," in *Republicanism: A Shared European Heritage*, ed. Quentin Skinner and Martin Van Gelderen (Cambridge: Cambridge

University Press, 2002), 2:227–47; Liana Vardi, *The Physiocrats and the World of the Enlightenment* (Cambridge: Cambridge University Press, 2012). For the producerist label in American settings, see Eric Foner, *Free Soil, Free Labor, Free Men: The Ideology of the Republican Party before the Civil War* (New York: Oxford University Press, 1995); Rosanne Currarino, *The Labor Question in America: Economic Democracy in the Gilded Age* (Champaign: University of Illinois Press, 2011); Alex Gourevitch, Review of *The Labor Question in America*, *Historical Materialism* 21 (February 2013): 179–90; Alex Gourevitch, *From Slavery to the Co-operative Commonwealth: Labor and Republican Liberty in the Nineteenth Century* (Cambridge: Cambridge University Press, 2013); Noam Maggor, *Brahmin Capitalism: Frontiers of Wealth and Populism in America's First Gilded Age* (Cambridge, MA: Harvard University Press, 2017).

20. Thomas Paine, "Agrarian Justice," in *Thomas Paine Reader*, ed. Michael Foot and Isaac Kramnick (Harmondsworth, UK: Penguin, 1987), 475; C. J. Merriam, "Thomas Paine's Political Theories," *Political Science Quarterly* 14, no. 3 (1899): 389–403. Money relief was usually confined to payments to pensioners, indigent populations, or the disabled.

21. Jonathan Levy, *Ages of American Capitalism: A History of the United States* (New York: Random House, 2021), 270–75; Nelson Lichtenstein, *State of the Union: A Century of American Labor* (Princeton, NJ: Princeton University Press, 2002), 65–66; David Montgomery, *The Fall of the House of Labor: The Workplace, the State, and American Labor Activism, 1865–1925* (Cambridge: Cambridge University Press, 1987).

22. See Quentin Skinner, "Language and Political Change," in *Political Innovation and Conceptual Change*, ed. Terrence Ball and James Farr (Cambridge: Cambridge University Press, 1989), 1–23. For contextualist treatments of these topics, see, among others, John Dunn, *Democracy: A History* (New York: Atlantic Monthly Press, 2005); Duncan Bell, "What Is Liberalism?," *Political Theory* 42 (2014): 682–715; Mark Goldie, "Ideology," in *Political Innovation and Conceptual Change*, ed. Terrence Ball and James Farr (Cambridge: Cambridge University Press, 1989), 266–91.

23. See Thomas Paine, *Agrarian Justice Opposed to Agrarian Law, and to Agrarian Monopoly: Being a Plan for Meliorating the Condition of Man, by Creating in Every Nation a National Fund, to Pay to Every Person, When Arrived at the Age of Twenty-One Years, the Sum of Fifteen Pounds Sterling, to Enable Him or Her to Begin the World* (Paris: W. Adlard, 1797). For contextualization, see Gregory Claeys, *Thomas Paine: Social and Political Thought* (Boston: Unwin, 1989); Yannick Bosc, "Thomas Paine as a Theorist of the Right to Existence," *Journal of Early American History* 6, no. 2 (2011): 113–23; Andrew Gamble and Rajiv Prabhakar, "Assets and Poverty," *Theoria: A Journal of Social and Political Theory* 107 (August 2005): 3–5.

24. Paine, *Agrarian Justice*, 16.

25. Paine, *Agrarian Justice*, 16.

26. Paine, *Agrarian Justice*, 16.

27. Paine, *Agrarian Justice*, 26.

28. Paine, *Agrarian Justice*, 26.

29. Paine, *Agrarian Justice*, 26.

30. Paine, *Agrarian Justice*, 26.

31. For discussion, see Michael Kennedy, *The Jacobin Clubs in the French Revolution, 1793–1795* (New York: Berghahn Books, 2000), 139.

32. See Carine Lounissi, *Thomas Paine and the French Revolution* (New York: Springer, 2018), 185–86; J. C. D. Clark, *Thomas Paine: Britain, America, and France in the Age of Enlightenment and Revolution* (London: Oxford University Press, 2018).

33. Michel Troper, *Terminer la Révolution: La Constitution de 1795* (Paris: Fayard, 2006). See also Michael Sonenscher, "Introduction," in *Emmanuel Joseph Sieyès: Political Writings*, ed. Michael Sonenscher (Indianapolis, IN: Hackett, 2003), vii–lxiv.

34. Claeys, *Thomas Paine*, 121.

35. Gareth Stedman Jones, *An End to Poverty? A Historical Debate* (New York: Columbia University Press, 2004), 114. Gregory Claeys, "Thomas Paine's *Agrarian Justice* (1796) and The Secularization of Natural Jurisprudence," *Bulletin of the Society for the Study of Labour History* 52, no. 3 (1988): 21–31; Mark Ravallion, *The Economics of Poverty: History, Measurement, and Policy* (London: Oxford University Press, 2016), 583–84.

36. Henry Phelps Brown, *Egalitarianism and the Generation of Inequality* (New York: Oxford University Press, 1988), 141.

37. Ronald T. Ridley, "Leges Agrariae: Myths Ancient and Modern," *Classical Philology* 95 (2000): 459–67.

38. Kurt A. Rauflaub, *Social Struggles in Archaic Rome: New Perspectives on the Conflict of the Orders* (New York: John Wiley, 2008), 153.

39. Geza Alfoldy, *The Social History of Rome* (London: Routledge, 2014), 22.

40. Jean-Jacques Aubert, "The *Lex Agraria* of 111 B.C.," in *The Cambridge Companion to the Roman Republic*, ed. Harriet I. Flower (New York: Cambridge University Press, 2014), 179–83.

41. Aubert, "*Lex Agraria*," 183–85.

42. See Eric Nelson, *The Hebrew Republic: Jewish Sources and the Transformation of European Political Thought* (Cambridge, MA: Harvard University Press, 2010), 60–65; "'For the land Is Mine': The Hebrew Commonwealth and the Rise of Redistribution," unpublished paper. Historians from Livy to Florus to Lucan equally condemned these laws as injurious—as Nelson notes, it was "an article of faith in the surviving Latin sources . . . that these agrarian laws constituted unjust expropriations of private property, and that the controversy surrounding their proposal and passage ultimately brought about the fall of the republic" (60–61).

43. Cicero, *On Duties* (Cambridge: Cambridge University Press, 2011), 174–85; Cicero, *The Orations of Marcus Tullius Cicero: Three Orations on the Agrarian*

Law, the Four against Catiline, the Orations for Rabirius, Murena, Sylla, Archias, Flaccus, Scaurus, Etc. (London: Bell and Daldy, 1867). See also Neal Wood, *Cicero's Social and Political Thought* (Berkeley: University of California Press, 1991).

44. Annie Lowrey, *Give People Money: The Simple Idea to Solve Inequality and Revolutionize Our Lives* (New York: Random House, 2018), 18–19; Philippe Van Parijs, "More et Vives à l'origine du revenue garanti?" in *Chemins d'Utopie: Thomas More à Louvain, 1516–2016*, ed. Paul-Augustin Deproost, Charles-Henri Nyns, and Christophe Vielle (Louvain: Ciaco, 2015), 56–57.

45. Cited in Eric Nelson, *The Greek Tradition in Republican Thought* (London: Cambridge University Press, 2004), 178. For the original Hebrew laws, see Jeffrey A. Fager, *Land Tenure and the Biblical Jubilee: Uncovering Hebrew Ethics through the Sociology of Knowledge* (New York: Black, 1993), 119–30.

46. Harvey Mansfield, *Machiavelli's New Modes and Orders: A Study of the Discourses on Livy* (Chicago: University of Chicago Press, 2001), 69–70.

47. Robert C. Palmer, *English Law in the Age of the Black Death, 1348–1381: A Transformation of Governance and Law* (Chapel Hill: University of North Carolina Press, 2002); Lawrence Wilde, *Thomas More's Utopia: Arguing for Social Justice* (London: Routledge, 2016).

48. Thomas More, *Utopia*, trans. Paul Turner (London: Penguin Books, 2003), 22.

49. See Van Parijs and Vanderborght, *Basic Income*, 264n. "Cum potius multo fuerit providendum, uti aliquis esset proventus vitae, ne cuiquam tam dira sit furandi primum, dehinc pereundi necessitas," in Thomas More, *De optimo rei publicae statu, deque nova insula Utopia* (Cambridge: Cambridge University Press, 1995), 56. Translation from Nelson, *Greek Tradition*, 39.

50. For linguistic clarification of *proventus* as referring to yields of corn in a Renaissance setting, see William Smith, *A Copius and Critical English-Latin Dictionary, to Which Is Added a Dictionary of Proper Names* (New York: American Book Company, 1871), 172.

51. More, *De optimo rei publicae statu*, 56.

52. Van Parijs and Vanderborght, *Basic Income*, 189.

53. Thomas Skidmore, *The Rights of Man to Property: Being a Proposition to Make It Equal among the Adults of the Present Generation; and to Provide for Its Equal Transmission to Every Individual of Each Succeeding Generation, on Arriving at the Age of Maturity. Addressed to the Citizens of the State of New York Particularly, and to the People of Other States and Nations Generally* (New York: Burt Franklin, 1829), 23.

54. Skidmore, *Rights of Man to Property*, 23.

55. Gamble, "Assets and Poverty," passim; Jones, *End to Poverty*, passim; Gourevitch, *From Slavery to the Co-operative Commonwealth*.

56. Skidmore, *Rights of Man to Property*, 23.

57. Thomas Spence, *The Political Works of Thomas Spence* (London: Avero, 1982), 51.

58. Thomas Spence, "The Rights of Infants," in *The Origins of Universal Grants: An Anthology of Historical Writings on Basic Capital and Basic Income*, ed. J. Cunliffe and G. Erreygers (New York: Springer, 2004), 83.

59. Mark Huillung, *Citizens and Citoyens: Republicans and Liberals in America and France* (Cambridge, MA: Harvard University Press, 2002), 29.

60. See Orestes Augustus Brownson, *The Works of Orestes A. Brownson: Civilization* (New York: T. Nourse, 1884), 574–75; Christopher Lasch, *The True and Only Heaven: Progress and Its Critics* (New York: W. W. Norton, 1991), e-book, 189–200. Even these versions regularly called forth objections of "agrarianism" and pointed up the controversial status of the plan (the financial radical William Leggett, for instance, preferred monetary reform over requisitioning); James Simeone, "Reassessing Jacksonian Political Culture: William Leggett's Egalitarianism," *American Political Thought* 4, no. 3 (Summer 2015): 359–90.

61. Orestes Brownson, *The Laboring Classes* (Boston: Benjamin Greene, 1840), 78. For more context on Brownson, see Arthur Schlesinger Jr., *Orestes Brownson: A Pilgrim's Progress* (New York: Octagon Books, 1963).

62. Cited in John Cunliffe and Guido Erreygers, "Orestes Brownson," in *Inherited Wealth, Justice and Equality* (London: Routledge, 2013), 60.

63. Cunliffe and Erreygers, "Orestes Brownson," 84.

64. Cunliffe and Erreygers, "Orestes Brownson," 81.

65. Cunliffe and Erreygers, "Orestes Brownson," 81.

66. Louis F. Post, *The Prophet of San Francisco: Personal Memories and Interpretations of Henry George* (New York: Minerva Group, 2002), 226.

67. Henry George, *Progress and Poverty: An Inquiry into the Cause of Industrial Depressions and of Increase of Want with Increase of Wealth; the Remedy* (New York: National Single Tax League Publishers, 1879). For context, see Edward O'Donnell, *Henry George and the Crisis of Inequality: Progress and Poverty in the Gilded Age* (New York: Columbia University Press, 2017), 130–35; Louis F. Post, *The Prophet of San Francisco: Personal Memories and Interpretations of Henry George* (New York: Minerva Group, 2002), 226.

68. Edward Bellamy, *Looking Backward: From 2000 to 1887* (Bedford, MA: Applewood Books, 2000).

69. Bellamy, *Looking Backward*, 77.

70. Bellamy, *Looking Backward*, 77.

71. Jamie Bronstein, "A History of the BIG Idea: Winstanley, Paine, Skidmore and Bellamy," *Journal of Evolution and Technology* 24, 1 (February 2014): 62–69.

72. Peter Garnsey, *Thinking about Property: From Antiquity to the Age of Revolution* (London: Cambridge University Press, 2007), 126–30; Daniel Bell, *Marxian Socialism in the United States* (Ithaca, NY: Cornell University Press, 1995), 17–20. For the French tradition, see Roberto Romani, "The Republican Foundations of

Sismondi's 'Nouveaux principes d'économie politique," *History of European Ideas* 31, no. 1 (2005): 17-33; Pierre-Joseph Proudhon, *What Is Property?*, ed. Donald Kelley (Cambridge: Cambridge University Press, 1994), 43-45; Nelson, *Hebrew Republic*, 87; Jocelyn Betts, "After the Freeholder: Republican and Liberal Themes in the Works of Samuel Laing," *Modern Intellectual History* 10 (2017): 1-30; James Simeone, "Reassessing Jacksonian Political Culture: William Leggett's Egalitarianism," *American Political Thought* 4, no. 3 (Summer 2015): 359-90.

73. Nelson, *Hebrew Republic*, 187.

74. Nelson, *Hebrew Republic*, 141. See also David McNally, *Against the Market: Political Economy, Market Socialism and the Marxist Critique* (London: Verso Books, 1993), 141-48.

75. Carl Guarneri, *The Utopian Alternative: Fourierism in Nineteenth-Century America* (Ithaca, NY: Cornell University Press, 2018), 478; Kathy E. Ferguson, *Emma Goldman: Political Thinking in the Streets* (New York: Rowman and Littlefield, 2011), 153.

76. Pierre-Joseph Proudhon, "Address to the Constituent Assembly," in *Property Is Theft! A Pierre-Joseph Proudhon Anthology*, ed. Iain McKay (Edinburgh: Edinburgh University Press, 2011), 349.

77. Nicholas V. Riasanovsky, *The Teaching of Charles Fourier* (Berkeley: University of California Press, 2020), 8-9.

78. Charles Fourier, *La fausse industrie morcellée* (Paris: Bossange, 1836), 491.

79. Fourier, *Fausse industrie morcellée*, 467.

80. Fourier, *Fausse industrie morcellée*, 466.

81. Ragip Epe and Sylvie Rirot, "Charles Fourier: A 'Non-scientistic Conception of Justice," in *The Individual and the Other in Economic Thought: An Introduction*, ed. Ragip Epe (London: Routledge, 2018), 118.

82. Édouard de Pompery, *Théorie de l'Association et de l'Unité universelle de C. Fourier: Introduction religieuse at philosophique* (Paris: Capelle, 1841), 59.

83. Quoted in Van Parijs and Vanderborght, *Basic Income*, 255.

84. Quoted in Van Parijs and Vanderborght, *Basic Income*, 91.

85. Serge Audier, *L'âge productiviste: Hégémonie prométhéenne, brèches et alternatives écologiques* (Paris: Découverte, 2019), 191.

86. Serge Audier, *La société écologique et ses ennemis: Pour une histoire alternative de l'émancipation* (Paris: Découverte, 2017), 117.

87. Joseph Charlier, *Solution du problème social, ou Constitution humanitaire, basée sur la loi naturelle et précédée de l'exposé des motifs* (Brussels: Imprimerie Geuse, 1848).

88. Charlier, *Solution*, 103.

89. Charlier, *Solution*, 103.

90. John Cunliffe and Guido Erreygers, "Joseph Charlier and Basic Income," *History of Political Economy* 33, no. 3 (2001): 459-84.

91. Charlier, *Solution*, 110.

92. Charlier, *Solution*, 110.

93. Samuel P. Orth, *Socialism and Democracy in Europe* (London: BoD, 2018), 83.

94. John Cunliffe and Guido Erreygers, "Joseph Charlier," in *Inherited Wealth, Justice and Equality* (London: Routledge, 2013),43.

95. Guy Standing, *Promoting Income Security as a Right: Europe and North America* (London: Anthem, 2004), 431.

96. Karl Marx, *Capital: The Process of Capitalist Production*, translated from the 3rd German ed. by S. Moore and E. Aveling (Moscow: International Publishers, 1974), 602.

97. David Raventos, *Basic Income: The Material Conditions of Freedom* (London: Pluto Press, 2007), 201.

98. Karl Marx and Friedrich Engels, *Karl Marx, Frederick Engels: Collected Works*, vol. 47 (New York: International Publishers, 1995), 68, 567. Engels commissioned the introduction from Bernstein.

99. François Guedj and Gérard Vindt, *Le temps de travail: Une histoire conflictuelle* (Paris: Fenixx, 2008).

100. Leslie Derfler, *Paul Lafargue and the Founding of French Marxism, 1842–1882* (Cambridge, MA: Harvard University Press, 1991), 158–59.

101. Derfler, *Paul Lafargue*, 158.

102. Derfler, *Paul Lafargue*, 303.

103. Hans Achterhuis, *Arbeid, een eigenaardig medicijn* (Amsterdam: Ambo, 1984), 145.

104. F. Domela Nieuwenhuis, *Rede van F. Domela Nieuwenhuis over de belastingkwestie met de daarbij gevoerde debatten, gehouden in de Kamerzitting van Zaterdag 22 December 1888* (1889), 1.

105. Rosa Luxemburg, "Speeches and Letters on War and Revolution, 1918–1919," in *The Rosa Luxemburg Reader*, ed. Kevin Anderson (New York: New York University Press, 2004), 347.

106. Luxemburg, "Speeches and Letters," 347.

107. See Vladimir Ulyanov Lenin, *Collected Works*, vol. 30 (Moscow: Progress Publishers, 1965), 500.

108. E. Mabel Milner and Dennis Milner, *Scheme for a State Bonus* (London: Simpkin, Marshall, 1918), 7.

109. For contextualization see Sloman, *Transfer State*, 66–68.

110. E. Mabel Milner and Dennis Milner, "Scheme for a State Bonus," in *The Origins of Universal Grants: An Anthology of Historical Writings on Basic Capital and Basic Income*, ed. J. Cunliffe and G. Erreygers (New York: Springer, 2004), 121–33.

111. Milner and Milner, "Scheme for a State Bonus," 62. See also D. Milner and E. Mabel Milner, *Scheme for a State Bonus: A Rational Method of Solving the Social Problem* (Darlington, UK: North of England Newspaper Company, 1918).

112. Milner and Milner, "Scheme for a State Bonus," 62.

113. Milner and Milner, "Scheme for a State Bonus," 62.

114. Milner and Milner, "Scheme for a State Bonus," 62. See also Van Trier, *Every One a King*, 37-38.

115. Cited in Sloman, "Basic Income," 25.

116. See Philip Ironside, *The Social and Political Thought of Bertrand Russell: The Development of an Aristocratic Liberalism* (Cambridge: Cambridge University Press, 2006), 140; Royden Harrison, "Bertrand Russell: From Liberalism to Socialism?," *Russell* 6, no. 1 (1986): 5-38; Alan Ryan, *Bertrand Russell: A Political Life* (Oxford: Oxford University Press, 1988).

117. Douglas's argument, however, was based on a prior argument in the *English Review* in 1918. See Van Trier, *Every One a King*, 159-94.

118. C. Marshall Hattersley, *The Community's Credit: A Consideration of the Principles and Proposals of the Social Credit Movement* (London: Credit Power Press, 1922).

119. Hattersley, *Community's Credit*, 22.

120. Brian Burkitt, *The Political Economy of Social Credit and Guild Socialism* (London: Routledge, 2006), 98.

121. G. D. H. Cole, *Principles of Economic Planning* (London: Macmillan, 1935), 225.

122. G. D. H. Cole, *The Next Ten Years in British Social and Economic Policy* (London: Garland, 1929), 278.

123. Cole, *Principles of Economic Planning*, 252.

124. Cole, *Principles of Economic Planning*, 252.

125. Cole, *Principles of Economic Planning*, 250-55.

126. Ben Jackson, *Equality and the British Left: A Study in Progressive Political Thought, 1900-1964* (Manchester: Manchester University Press, 2007), 64; Sloman, "Basic Income," 23.

127. George Wansbrough to J. M. Keynes, December 11, 1939, Papers of John Maynard Keynes, King's College Archives, University of Cambridge, folder 87, HP/1/87-9, GB 272 JMK.

128. J. M. Keynes to George Wansbrough, December 14, 1939 (copy), Papers of John Maynard Keynes, King's College Archives, University of Cambridge, folder 87, HP/1/87-9, GB 272 JMK.

129. J. M. Keynes to George Wansbrough, December 14, 1939.

130. H. A. Kane, *Huey Long's Louisiana Hayride* (London: Pelican, 1971), 57-58.

131. Monica Prasad, *The Land of Too Much: American Abundance and the Paradox of Poverty* (Cambridge, MA: Harvard University Press, 2012), 188; Robin D. G. Kelley, *Hammer and Hoe: Alabama Communists during the Great Depression* (Chapel Hill: University of North Carolina Press, 2015), 236-43; Alan Brinkley, *Voices of Protest: Huey Long, Father Coughlin, and the Great Depression* (New York: Knopf Doubleday, 2011).

132. Cited in Arthur Schlesinger, *The Politics of Upheaval: 1935–1936, the Age of Roosevelt* (London: Houghton Mifflin, 2003), 3:64; Van Trier, *Every One a King*, passim.

133. Juliet Rhys-Williams, *Something to Look Forward To: A Suggestion for a New Social Contract* (London: Macdonald, 1943), 146.

134. Sloman, *Transfer State*, 65. See also Peter Sloman, "Beveridge's Rival: Juliet Rhys-Williams and the Campaign for Basic Income, 1942–55," *Contemporary British History* 30, no. 2 (2018): 203–23; Peter Sloman, " 'The Jehovah's Witnesses of Social Policy'? Explaining the Rise, Fall, and Revival of Universal Basic Income in Britain since 1918," working paper, POLIS, University of Cambridge, 2019), 1–14: Alisa McKay, *The Future of Social Security Policy: Women, Work and a Citizens' Basic Income* (New York: Routledge, 2005), 146–47.

135. Cited in Brandon Rhys-Williams, *Stepping Stones to Independence: National Insurance after 1990* (Aberdeen: Aberdeen University Press, 1989), 7; Juliet Rhys-Williams, *A New Look at Britain's Economic Policy* (Harmondsworth, UK: Penguin, 1965); Juliet Rhys-Williams, *Something to Look Forward To: A Suggestion for a New Social Contract* (London, 1943). See also the later Juliet Rhys-Williams, *Taxation and Incentive* (London: Oxford University Press, 1953).

136. Rhys-Williams, *Something to Look Forward To*, 7.

137. Rhys-Williams, *Something to Look Forward To*, 7.

138. Sloman, *Transfer State*, 78.

139. Bertrand de Jouvenel, *The Ethics of Redistribution* (Indianapolis, IN: Liberty Fund, 1972), 9. Gáspár Miklós Tamás similarly notes that this tradition "did not aim at the obliteration of property, only at the rehabilitation of *ager publicus*, and handouts to the indigent and the preservation of an independent counterpower." See G. M. Tamás, "Communism on the Ruins of Socialism," *The Idea of Communism Conference* (June 26, 2012), transcript.

140. Jouvenel, *Ethics of Redistribution*, 7.

Chapter Two

1. On anti-Semitism in American academia in the thirties, see Milton Friedman and Rose Friedman, *Two Lucky People* (Chicago: University of Chicago Press, 1998), 58; George J. Stigler, *Memoirs of an Unregulated Economist* (Chicago: University of Chicago Press, 1988), 31; Kenneth Arrow, *On Ethics and Economics* (London: Routledge, 2017), 29; E. Roy Weintraub, "Keynesian Historiography and the Anti-Semitism Question," *History of Political Economy* 44, no. 1 (2012): 41–67.

2. Details of the "Milton Friedman affair" can be found in Friedman and Friedman, *Two Lucky People*, 95–102.

3. Friedman and Friedman, *Two Lucky People*, 64.

4. Lanny Ebenstein, *Milton Friedman: A Biography* (London: Palgrave Macmillan, 2007), 34. On Friedman's relation to the New Deal, see Edward Nelson, *Milton*

Friedman and Economic Debate in the United States, 1932–1972, vol. 1 (Chicago: University of Chicago Press, 2020), 65, and Friedman and Friedman, *Two Lucky People*, 58–61.

5. For Friedman's opinions about the New Deal see Ebenstein, *Milton Friedman*, 1:34, and Friedman and Friedman, *Two Lucky People*, 59.

6. Ebenstein, *Milton Friedman*, 1:35.

7. On Friedman's role in implementing withholding tax see Friedman and Friedman, *Two Lucky People*, 120–23.

8. On these formative years see in particular Béatrice Cherrier, "The Lucky Consistency of Milton Friedman's Science and Politics, 1933–1963," in *Building Chicago Economics: New Perspectives on the History of America's Most Powerful Economics Program*, ed. Robert Van Horn, Philip Mirowski, and Thomas A. Stapleford (Cambridge: Cambridge University Press, 2011), 338; Angus Burgin, *The Great Persuasion: Reinventing Free Markets since the Depression* (Cambridge: Cambridge University Press, 2012), 152–85.

9. For citizens whose income rose and fell from one year to another, the tax system was making them pay more than those receiving the same amount but whose income was steady. This problem was particularly acute for low-income workers, constantly moving from a zero-tax bracket to another one. To compensate for this unequal treatment, Friedman first conceived a restrictive version of his "negative income tax" so that in a bad year the taxpayer would receive money from the Treasury rather than pay. See Letter to Melvin Rosen, March 4, 1969, Negative Income Tax, 1965–92, Milton Friedman Papers, Hoover Institution, box 201, file 201.9. Friedman would later explain that he first came up with the idea at the Treasury Department in a 1996 letter to Dennis J. Ventry, where he confirmed that "negative income taxes were probably discussed at the treasury in 1941 to 1943 when I was a member of the Tax Research staff." Milton Friedman, Letter to Dennis Ventry Jr., December 3, 1996, Milton Friedman Papers, Hoover Institution, Negative Income Tax, 1966–2004, box 201, file 201.7. Moreover, the episode was reported in Christopher Green, *Negative Taxes and the Poverty Problem* (Washington, DC: Brookings Institution, 1967), 57; Robert J. Lampman, "The Decision to Undertake the New Jersey Experiment," in *The New Jersey Income-Maintenance Experiment*, ed. David Kershaw and Jerilyn Fair, vol. 1 (New York: Academic Press, 1977), xiii; Daniel Moynihan, *The Politics of a Guaranteed Income* (New York: Academic Press, 1973), 50; and Dennis J. Ventry, Letter to Milton Friedman, November 22, 1996, Milton Friedman Papers, Hoover Institution, Negative Income Tax, 1966–2004, box 201, file 201.7.

10. Friedman mentions discussing the proposal with Vickrey in a letter to Christopher Green: "I suspect we must have talked about it at that time but when I checked up on it, I found no reference to it." Milton Friedman, Letter to Christopher Green, January 20, 1966, Milton Friedman Papers, Hoover Institution, Negative Income Tax, 1966–80, box 201, file 201.6 and 7.

11. Friedman, Letter to Melvin Rosen.

12. Friedman would discuss his NIT as a more general tool for social policy at the first Mont Pèlerin conference in April 1947 and then, a few months later, in a draft of his paper "A Monetary and Fiscal Framework for Economic Stability," where he mentions "transfer payments" in the form of "negative revenues" and notes that he will share the idea widely with his colleagues. See "Taxation, Poverty and Income Distribution," Tuesday April 8th, 8:30 p.m., Mont Pèlerin Society Records, Hoover Institution Archives, Stanford University, 5.12 meeting file—Mont Pèlerin, Minutes, 1947; Milton Friedman, "A Monetary and Fiscal Framework for Economic Stability," typescript, first draft, April 18, 1947, Friedman Papers, Hoover Institution, box 38, file 38.9.

13. The statement was circulated in May 1968 to 275 universities and research organizations. It received signatures from, among others, Paul Samuelson, Harold Watts, James Tobin, John Kenneth Galbraith, and Robert Lampman, but it also included Abba P. Lerner, Kenneth Arrow, T. C. Koopmans, and Joseph Stiglitz. See "A Statement by Economists on Income Guarantees and Supplements, May 27, 1968, in Income Maintenance Programs," *Hearings before the Subcommittee on the Fiscal Policy of the Joint Economic Committee Congress of the United States*, Ninetieth Congress, volume 2, Appendix Materials, Appendix 17 (1968), 676.

14. Friedman, Letter to Christopher Green, January 20, 1966.

15. For a detailed account of the interwar debates about welfare see Peter Sloman, *Transfer State: The Idea of a Guaranteed Income and the Politics of Redistribution in Modern Britain* (Oxford: Oxford University Press, 2019), 63–94.

16. Friedman mentions Douglas's, Pigou's, and Bellamy's ideas in Milton Friedman, Lecture notes at the University of Wisconsin, October 1940, Milton Friedman Papers, Hoover Institution, box 75, file 5; Friedman, Letter to Christopher Green, January 20, 1966.

17. Friedman, Letter to Christopher Green, January 20, 1966.

18. On Oskar Lange's relationship with Friedman, see Nelson, *Milton Friedman and Economic Debate in the United States, 1932–1972*, 1:249.

19. See in particular Oskar Lange, "On the Economic Theory of Socialism: Part I," *Review of Economic Studies* 4, no. 1 (1936): 53–71; Abba P. Lerner, *The Economics of Control* (New York: Macmillan, 1946), 267–68.

20. Arrow, *On Ethics and Economics*, 195.

21. Later both Stigler and Friedman published accounts of *The Economics of Control* (1944) where Stigler is even thanked at the beginning of the book for "reading the manuscript and correcting a number of errors." See George J. Stigler, Review of *The Economics of Control: Principles of Welfare*, *Political Science Quarterly* 60, no. 1 (1945): 113–15; Milton Friedman, "Lerner on the Economics of Control," *Journal of Political Economy* 55, no. 5 (1947): 405–16.

22. Milton Friedman, Letter to Martin Bronfenbrenner, March 30, 1964, Milton Friedman Papers, Hoover Institution, box 21, file 21.35.

23. Peter Sloman, "'Beveridge's Rival: Juliet Rhys-Williams and the Campaign for Basic Income, 1942–1955," *Contemporary British History* 30, no. 2 (2016): 207; Juliet Rhys-Williams, *Something to Look Forward To: A Suggestion for a New Social Contract* (London: Macdonald, 1943), 167.

24. See Juliet Rhys-Williams, *Taxation and Incentive* (Oxford: Oxford University Press, 1953); Juliet Rhys-Williams, *A New Look at Britain's Economic Policy* (Harmondsworth, UK: Penguin, 1965).

25. Milton Friedman, "An Objective Method of Determining a 'Minimum Standard of Living,'" 1939, Milton Friedman Papers, Hoover Institution, box 37, file 37.8.

26. See in particular Daniel P. Moynihan, *The Politics of a Guaranteed Income* (New York: Vintage Books, 1973); Leslie Lenkowsky, *Politics, Economics and Welfare Reform: Failure of the Negative Income Tax in Britain and the United States* (New York: University Press of America, 1986); Dennis J. Ventry, "The Negative Income Tax: An Intellectual History," *Tax Notes* 27 (1997); Alice O'Connor, *Poverty Knowledge* (Princeton, NJ: Princeton University Press, 2001); Brian Steensland, *The Failed Welfare Revolution* (Princeton, NJ: Princeton University Press, 2008); Melinda Cooper, *Family Values: Between Neoliberalism and the New Social Conservatism* (New York: Zone Books, 2017); Romain D. Huret, *The Experts' War on Poverty: Social Research and the Welfare Agenda in Postwar America* (Ithaca, NY: Cornell University Press, 2018).

27. See in particular Sonia M. Amadae, *Rationalizing Capitalist Democracy: The Cold War Origins of Rational Choice Liberalism* (Chicago: University of Chicago Press, 2003); Béatrice Cherrier and Jean-Baptiste Fleury, "Economists' Interest in Collective Decision after World War II: A History," *Public Choice*, 172, no. 1–2 (2017): 23–44.

28. See especially Alfred Marshall, *The Principles of Economics* (London, 1890), and A. C. Pigou, *The Economics of Welfare* (London: Macmillan, 1920). These two authors and the debates they shaped in the thirties were crucial for Friedman. Not only was his first paper a criticism of Pigou, but most of his assignments for his courses in the forties were filled with discussions on the "old" welfare economics. See, for example, his courses at the University of Wisconsin in 1940–41, in Minnesota in 1945–46, and at Columbia from 1937 to 1940. See in particular Notes on Friedman's lecture, 1939, 2, Milton Friedman Papers, Hoover Institution, box 75, file 75.1; Assignments in course given at Columbia by M. Friedman titled "Structure of Neo-classical Economics," 1939–40, Milton Friedman Papers, Hoover Institution, box 75, file 75.12.

29. Jeremy Bentham, *A Fragment on Government, or A Comment on the Commentaries* (London, 1823).

30. See Martin Ravallion, *The Economics of Poverty: History, Measurement, and Policy* (Oxford: Oxford University Press, 2016), 55–57, 74–75.

31. David Grewal, "Utility and Interpersonal Comparability: Skepticism about 'Other Minds' in Neoclassical Economics," unpublished paper, 3.

32. Pigou, *Economics of Welfare*, 89.

33. Robert Cooter and Peter Rappoport, "Were the Ordinalists Wrong about Welfare Economics?," *Journal of Economic Literature* 22, no. 2 (1984): 507–30.

34. Cooter and Rappoport, "Were the Ordinalists Wrong about Welfare Economics?," 519.

35. Pigou, *Economics of Welfare*, 17.

36. Pigou, *Economics of Welfare*, 17.

37. Pigou, *Economics of Welfare*, 756.

38. See, for example, Pigou: "some defined quantity and quality of house accommodation, of medical care, of education, of food, of leisure, of the apparatus of sanitary convenience and safety where work is carried on, and so on," in Pigou, *Economics of Welfare*, 759.

39. Sloman, *Transfer State*, 41.

40. Lionel Robbins, *An Essay on the Nature and Significance of Economic Science* (London: Macmillan, 1932).

41. In fact, Pareto's principle had already abandoned interpersonal comparisons. See Vilfredo Pareto, *Cours d'économie politique* (Lausanne, 1896).

42. For a detailed account of the debates about welfare economics at that period, see Antoinette Baujard, "Welfare Economics" (working paper, GATE, 1333, 2013); SSRN: https://ssrn.com/abstract=2357412.

43. Lionel Robbins, "Interpersonal Comparisons of Utility: A Comment," *Economic Journal* 48, no. 192 (1938): 636.

44. Robbins, *Essay on the Nature and Significance of Economic Science*, 140.

45. See Grewal, "Utility and Interpersonal Comparability."

46. On this see especially Roger E. Backhouse, "Robbins and Welfare Economics: A Reappraisal," *Journal of the History of Economic Thought* 31, no. 4 (2009): 474–84.

47. Niklas Olsen, *The Sovereign Consumer: A New Intellectual History of Neoliberalism* (Cham: Palgrave Macmillan Switzerland, 2018), 128–29.

48. Susan Howson, *Lionel Robbins* (Cambridge: Cambridge University Press, 2011), 215.

49. Robbins, *Essay on the Nature and Significance of Economic Science*, 151.

50. As opposed as the "cardinalist" view implied by Pigou, ordinalists then referred to the idea that only comparisons between goods (and their "rates of substitution" or "elasticities of demand") could be made. See John R. Hicks and Roy G. D. Allen, "A Reconsideration of the Theory of Value, Part I," *Economica* 1, no. 1 (1934): 52–76.

51. See, for example, the compensation principle derived from Pareto's work and developed by Nicholas Kaldor and John Hicks.

52. Roger E. Backhouse, "The Origins of the New Welfare Economics," unpublished paper (2016).

53. See in particular Maxime Desmarais-Tremblay, "The Normative Problem of Merit Goods in Perspective," *Forum for Social Economics* 48, no. 3 (2019): 219–47.

54. Thomas Wilson, "Welfare Economics and the Welfare State," *Hem* 83, no. 5 (1980).

55. Notes on Friedman's lecture, October 5, 1939, 2. Milton Friedman Papers, Hoover Institution, box 75, file 75.12.

56. Philip Mirowski and Wade D. Hands, "A Paradox of Budgets: The Postwar Stabilization of American Neoclassical Demand Theory," *History of Political Economy* 30, supplement (1998): 272.

57. Milton Friedman, "Lerner on *The Economics of Control*," early draft, Milton Friedman Papers, Hoover Institution, box 33, file 33.36 (probably drafted in 1946). The piece would be published in a substantially shorter version in 1947 in the *Journal of Political Economy*.

58. For a good summary of Lerner's argument and ensuing debates see Paul A. Samuelson, "A. P. Lerner at Sixty," *Review of Economic Studies* 31, no. 3 (June 1964): 172–76.

59. Lerner, *Economics of Control*, 28.

60. Lerner, *Economics of Control*, 29.

61. Lerner, *Economics of Control*, 29.

62. Friedman, "Lerner on the Economics of Control," draft.

63. Milton Friedman, "Notes on 'The Optimum Division of Income,'" Milton Friedman Papers, Hoover Institution, box 161, file 161.2, 22–23.

64. Friedman, "Lerner on the Economics of Control," draft.

65. Milton Friedman, "What All Is Utility?," *Economic Journal* 65, no. 259 (1955): 407.

66. Friedman, "What All Is Utility?, 409.

67. Milton Friedman, "The Methodology of Positive Economics," in Milton Friedman, *Essays in Positive Economics* (Chicago: University of Chicago Press, 1953), 4.

68. Friedman, "Methodology of Positive Economics."

69. Milton Friedman, Letter to Earl E. Rolph and George F. Break, April 8, 1952, Milton Friedman Papers, Hoover Institution, box 32, file 33.10.

70. Thanks to Peter Sloman for alerting us to the existence of this presentation. See "Taxation, Poverty and Income Distribution," presented Tuesday April 8, 8:30 p.m., Mont Pèlerin Society records, Hoover Institution Archives, Stanford University, 5.12 Meeting file—Mont Pèlerin, Minutes, 1947.

71. Milton Friedman, Letter to Robert de Fremery, December 18, 1947, Milton Friedman Papers, Hoover Institution, box 25, file 25.15.

72. Olsen, *Sovereign Consumer*, 128–29.

73. Friedrich A. Hayek, *The Road to Serfdom: Text and Documents; The Definitive Edition* (New York: Routledge, 2008), 67.

74. Friedman, "Objective Method of Determining a 'Minimum Standard of Living.'" See also Jennifer Burns, "Stanford Scholar Explores Pros, Cons of 'Basic

Income,'" *Stanford News*, August 8, 2018. I especially thank Jennifer Burns for pointing out the existence of this document and spurring me to explore the archives at the Hoover Institution.

75. Friedman met Gunnar Myrdal in New York to discuss his piece. He had also met him earlier through seminars and events organized by students at Columbia University, where Friedman was teaching from 1937 to 1940. See Richard Sterner, Letter to Milton Friedman, June 9, 1939, Milton Friedman Papers, Hoover Institution, box 37, file 37.8; Friedman and Friedman, *Two Lucky People*, 77-78.

76. See, for example, Milton Friedman, "The Regression Analysis of Family Expenditure Data," typescript for presentation at the meetings of the American Statistical Association, Atlantic City, December 1937, Milton Friedman Papers, Hoover Institution, box 109, file 109.7.

77. See in particular Thomas A. Stapleford, *The Cost of Living in America: A Political History of Economic Statistics, 1880-2000* (Cambridge: Cambridge University Press, 2009).

78. Although at first they decided it should not, after analyzing French diets they changed their minds. See Friedman and Friedman, *Two Lucky People*, 62.

79. Milton Friedman, "An Objective Method of Determining a 'Minimum Standard of Living'" (1939), Milton Friedman Papers, Hoover Institution, box 37, file 37.8, 5.

80. Milton Friedman, "The Case for the Negative Income Tax: A View from the Right," *Proceedings of the National Symposium on Guaranteed Income* (1966), 114.

81. Friedman, "Objective Method," 5-6.

82. Friedman, "Objective Method," 5-6.

83. Friedman, "Objective Method," 3.

84. Friedman, "Objective Method," 7.

85. Milton Friedman, "The Distribution of Income and the Welfare Activities of Government," Lecture, Wabash College, 20 June 1956, 7, https://miltonfriedman .hoover.org/internal/media/dispatcher/215144/full.

86. T. H. Marshall, "*Citizenship and Social Class*," *and Other Essays* (Cambridge University Press, 1950), 9.

87. Marshall, "*Citizenship and Social Class*," 47.

88. Richard H. Tawney, *Equality* (1931; repr., Oakville, ON: Capricorn Books, 1952), 130-31.

89. William H. Beveridge, *Full Employment in a Free Society* (London: Allen and Unwin, 1944), 186.

90. Beveridge, *Full Employment*, 186.

91. For discussions about needs and planning see in particular Kate Soper, *On Human Needs: Open and Closed Theories in a Marxist Perspective* (Brighton, UK: Harvester Press, 1981), 203-19.

92. Robert M. Collins, *The Business Response to Keynes, 1929-1964* (New York: Columbia University Press, 1981), 51.

93. Hansen quoted in Collins, *Business Response to Keynes*, 183.

94. John Kenneth Galbraith, *The Affluent Society* (Boston: Houghton Mifflin, 1958), 280.

95. Galbraith, *Affluent Society*, 189.

96. Galbraith, *Affluent Society*, 392.

97. O'Connor, *Poverty Knowledge*, 145.

98. On the socialist calculation debate and collective decision-making see Peter Boettke, ed., *Socialism and the Market: The Socialist Calculation Debate Revisited* (London: Routledge, 2000).

99. Friedrich A. Hayek, "The Use of Knowledge in Society," *American Economic Review* 35, no. 4 (September 1945): 519–30.

100. Hayek, "Use of Knowledge in Society," 519.

101. Sloman, *Transfer State*, 48.

102. James Meade, *Planning and the Price Mechanism* (London: Allen and Unwin, 1948).

103. James Meade, "Poverty in the Welfare State," *Oxford Economic Papers* 24, no. 3 (November 1972): 303.

104. Milton Friedman, Letter to Martin Bronfenbrenner, July 18, 1947, Milton Friedman Papers, Hoover Institution, box 21, file 21.35.

105. Milton Friedman and George J. Stigler, *Roofs or Ceilings? The Current Housing Problem* (Irvington-on-Hudson, UK: Foundation for Economic Education, 1946), 10.

106. Milton Friedman, "Neoliberalism and Its Prospects," *Farmand* (Oslo), February 17, 1951, 89–93.

107. "Taxation, Poverty and Income Distribution," presented Tuesday April 8, 8:30 p.m., Mont Pèlerin Society Records, Hoover Institution Archives, Stanford University, 5.12 Meeting file—Mont Pèlerin, Minutes, 1947.

108. "Taxation, Poverty and Income Distribution."

109. Milton Friedman correspondence with John V. Van Sickle, "Agenda for the Conference of Fifteen," December 9, 1954, Milton Friedman Papers, Hoover Institution, box 34, file 34.29.

110. Friedman, "Distribution of Income and the Welfare Activities of Government."

111. Milton Friedman, Letter to Don Patinkin, November 8, 1948, Milton Friedman Papers, Hoover Institution, box 31, file 31.24.

112. Friedman, "Distribution of Income and the Welfare Activities of Government."

113. Milton Friedman, Letter to Robert de Fremery, December 18, 1947, Milton Friedman Papers, Hoover Institution, box 25, file 25.15.

114. See in particular Friedman and Stigler, *Roofs or Ceilings?*

115. Milton Friedman, Letter to Martin Bronfenbrenner, July 18, 1947, Milton Friedman Papers, Hoover Institution, box 21, file 21.35.

116. Friedman, "Case for the Negative Income Tax," 111.

117. Annelien De Dijn, *Freedom: An Unruly History*, (Cambridge, MA: Harvard University Press, 2020), 345.

118. Cherrier, "Lucky Consistency of Milton Friedman's Science and Politics," 359.

119. Milton Friedman, *Capitalism and Freedom* (Chicago: University of Chicago Press, 1962), 15.

120. Milton Friedman and Rose Friedman, *Tyranny of the Status Quo* (New York: Harcourt Brace Jovanovich, 1984), 66.

121. Abba P. Lerner, "Review of *Capitalism and Freedom* by Milton Friedman," *American Economic Review*, 53, no. 3 (1963): 459.

122. Friedman, "Distribution of Income and the Welfare Activities of Government."

123. Gary Gerstle, *Liberty and Coercion: The Paradox of American Government; From the Founding to the Present* (Princeton, NJ: Princeton University Press, 2015), 272.

124. James T. Sparrow, *Warfare State: World War II Americans and the Age of Big Government* (Oxford: Oxford University Press, 2011), 123.

125. Ventry, "Negative Income Tax," 2.

126. Collins, *Business Response to Keynes*, 146.

127. Romain Huret, *La fin de la pauvreté? Les experts sociaux en guerre contre la pauvreté aux États-Unis (1945–1974)* (Paris: Éditions EHESS, 2004), 109.

128. See the list in Materials Available for Distribution by the Division of Tax Research. U.S. Treasury Department, January 1, 1946, Milton Friedman Papers, Hoover Institution, Tax Division, box 101, file 101.12.

129. George Stigler is therefore the first writer to mention an NIT proposal in a published piece. He advocated a tax "with negative rates" for the lowest incomes brackets in order to struggle against poverty without imposing minimum wages on the labor market. See George J. Stigler, "The Economics of Minimum Wage Legislation," *American Economic Review* 36, no. 3 (1946): 358–65.

130. Walter Heller, *New Dimensions of Political Economy* (Cambridge, MA: Harvard University Press, 1966), 115.

131. William D. Grampp and Emanuel T. Weiler, *Economic Policy: Readings in Political Economy* (Homewood, IL: Richard D. Irwin, 1953), 284–92; H. S. Booker, "Lady Rhys Williams' Proposal for the Amalgamation of Direct Taxation with Social Insurance," *Economic Journal* 56, no. 222 (June 1946): 230–43; Richard Musgrave, *The Theory of Public Finance: A Study in Public Economy* (New York: McGraw-Hill, 1959);, Earl Rolph and George Break, *Public Finance* (New York: Ronald Press, 1961), 404; James Buchanan, *The Public Finances: An Introductory Textbook* (Homewood, IL: Richard D. Irwin, 1965), 157–58.

132. Robert Rudolph Schutz, "Transfer Payments and Income Inequality" (PhD diss., University of California, Berkeley, 1952).

133. Schutz, "Transfer Payments and Income Inequality," 11.

134. Milton Friedman interview with Eduardo Suplicy, "News on the Basic Income Guarantee," June 2000; https://usbig.net/newsletters/june.html.

135. Lerner relied on a 1929 proposal by the American economist Fred M. Taylor for this book-length argument. In his article for the *American Economic Review*, Taylor had proposed publicly controlled investment coupled with income grants to consumers. Taylor did insist on a strong work requirement, however: "That conditions of some sort should be attached to the receiving of an income," he claimed, "cannot be questioned." Abba Lerner, *The Economics of Control: Principles of Welfare Economics* (London: Macmillan, 1944), 95. See also Lerner, "Statics and Dynamics in Socialist Economics," *Economic Journal* 47 (1937): 253–70; Oskar Lange and Fred M. Taylor, *On the Economic Theory of Socialism* (Minneapolis: University of Minnesota Press, 1938).

136. Nancy Ruggles, "Recent Developments in the Theory of Marginal Cost Pricing," *Review of Economic Studies* 17 (1949): 107–26; George J. Stigler, "The New Welfare Economics," *American Economic Review* 33 (1943): 355–59; Oskar Lange, "The Foundations of Welfare Economics," *Econometrica* 10 (1942): 215–28; Nancy Ruggles, "The Welfare Basis of the Marginal Cost Pricing Principle," *Review of Economic Studies* 17, no. 1 (1949–50): 29–46.

137. William H. Hutt, *Plan for Reconstruction: A Project for Victory in War and Peace* (London: Kegan Paul, Trench, Trubner, 1944), 173.

138. Gosta Esping-Andersen, *The Three Worlds of Welfare Capitalism* (London: John Wiley, 2013); Steven Pinch, *Worlds of Welfare: Understanding the Changing Geographies for Social Welfare Provision* (London: Routledge, 2002).

139. Anton Jäger and Daniel Zamora, "Welfare without the Welfare State": The Death of the Postwar Welfarist Consensus," *New Statesman*, February 2021.

Chapter Three

1. James A. Ward, *Ferrytale: The Career of W. H. "Ping" Ferry* (Stanford, CA: Stanford University Press, 2001), 93.

2. *The Triple Revolution* (Santa Barbara, CA: Ad Hoc Committee on a Triple Revolution, 1964).

3. *Triple Revolution.*

4. *Triple Revolution.*

5. Milton Friedman, quoted in Austin C. Wehrwein, "Economist Says Negative Tax Should Replace All Poverty Aid," *New York Times*, December 16, 1965, 41.

6. *Triple Revolution.*

7. Ward, *Ferrytale*, 94.

8. Brian Steensland, *The Failed Welfare Revolution* (Princeton, NJ: Princeton University Press, 2008).

9. Alice O'Connor, *Poverty Knowledge* (Princeton, NJ: Princeton University Press, 2001), 139.

10. Edward D. Berkowitz, *Mr. Social Security: The Life of Wilbur J. Cohen* (Lawrence: University Press of Kansas, 1995), 110.

11. Romain D. Huret, *La fin de la pauvreté? Les experts sociaux en guerre contre la pauvreté aux États-Unis (1945–1974)* (Paris: Éditions EHESS, 2004), 84.

12. Berkowitz, *Mr. Social Security*, 146.

13. Conference on Economic Progress, *Poverty and Economic Deprivation: The Plight of Two-Fifths of a Nation* (Washington, DC: Conference on Economic Progress, 1962), 72–82.

14. Robert A. Caro, *The Years of Lyndon Johnson: The Passage of Power* (New York: Vintage Books, 2012), 540.

15. Huret, *La fin de la pauvreté?*, 119.

16. Lyndon B. Johnson, *Annual Message to the Congress on the State of the Union*, January 8, 1964.

17. Leslie Lenkowsky, *Politics, Economics, and Welfare Reform: Failure of the Negative Income Tax in Britain and the United States* (New York: University Press of America, 1986), 16.

18. Walter Heller, "Progress and Poverty," memorandum to the president, May 1, 1963, Robert Lampman Papers, University of Wisconsin.

19. Daniel P. Moynihan, *The Politics of a Guaranteed Income* (New York: Vintage Books, 1973), 81–86.

20. Robert Lampman, "The Effectiveness of Some Institutions in Changing the Distribution of Income," *American Economic Review* 47, no. 2 (1957): 519–28.

21. Huret, *Fin de la pauvreté?*, 91.

22. Robert Lampman, "One-Fifth of a Nation," *Challenge* 12, no. 7 (April 1964): 11.

23. Robert Lampman, "Recent Changes in Income Inequality Reconsidered," *American Economic Review* 25 (June 1954): 251–68.

24. John Kenneth Galbraith, *The Affluent Society* (Boston: Houghton Mifflin, 1958).

25. Leon Keyserling, "Eggheads and Politics," *New Republic*, October 27, 1958, 15.

26. Nicholas Lemann, *The Promised Land* (New York: Vintage Books, 1992), 118.

27. Robert Lampman, "The Low-Income Population and Economic Growth," Study Paper 12, US Congress, joint economic committee, 1959.

28. Michael Harrington, "Our Fifty Million Poor," *Commentary*, July 1959, 19.

29. Franklin Delano Roosevelt, "One Third of a Nation Ill-Housed, Ill-Clad, Ill-Nourished," Second Inaugural Address, January 20, 1937.

30. Huret, *Fin de la pauvreté?*, 82.

31. *Fin de la pauvreté?*, 89.

32. Dwight Macdonald, "Our Invisible Poor," *New Yorker*, January 19, 1963, 130–39; https://www.newyorker.com/magazine/1963/01/19/our-invisible-poor.

33. Carl M. Brauer, "Kennedy, Johnson, and the War on Poverty," *Journal of American History* 69 (1982): 98–119; Linda M. Keefe, "Dwight Macdonald and Poverty Discourse, 1960–1965: The Art and Power of a Seminal Book Review," *Poverty and Public Policy* 2, no. 2 (2010): 145–88.

34. Harrington, "Our Fifty Million Poor," 25–27.

35. Oscar Lewis, *Five Families: Mexican Case Studies in the Culture of Poverty* (New York: Basic Books, 1959).

36. Oscar Lewis, "The Culture of Poverty in Mexico City: Two Case Studies," *Economic Weekly*, June 1960, 965.

37. Michael Harrington, *The Other America* (Baltimore: Penguin, 1962), 18.

38. Harrington, *Other America*, 18.

39. Harrington, *Other America*, 168.

40. Macdonald, "Our Invisible Poor," 130–39.

41. Macdonald, "Our Invisible Poor," 130–39.

42. Robert Lampman's report to the president on June 10, 1963. Quoted in Lemann, *Promised Land*, 131.

43. Harrington, *Other America*, 168–69.

44. Lenkowsky, *Politics, Economics and Welfare Reform*, 52.

45. Lewis, "Culture of Poverty in Mexico City," 965.

46. Harrington, *Other America*, 169.

47. Lampman, "One-Fifth of a Nation," 11–13.

48. Robert Theobald, ed., *The Guaranteed Income: Next Step in Economic Evolution?* (New York: Doubleday, 1965).

49. Robert Theobald, *Free Men and Free Markets* (New York: Doubleday, 1963), 68–69, 111.

50. Ralph Helstein, Gerard Piel, and Robert Theobald, *Jobs, Machines and People* (Santa Barbara, CA: Center for the Study of Democratic Institutions, 1964), 3.

51. Theobald, *Free Men and Free Markets*, 115.

52. Steven B. Wolinetz, "Friedman, Harrington and Poverty," *Cornell Daily Sun*, December 16, 1964, 4.

53. Wolinetz, "Friedman, Harrington and Poverty."

54. Wolinetz, "Friedman, Harrington and Poverty."

55. The term was coined by Robert Lachman. See Lachman, *The Age of Keynes* (New York: Vintage Books, 1966), 287.

56. Jacqueline Best, "Hollowing Out Keynesian Norms: How the Search for a Technical Fix Undermined the Bretton Woods Regime," *Review of International Studies* 30, no. 3 (July 2004): 386.

57. James Tobin, *The New Economics One Decade Older* (Princeton, NJ: Princeton University Press, 1974), 5.

58. Lemann, *Promised Land*, 130.

59. Binyamin Appelbaum, *The Economists' Hour* (New York: Little, Brown, 2019), e-book.

60. Allen Schick, "The Cybernetic State," *Trans-action* 7 (1970): 14–26.

61. Walter W. Heller, Brief book on economic matters, December 20, 1962, 3. Folder identifier, JFKPOF-063a-009-p014; https://www.jfklibrary.org/asset-viewer /archives/JFKPOF/063a/JFKPOF-063a-009.

62. Heller, Brief book on economic matters.

63. Heller, Brief book on economic matters, 4.

64. Cathie J. Martin, *Shifting the Burden: The Struggle over Growth and Corporate Taxation* (Chicago: University of Chicago Press, 1991), 52.

65. James Tobin, "Raising the Incomes of the Poor," in *Agenda for the Nation*, ed. Kermit Gordon (Washington, DC: Brookings Institution, 1968), 86–87.

66. Tobin, "Raising the Incomes of the Poor," 86–87.

67. Aaron Major, *Architects of Austerity* (Stanford, CA: Stanford University Press, 2014), 129.

68. Major, *Architects of Austerity*, 130.

69. Best, "Hollowing Out Keynesian Norms," 394.

70. Walter Heller, Letter to Milton Friedman, March 28, 1961, Milton Friedman Papers, Hoover institution Archives, box 28, file 28–5.

71. Herbert Stein, *The Fiscal Revolution in America: Policy in Pursuit of Reality* (Washington, DC: American Enterprise Institute Press, 1990), 381–82.

72. Milton Friedman, "Letter: Friedman and Keynes," *Time*, February 4, 1966, 13.

73. Edmund F. Wehrle, "Guns, Butter, Leon Keyserling, the AFL-CIO, and the Fate of Full Employment Economics," *Faculty Research and Creative Activity* 18 (2004): 9.

74. Caro, *Years of Lyndon Johnson*, 538.

75. Major, *Architects of Austerity*, 131.

76. Kim McQuaid, *Uneasy Partners: Big Business in American Politics, 1945–1990* (Baltimore: Johns Hopkins University Press, 1994), 124.

77. Berkowitz, *Mr. Social Security*, 292.

78. Berkowitz, *Mr. Social Security*, 292.

79. Odin Anderson, "The Politics of the Welfare State as Seen by Wilbur J. Cohen," manuscript, 2012.

80. Robert Lampman, "Approaches to the Reduction of Poverty," *American Economic Review* 55, no. 1 (March 1965): 521–29.

81. Lemann, *Promised Land*, 149.

82. John Kenneth Galbraith, *The Affluent Society*, 2nd ed. (London: Hamish Hamilton, 1969), 264. For a detailed account of Galbraith's shifting views about basic income see Philippe Van Parijs and Yannick Vanderborght, *Basic Income: A Sane Proposal for a Free Society* (Cambridge, MA: Harvard University Press, 2017), 87–89.

83. Drucker quoted in Margaret Wiley Marshall, "'Automation' Today and in 1662," *American Speech* 32, no. 2 (May 1957): 149.

84. Gregory R. Woirol, *The Technological Unemployment and Structural Unemployment Debates* (London: Greenwood Press, 1996) 78.

85. For a detailed list of the articles written during the mid-1950s see Woirol, *Technological Unemployment and Structural Unemployment*, 161.

86. Clarence Long, *Unemployment Problems*, Hearings before the Senate Special Committee on Unemployment Problems, 86th Cong., 1959, 182.

87. Philip Taft and Merton Stoltz, Statement, *Employment, Growth and Price Levels*, Hearings before the Joint Economic Committee, Eighty-sixth Congress, 1959, Part 8, 2707–8.

88. John T. Dunlop, *Public Policy and Unemployment*, in Hearings before the Senate Special Committee on Unemployment Problems, Studies in Unemployment, 1960, 1–2, 14.

89. Dunlop, *Public Policy and Unemployment*, 14.

90. O'Connor, *Poverty Knowledge*, 141.

91. Lachman, *Age of Keynes*, 201–3.

92. Adolph Reed, "When Compromises Come Home to Roost II: The Triumph of Culture over Political Economy," manuscript.

93. Charles C. Killingsworth, "Automation, Jobs, and Manpower: The Case for Structural Unemployment" in *Men without Work*, ed. Stanley Lebergott (Englewood Cliffs, NJ: Prentice-Hall, 1964), 90.

94. In particular Donald N. Michael, *Cybernation: The Silent Conquest*, Report for the Center for the Study of Democratic Institutions (Santa Barbara, CA, 1962).

95. The first use of the concept came from Michael, *Cybernation*.

96. Norbert Wiener, *Cybernetics, or Control and Communication in the Animal and the Machine* (Cambridge, MA: MIT Press, 1948).

97. Norbert Wiener, *The Human Use of Human Beings* (New York: Houghton Mifflin, 1950), 163.

98. Wiener, *Human Use of Human Beings*, 153–54.

99. Wiener, *Human Use of Human Beings*, 154.

100. Wiener, *Human Use of Human Beings*, 162.

101. Wiener, *Human Use of Human Beings*, 162.

102. Wilbur H. Ferry, "The Dilemmas of Abundance," speech delivered at San Francisco State College, October 3, 1961, quoted in Ward, *Ferrytale*, 88. See also Wilbur H. Ferry, *Caught on the Horn of Plenty*, Bulletin, January (Santa Barbara, CA: Center for the Study of Democratic Institutions, 1962).

103. Ferry, *Caught on the Horn of Plenty*.

104. *Triple Revolution*.

105. *Triple Revolution*.

106. Robert Theobald, " 'Technological Change, Threat or Promise?,' " Presented at the 1965 Annual Meeting of the American Orthopsychiatric Association, New York, 1965.

107. Ralph Helstein, Gerard Piel, and Robert Theobald, *Jobs, Machines and People: A Conversation* (Santa Barbara, CA: Center for the Study of Democratic Institutions, 1964), 13.

108. See Stephen M. Ward, *In Love and Struggle: The Revolutionary Lives of James and Grace Lee Boggs* (Chapel Hill: University of North Carolina Press, 2016).

109. Ward, *In Love and Struggle*.

110. Letter from Todd Gitlin to James Boggs, September 22, 1964, James and Grace Lee Boggs Papers, Walter P. Reuther Library, Detroit.

111. Cedric Johnson, "James Boggs, the 'Outsiders,' and the Challenge of Postindustrial Society," *Souls* 13, no. 3 (2011): 303–26.

112. Johnson, "James Boggs."

113. Stephen M. Ward, "An Ending and a Beginning: James Boggs, C. L. R. James, and the American Revolution," in *A New Insurgency: The Port Huron Statement and Its Times*, ed. Howard Brick and Gregory Parker (Ann Arbor: University of Michigan Library, 2015).

114. James Boggs, Foreword, "Monroe, North Carolina . . . Turning Point in American History," 1962, in *Pages from a Black Radical's Notebook: A James Boggs Reader*, ed. Stephen M. Ward (Detroit: Wayne State University Press, 2011), 72.

115. Stephen M. Ward, ed., *Pages from a Black Radical's Notebook: A James Boggs Reader* (Detroit: Wayne State University Press, 2011), 104.

116. James Boggs, "Practical Applications of Automation," paper prepared for the Automation Seminar in Detroit," Tuesday, March 23, 1965, 2. James and Grace Lee Boggs Papers, Walter P. Reuther Library, Detroit.

117. Ward, *Pages from a Black Radical's Notebook*, 114.

118. Ward, *Pages from a Black Radical's Notebook*, 113.

119. Ward, *Pages from a Black Radical's Notebook*, 113.

120. Ward, *Pages from a Black Radical's Notebook*, 109–10.

121. Ward, *Pages from a Black Radical's Notebook*, 109.

122. See William P. Jones, *The March on Washington: Jobs, Freedom and the Forgotten History of Civil Rights* (New York: W. W. Norton, 2014), 1–40.

123. A. Philip Randolph, "March on Washington Movement Presents Program for the Negro," in *What the Negro Wants*, ed. Rayford Logan (Notre Dame, IN: University of Notre Dame Press, 2001), 141.

124. Reed, "When Compromises Come Home to Roost II."

125. Bayard Rustin, "From Protest to Politics: The Future of the Civil Rights Movement," *Commentary*, February 1965, 27–28.

126. Rustin, "From Protest to Politics," 1965, 27–28.

127. James Boggs, "Cybernation, Society and the Negro," paper presented at the Conference on "Cybernation, Society and the Negro," Morgan State College, March 16, 1965, 3. James and Grace Lee Boggs Papers, Walter P. Reuther Library, Detroit.

128. James Boggs, "The Negro and Cybernation," in *The Evolving Society*, ed. Alice Mary Hilton (New York: Institute for Cybercultural Research, 1966), 171–72.

129. Wilbur Ferry, "Farewell to Integration," 1967, Wilbur Ferry Papers, Center for the Study of Democratic Institutions Collection, Vanderbilt University, box 352, 18.

130. Quoted in Christopher Lasch, *The True and Only Heaven: Progress and Its Critics* (New York: W. W. Norton, 1991), e-book.

131. Martin Luther King Jr., *Where Do We Go from Here: Chaos or Community?* (Boston: Beacon Press, 1967).

132. *A "Freedom Budget" for All Americans: Budgeting Our Resources, 1966–1975, to Achieve "Freedom from Want"* (New York: A. Philip Randolph Institute, 1966).

133. Milton Friedman, "The Case for the Negative Income Tax: A View from the Right," *Proceedings of the National Symposium on Guaranteed Income*, December 9, 1966, 115.

134. Robert Lampman, Nixon's Choices on Cash for the Poor, May 1969, Notes and Comments, Lampman Archives, Institute for Research on Poverty, University of Wisconsin.

135. Milton Friedman, "The Distribution of Income and the Welfare Activities of Government," 1956, 7, https://miltonfriedman.hoover.org/internal/media/dispatcher/215144/full.

136. Frank C. Porter, "Incentive Unresolved in Income Debate," *Washington Post*, December 10, 1966.

137. Robert Theobald, "Towards Full Unemployment," in *Increasing Understanding of Public Problems and Policies* (Chicago: Farm Foundation, 1967), 110.

138. "Assuring Decent Living Standard," *Newark (NJ) Evening News*, May 1, 1967.

139. Theobald, "Towards Full Unemployment," 110.

140. See in particular Robert J. Lampman, oral interview, May 24, 1983, by Michael L. Gillette, LBJ Library Oral Histories, LBJ Presidential Library, accessed June 11, 2020, 41.

141. Lampman, oral interview.

142. For a more detailed account of the programs see Michael L. Gillette, *Launching the War on Poverty: An Oral History* (Oxford: Oxford University Press, 2010).

143. Carl H. Madden, "The War on Poverty," *Law and Contemporary Problems* 31 (1966): 57.

144. Berkowitz, *Mr. Social Security*, 239.

145. Huret, *Fin de la pauvreté?*, 93–95.

146. Harrington, *Other America*, 67.

147. Harrington, *Other America*, 84.

148. Touré F. Reed, "Why Moynihan Was Not So Misunderstood at the Time," *Nonsite* 17 (September 2014).

149. Daniel P. Moynihan, "The Negro Family: The Case for National Action," in *The Moynihan Report and the Politics of Controversy* (Cambridge, MA: MIT Press, 1967), 47. See also Melinda Cooper, *Family Values: Between Neoliberalism and the New Social Conservatism* (Cambridge, MA: MIT Press, 2018).

150. Moynihan, "Negro Family."

151. Moynihan, *Politics of a Guaranteed Income*, 108.

152. James Tobin, "On Improving the Economic Status of the Negro," *Daedalus* 94, no. 4 (Fall 1965): 880.

153. Tobin, "On Improving the Economic Status of the Negro," 890.

154. Tobin, "On Improving the Economic Status of the Negro," 890.

155. James Tobin, "Raising the Incomes of the Poor," in *Agenda for the Nation*, ed. Kermit Gordon (Washington, DC: Brookings Institution, 1968), 96. Tobin's argument tapped into a broader debate about the effects of slavery on contemporary black life, evinced by the popularity of Stanley M. Elkins, *Slavery: A Problem in American Institutional and Intellectual Life* (Chicago: University of Chicago Press, 1968).

156. Tobin, "On Improving the Economic Status of the Negro," 880.

157. Tobin, "On Improving the Economic Status of the Negro," 889.

158. Tobin, "Raising the Incomes of the Poor," 97.

159. Tobin, "On Improving the Economic Status of the Negro," 887.

160. Tobin, "On Improving the Economic Status of the Negro."

161. Milton Friedman and Yale Brozen, *The Minimum Wage: Who Pays?* (Washington, DC: Free Society Association, 1966).

162. The idea was strongly promoted within the OEO since 1965, but was strongly blocked by Johnson and, perhaps more important, by Wilbur Cohen and Wilbur Mills, who were the key figures in social policy. See Walter Williams, "The Struggle for a Negative Income Tax: A Review Article," *Journal of Human Resources* 10, no. 4 (1975): 427–44; Robert Lampman, "The Negative Income Tax Experiment," extracts from the Archives Oral History Project, *Focus* (University of Wisconsin–Madison) 23, no. 2 (2004): 4–7.

163. Berkowitz, *Mr. Social Security*, 178.

164. Lemann, *Promised Land*, 197.

165. Reed, "When Compromises Come Home to Roost."

166. Reed, "When Compromises Come Home to Roost."

167. Reed, "When Compromises Come Home to Roost."

168. Adolph Reed Jr., "The Kerner Commission and the Irony of Antiracist Politics," *Labor Notes* 14, no. 4 (2017): 33.

169. Reed, "Kerner Commission," 33.

170. Frances Fox Piven and Richard A. Cloward, "The Weight of the Poor: A Strategy to End Poverty," *Nation* (May 2, 1966); https://www.thenation.com/article/archive/weight-poor-strategy-end-poverty/.

171. Premilla Nadasen, *Welfare Warriors: The Welfare Rights Movement in the United States* (London: Routledge, 2004).

172. *Hearings before the Subcommittee on Fiscal Policy of the Joint Economic Committee Congress of the United States*, 90th Cong., 2nd Sess., vol. 1, *Proceedings*, (Washington, DC: Government Printing Office, 1968), 77.

173. *Hearings before the Subcommittee on Fiscal Policy*, 67.

174. *Hearings before the Subcommittee on Fiscal Policy*, 77.

175. *Hearings before the Subcommittee on Fiscal Policy*, 77.

176. *Hearings before the Subcommittee on Fiscal Policy*, 81.

177. Herbert Marcuse, *One-Dimensional Man: Studies in the Ideology of Advanced Industrial Society* (Boston: Beacon Press, 1991), xxv.

178. See in particular Reuel Schiller, "The Curious Origins of Airline Deregulation: Economic Deregulation and the American Left," *Business History Review*, no. 93 (Winter 2019): 739.

179. Niklas Olsen, "Interview: How Neoliberalism Reinvented Democracy," *Jacobin*, June 4, 2019.

180. Theodore J. Lowi, *The End of Liberalism* (New York: W. W. Northon, 1969), 144, 147.

181. Robert Theobald, "The Background to the Guaranteed-Income Concept," in *The Guaranteed Income: Next Step in Economic Evolution?*, ed. Robert Theobald (New York: Doubleday, 1966), 94.

182. Theobald, "Background to the Guaranteed-Income Concept," 94.

183. Theobald, "Background to the Guaranteed-Income Concept."

184. Robert Theobald, "Food, Jobs and Human Rights," *Vital Speeches* 30, no. 2 (1963): 61–65.

185. Arthur Kemp, "Welfare without the Welfare State," *Il Politico* 31, no. 4 (1966): 716–30; Yale Brozen, "Welfare without the Welfare State," *Freemen* 16, no. 2 (1966): 40–52.

186. Kemp, "Welfare without the Welfare State," 729.

187. Moynihan, *Politics of a Guaranteed Income*, 54.

188. Moynihan, *Politics of a Guaranteed Income*," 54.

189. Otto Eckstein and Robert Harris, *Program Analysis: Income and Benefit Programs* (Washington DC: Office of the Assistant Secretary for Program Evaluation, 1966).

190. Otto Kerner (chairman), *Report of the National Advisory Commission on Civic Disorders*, (1967), 254. https://belonging.berkeley.edu/sites/default/files/kerner_commission_full_report.pdf?file=1&force=1.

191. Kerner (chairman), *Report of the National Advisory Commission on Civic Disorders*, 256.

192. "Assuring a Decent Living Standard," *Newark (NJ) Evening News*, May 1, 1967.

193. From 1967 to 1978, five experiments were held in US and Canadian cities: the New Jersey Graduated Work Incentive experiment (1968–72), the Rural Income Maintenance Experiment (1970–72), the Seattle/Denver Income Maintenance Experiments (1970–76), the Gary, Indiana, Experiment (1971–74), and the Manitoba Basic Annual Income Experiment (1975–78). For a detailed account of those experiments see David Kershaw and Jerilyn Fair, *The New Jersey Income-Maintenance Experiment*, vol. 1 (New York: Academic Press, 1976); Karl Widerquist,

"A Failure to Communicate: What (If Anything) Can We Learn from the Negative Income Tax Experiments?" *Journal of Socio-economics* 34, no. 1 (2005): 49–81.

194. The statement was circulated in May 1968 to 275 universities and research organizations. A list of those who signed it can be found in chapter 2, note 13. See "A Statement by Economists on Income Guarantees and Supplements, 27 May 1968," in Income Maintenance Programs," *Hearings before the Subcommittee on the Fiscal Policy of the Joint Economic Committee, Congress of the United States, 90th Cong.*, Second Session, vol. 2, Appendix Materials, appendix 17 (1968), 676.

195. Paul Samuelson, "Negative Income Tax," *Newsweek*, June 10, 1968, 76.

196. Moynihan, *Politics of a Guaranteed Income*, 86.

197. Cooper, *Family Values*, 43.

198. Lemann, *Promised Land*, 212.

199. Lemann, *Promised Land*, 212.

200. Lemann, *Promised Land*, 210.

201. Berkowitz, *Mr. Social Security*, 147.

202. Lemann, *Promised Land*, 211.

203. Daniel Moynihan, memo to the president, quoted in Lemann, *Promised Land*, 215.

204. Lemann, *Promised Land*, 215.

205. Lemann, *Promised Land*, 215.

206. On the reasons for his opposition see Milton Friedman and Rose Friedman, *Two Lucky People* (Chicago: University of Chicago Press, 1998), 382.

207. Friedman and Friedman, *Two Lucky People*, 176–77.

208. Lemann, *Promised Land*, 215.

209. Paul Pierson, *Dismantling the Welfare State? Reagan, Thatcher and the Politics of Retrenchment* (Cambridge: Cambridge University Press, 1994), 90.

210. John Kay, "Redistributive Market Liberalism," *New Statesman*, February 5, 1997.

211. Theobald, *Free Men and Free Markets*, 5, 118.

212. Samuel Brittan, *Capitalism with a Human Face* (Cheltenham, UK: Edward Elgar, 1995).

213. The proposal was essentially devised by James Tobin, who had become McGovern's economic adviser. See Robert W. Dimand, "On Limiting the Domain of Inequality: The Legacy of James Tobin," *Eastern Economic Journal* 29, no. 4 (Fall 2003): 559–64.

214. Huret, *Fin de la pauvreté?*, 190.

215. Theobald, *Free Men and Free Markets*, 149.

Chapter Four

1. For overviews and documents of the movement, see Achterhuis, *Arbeid: Een eigenaardig medicijn*, 54–55; Frank van Luijk, "Waarom werken wij? De betekenis

van werken, 1983–2008/2009" (PhD diss., Free University of Amsterdam, 2009), 24–25; René Didde, "Brandende trams en Bhagwan," *De Volkskrant*, April 11, 1998; K. G. Boon et al., *Het boek van de arbeid* (Amsterdam: De Arbeiderspers, 1957); H. G. Hamaker, ed., *Arbeid, beroep en samenleving* (Assen: Van Gorcum, 1981).

2. Eric Hobsbawm, "Birth of a Holiday: The First of May," in *May Day: A Short History of the International Workers' Holiday, 1886–1986*, ed. Philip S. Foner (New York: International, 1986).

3. See Rob Van Essen, *Kind van de verzorgingsstaat: Opgroeien in een tijdloos paradijs* (Amsterdam: Atlas Contact, 2016), 211; Herman Wigbold, *Bezwaren tegen de ondergang van Nederland* (Amsterdam: Arbeiderspers, 1998); Robert C. Kloosterman, "Amsterdamned: The Rise of Unemployment in Amsterdam in the 1980s," *Urban Studies* 31 (1994): 1325–44.

4. Cited in Didde, "Brandende trams," n.p.

5. Cited in Didde, "Brandende trams," n.p.

6. See Bo Bingel, "Achterhuis: Arbeid 'n vreemde ziekte," *Luie donder!* 2 (1984): 19–20. Collectif Charles Fourier Archives, Université Louvain-la-Neuve, box 22, folder 1981, and the International Institute for Social History, Amsterdam. All quotations of sources originally in French or Dutch have been translated by the authors.

7. Bingel, "Achterhuis," 20.

8. Nederlandse Bond tegen het Arbeidsethos, "Arbeidsplicht — Bah!," *Luie Donder* 5 (1984): 11.

9. Nederlandse Bond tegen het Arbeidsethos, "Arbeidsplicht — Bah!," 11.

10. Bingel, "Achterhuis," 19.

11. Bingel, "Achterhuis," 12. See also Marco Giugni, *The Politics of Unemployment in Europe: Policy Responses and Collective Action* (London: Routledge, 2016); D. Chabanet et al., *The Mobilization of the Unemployed in Europe: From Acquiescence to Protest?* (London: Springer, 2002).

12. See Walter Van Trier, "Who Framed Social Dividend?," USBIG Discussion Paper, March 26, 2002; Susanne Rehbein, *Das Grundeinkommen* (Munich: GRIN Verlag, 2009), 7; Jan Tinbergen, "Brief aan Koos Vorrink," Tinbergen Archives, University of Nijmegen, October 22, 1934 (available online). Tinbergen refers to a proposal put forward by E. Lewe van Middelstum, an unknown author who supposedly forwarded the idea for a *basis-inkomen* to the SDAP's leader Koos Vorrink. Tinbergen conversed with Lange and Lerner in the 1930s, although no evidence survives on issues pertaining to their dividends. See Erwin Dekker, *Jan Tinbergen (1903–1994) and the Rise of Economic Expertise* (Cambridge: Cambridge University Press, 2021), for a broader overview of Tinbergen's career.

13. Christian Roy, "Revolution, Work, Resistance: French Personalism's Connections with Eugen Rosenstock-Huessy," *Culture, Theory and Critique* 56 (2015); Jean-Louis Loubet del Bayle, *Les non conformistes des années* 30 (2001): 415–33;

John Hellman, *The Communitarian Third Way: Alexandre Marc and Ordre Nouveau, 1930–2000* (Montreal: McGill-Queen's University Press, 2002).

14. See in particular Alexandre Marc, "L'Amérique à quoi bon?," *L'Europe en formation* 114–55 (September-October 1969): 8–12; Alexandre Marc, "Redécouverte du minimum garanti," *L'Europe en formation* 143 (February 1972): 19–25.

15. Jürgen Habermas, "Conservative Politics, Work, Socialism and Utopia Today: Interview with Hans-Ulrich Beck, 2 April 1983," *Basler Zeitung*, January 7, 1984, 59–76.

16. Nanni Balestrini, "Afterword," in *We Want Everything* (London: Verso Books, 2022), 145.

17. See Kathleen Thelen, *Varieties of Liberalization and the New Politics of Social Solidarity* (London: Cambridge University Press, 2014), 162–65; Marc Van der Meer et al., eds., *Weg van het overleg? Twintig jaar na Wassenaar: Naar nieuwe verhoudingen in het Nederlandse model* (Amsterdam: Amsterdam University Press, 2003); Merijn Oudenampsen and Bram Mellink, *Neoliberalisme: een Nederlandse geschiedenis* (Amsterdam: Boom, 2022).

18. Servaas Storm and Ro Naastepad, "The Dutch Distress," *New Left Review* 20 (March/April 2003): 137–38. For a broader history of the Netherlands after the "permissive" turn of the 1960s, see James Kennedy, *Nieuw Babylon in aanbouw: Nederland in de jaren zestig* (Amsterdam: Boom, 2016).

19. See Milton Friedman and Rose Friedman, *Aan ons de Keus* (Brussels: Acropolis. Haasen, 1987); *Aan ons de Keus* (in four parts) available in *Het Archief*.

20. Kloosterman, "Amsterdamned."

21. See Annejet Van Der Zijl, *Een dag om nooit te vergeten: 30 april 1980—de stad, de krakers en de koningin* (Amsterdam: Singel Uitgeverijen, 2013).

22. Greetje Lubbi, "Wie zijn de werkelijke luchtfietsers?," in *Naar scheiding arbeid en inkomen* (Brussels: Werkgroep Arbeid en Milieu, 1985), 13–16.

23. Lubbi, "Wie zijn de werkelijke luchtfietsers?," 16.

24. See, inter alia, Richard Barbrook and Andy Cameron, "The Californian Ideology," *Science as Culture* 6 (1996): 44–72; Jasper Bernes, *The Work of Art in the Age of Deindustrialization* (Berkeley: University of California Press, 2016); Katja Diefenbach, "Alles läuft gut: Warum eine Politik des Wunsches nichts damit zu tun hat, sich etwas zu wollen," *DISKUS* (March 2003): 35–37.

25. Mary Mimi Howard, "Hannah Arendt's Contribution to a Critique of Political Economy," *New German Critique* 47 (2020): 74.

26. For overviews of this "cybernetic moment," see Eden Medina, *Cybernetic Revolutionaries: Technology and Politics in Allende's Chile* (Cambridge, MA: MIT Press, 2014); Andrew Pickering, *The Cybernetic Brain: Sketches of Another Future* (Chicago: University of Chicago Press, 2010); Alexander R. Galloway, "The Cybernetic Hypothesis," *differences* 25, no. 1 (2014): 107–31; Langdon Winner, *Autonomous Technology: Technics-out-of-Control as a Theme in Political Thought* (Cambridge, MA: MIT Press, 1978).

27. Cited in Alastair Hemmens, "The New Spirit of Capitalism and the Critique of Work in France since May '68," in Hemmens, *The Critique of Work in Modern French Thought* (London: Palgrave, 2019), 182–83.

28. Alastair Hemmens, "New Spirit of Capitalism," 182.

29. Alastair Hemmens, "New Spirit of Capitalism," 182.

30. Cited in David Broder, "The Autumn and Fall of Italian Workerism," *Catalyst* 3, no. 4 (2020): 30. See also Nanni Balestrini and P. Moron, *L'orda oro, 1968–1977* (Milan: Feltrinelli, 2005).

31. See Joachim Häberlen, "From TUNIX to Tuwat," in *The Emotional Politics of the Alternative Left: West Germany, 1968–1984* (London: Cambridge University Press, 2018), 240.

32. See Hans-Georg Betz, *Postmodern Politics in Germany* (London: Macmillan, 1991), 36–37; François Dosse, *Gilles Deleuze and Félix Guattari: Intersecting Lives* (New York: Columbia University Press, 2007), 294.

33. Ivan Illich, *Le chômage créateur: Postface à la convivialité* (Paris: Seuil, 1977).

34. Another important catalyst to a left antiwork and antistate sensibility was the 1972 publication of the Club of Rome's "Limits to Growth" report, issued on the eve of the global oil shock and the consequent financial slump. E. F. Schumacher's 1973 book *Small Is Beautiful*, for instance, issued a call for decreased and decentralized production and coupled it with an incentive to look for "work that really needs to be done ... the development of technologies by which ordinary, decent, hardworking, modest and all-too-often abused people can improve their lot." See E. F. Schumacher, *Small Is Beautiful: Economics as if People Mattered* (New York: Harper and Row, 1973).

35. Terence Renaud, *New Lefts: The Making of a Radical Tradition* (Princeton, NJ: Princeton University Press, 2021); Adrian Little, *Post-Industrial Socialism: Towards a New Politics of Welfare* (London: Routledge, 2004).

36. See Justin H. Vassallo, "The World Henry Ford Made," *Boston Review*, October 2020, n.p.; Greg Grandin, *Fordlandia: The Rise and Fall of Henry Ford's Forgotten Jungle City* (New York: Henry Holt, 2010); Stefan Link, "Business as Political Action: The Ford-GM Rivalry in the 1920s and the Limits of 'Embeddedness,'" unpublished manuscript, 1–41.

37. Andrea Muehlebach and Nitzan Shosan, "Post-Fordist Affect," *Anthropological Quarterly* 85, no. 2 (Spring 2012): 317.

38. Mario Tronti, *Workers and Capital*, trans. David Broder (London: Verso Books, 2019), 301.

39. See Carroll Pursell, ed., *A Companion to American Technology* (London: John Wiley, 2008), 65. Peter Drucker situates the coinage in 1951, although other reports situate it earlier. See Peter Drucker, *Innovation and Entrepreneurship* (London: Routledge, 2012), 99. For a representative view from Detroit, see Thomas J. Sugrue, *The Origins of the Urban Crisis: Race and Inequality in Postwar Detroit* (Princeton, NJ: Princeton University Press, 2014).

40. Stefan Link, "The Charismatic Corporation: Finance, Administration, and Shop Floor Management under Henry Ford," *Business History Review* 92 (Spring 2018): 85–115; "Refashioning Fordism," in *Forging Global Fordism: Nazi Germany, Soviet Russia, and the Contest over the Industrial Order* (Princeton, NJ: Princeton University Press, 2019), 209. For Marxist treatments, see Michel Aglietta, *A Theory of Capitalist Regulation: The US Experience* (London: New Left Books, 1979).

41. Friedrich Pollock, *Automation: A Study of Its Economic and Social Consequences* (New York: Praeger, 1957). Pollock already foresaw the presumed necessity of basic income schemes, referencing the worries of trade union radicals such as Walter Reuther. See John Diebold, *Automation: The Advent of the Automatic Factory* (New York: Van Nostrand, 1952). For a discussion of Pollock's work in context, see Jason E. Smith, *Smart Machines and Service Work: Automation in an Age of Stagnation* (Chicago: Reaktion Books, 2020), 18–21.

42. Friedrich Pollock, "State Capitalism: Its Possibilities and Limitations," in *Critical Theory and Society: A Reader*, ed. Stephen Bronner and Douglas Kellner (New York: Routledge, 1989), 115–20; "Is National Socialism a New Order?," *Studies in Philosophy and Social Science* 4 (1941): 453.

43. Quoted in Reuel Schiller, "The Curious Origins of Airline Deregulation: Economic Deregulation and the American Left," *Business History Review* 93 (Winter 2019): 729–53.

44. Nicola Pizzolato, "Transnational Radicals: Labour Dissent and Political Activism in Detroit and Turin (1950–1970)," *International Review of Social History* 56, no. 1 (April 2011): 1–30; Nanni Balestrini, *The Golden Horde: Revolutionary Italy, 1960–1977* (New York: Seagull Books, 2021). Boggs's work was translated into Italian in 1968, at the start of the country's industrial tumult; see James Boggs, *La rivoluzione americana* (Turin: Jaca Books, 1968).

45. J. Jesse Ramirez, "Marcuse among the Technocrats: America, Automation, and Postcapitalist Utopias, 1900–1941," *Amerikastudien/American Studies* 57 (2012): 31–50. See also Harry Braverman, *Labor and Monopoly Capital: The Degradation of Work in the Twentieth Century* (New York: Monthly Review Press, 1974), for a later discussion of this trend.

46. See Frederick Harry Pitts, "Escape by Approximation: The Contemporary Relevance of Marcuse's Conceptualization of Labor," *Telos Scope*, July 17, 2012. For the original, see Douglas Kellner, "Introduction to 'On the Philosophical Foundation of the Concept of Labor,'" in *Telos* 16 (Summer 1973): 2–8. Herbert Marcuse, "On the Philosophical Foundation of the Concept of Labor in Economics," *Telos* 16 (Summer 1973). See also Rakesh Bandari, "On the Continuing Relevance of Mattick's Critique of Marcuse," *International Journal of Political Economy* 29 (Winter 1999/2000): 56; Paul Mattick, *Critique of Marcuse* (New York: Herder and Herder, 1972); Howard Brick, *Transcending Capitalism: Visions of a New Society in Modern American Thought* (Ithaca, NY: Cornell University Press, 2015).

47. See Hannah Arendt, *The Human Condition* (Chicago: University of Chicago Press, 1958). Arendt's distinction between "vita activa" and "vita contemplativa"—the former associated with repetitive toil, the latter with agentive action—provided a later source of inspiration for Dutch postwork writers such as Hans Achterhuis.

48. Philip Walsh, *Arendt contra Sociology: Theory, Society and Its Science* (London: Routledge, 2016), 140.

49. Douglas Kellner, *Herbert Marcuse and the Crisis of Marxism* (New York: University of California Press, 1984), 253; Renaud, *New Lefts*.

50. Cited in Kevin Anderson, ed., *The Dunayevskaya-Marcuse-Fromm Correspondence, 1954–1978: Dialogues on Hegel* (London: Lexington Books, 2012), xxxiii; Herbert Marcuse, "The End of Utopia," in "Psychoanalyse und Politik," Lecture delivered at the Free University of West Berlin, July 1967.

51. Ramirez, "Marcuse among the Technocrats," 35; George Terborgh, *The Automation Hysteria* (New York: Norton, 1966).

52. See Erich Fromm, "The Psychological Aspects of the Guaranteed Income," in *The Guaranteed Income*, ed. Robert Theobald (New York: Doubleday, 1966). See also Herbert Marcuse, *One-Dimensional Man* (London: Routledge, 2002); Charlotte Mohs, Marco Bonavena, and Johannes Hauer, "Abschied von der Klassenmetaphysik: Formwandel der Klassengesellschaft, Paralyse der Kritik," *Phase* 2 (2018): 51–52; Alberto Toscano, "Liberation Technology: Marcuse's Communist Individualism" (working paper, Goldsmiths, 2005), 6–22; R. Moore, "Eros and Civilization for a Jobless Future: Herbert Marcuse and the Abolition of Work," in *Heathwood Journal of Critical Theory* 1 (2016): 2; Bernes, *Work of Art*, passim.

53. Cited in Bernes, *Work of Art*, 161. For the original, see Herbert Marcuse, *Eros and Civilization* (New York: Beacon Press, 2015), 156.

54. See Serge Crozier, "L'ère du prolétariat s'achève," *Arguments* 12–13 (February-March 1959): 281–83. Especially popular was John Goldthorpe, *The Affluent Worker: Political Attitudes and Behaviour* (Cambridge: Cambridge University Press, 1963). Later exponents include Daniel Bell and his own 1976 *The Coming of Post-Industrial Society*, where Marx's "labor theory of value" was declared historically obsolete in the age of the supercomputer.

55. Jean Baudrillard, *The Consumer Society* (London: Sage, 2016), passim.

56. Baudrillard, *Consumer Society*, 89.

57. See Jean-François Lyotard, *Libidinal Economy* (New York: A and C Black, 2004), 211.

58. See Cedric Johnson, "James Boggs, the 'Outsiders,' and the Challenge of Postindustrial Society," *Souls* 13, no. 3 (2008): 303–26.

59. Raoul Vaneigem, *The Revolution of Everyday Life* (New York: PM Press, 2009), 39. See also Anselm Jappe, *Guy Debord* (London: PM Press, 2017), for an overview of the movement.

60. Vaneigem, *Revolution of Everyday Life*, 39.

61. Vaneigem, *Revolution of Everyday Life*, 39.

62. Vaneigem, *Revolution of Everyday Life*, 39.

63. Vaneigem, *Revolution of Everyday Life*, 39.

64. Jean Fourastié, *Les 40.000 heures* (Paris: Denoël, 1965). See also Kristin Ross, "Henri Lefebvre on the Situationist International," *October* 79 (Winter 1997); Kristin Ross, *Fast Cars, Clean Bodies: Decolonization and the Reordering of French Culture* (Cambridge, MA: MIT Press, 1996).

65. See Miriam R. Levin, ed., *Cultures of Control* (London: Routledge, 2005), 249. The phrase was coined by Dominican friar Père Dubarle, who reviewed Norbert Wiener's book in *Le Monde* in 1948.

66. See Raoul Vaneigem, *Traité de savoir-vivre à l'usage des jeunes générations* (Paris: Gallimard, 1967). See also Alexandre Moatti, "Vocabulaire et controverses autour de la cybernétique et du transhumain, années 1960–1970," *L'Homme et la société* 205 (2017): 109–31.

67. Scott Lasch and John Ury, *The End of Organized Capitalism* (London: Polity, 1987).

68. Gianfranco Marelli, *L'amère victoire du situationnisme: Pour une histoire critique de l'internationale situationniste, 1956–1971* (Paris: Éditions Sulliver, 1998), 322; Rene Viénet et al., *May 68'—A Compendium: Situationist Reflections on the Uprisings in France, May 1968* (London: Bread and Circuses, 2018).

69. David Broder, "A Long-Established Disorder?," *Weekly Worker* 1368 (October 2021): 9.

70. Vaneigem, *Traité*, 36.

71. Vaneigem, *Traité*, 36. For the situationists' "cybernetic welfare state," see John Beck and Ryan Bishop, *Technocrats of the Imagination: Art, Technology, and the Military-Industrial Avant-Garde* (Durham, NC: Duke University Press, 2020), 18–20; Raoul Vaneigem, "Totality for Kids," in *Beneath the Paving Stones: Situationists and the Beach, May 1968*, ed. Dark Star (London: AK Press, Dark Star, 2001), 40. Vaneigem came out as a UBI proponent later in the century. See Raoul Vaneigem, *A Declaration of the Rights of Human Beings: On the Sovereignty of Life as Surpassing the Rights of Man* (London: PM Press, 2018); Raoul Vaneigem, "Raoul Vaneigem, "Sauver les acquis sociaux? Ils sont déjà perdus," *Ballast*, June 7, 2019, 12.

72. Vaneigem, *Traité*, 36.

73. In the mid-1960s, André Gorz would become one of the first editors to put out a more complete version of the text. See Helmut Reinicke and Moishe Postone, "On Nicolaus 'Introduction' to the *Grundrisse*," *Telos* 22 (Winter 1974–75): 130–48; Martin Nicolaus, "The Unknown Marx," *New Left Review* 48 (March–April 1968); Finn Bowring, *André Gorz and the Sartrean Legacy: Arguments for a Person-Centered Social Theory* (New York: Springer, 2000).

74. See Ramirez, "Marcuse and the Technocrats," 188; Loren Goldner, "Amadeo Bordiga, the Agrarian Question and the International Revolutionary Movement,"

Critique 23, no. 1 (1995): 73–100; David Broder, "Wrongly Overlooked Thinker," *Weekly Worker* 1309 (July 2020): 6.

75. See Gavin Mueller, *Breaking Things at Work* (London: Verso Books, 2020), 72; Raya Dunayevskaya, "Marx's Grundrisse and the Dialectic in Life and in Thought," in *Marx's Philosophy of Revolution in Permanence* (Leiden: Brill, 2019), 91–99; "The Dialectic of Marx's *Grundrisse* (excerpts from critique of Martin Nicolaus' Introduction to the *Grundrisse*)," *New Letters* 9–10 (1973): 1–9.

76. See Mike Davis, *Old Gods, New Enigmas: Marx's Lost Theory* (London: Verso Books, 2017), 111. For overviews, see Frederick Harry Pitts, *Critiquing Capitalism Today: New Ways to Read Marx* (London: Springer, 2017); Jan Hoff, *Marx Worldwide: On the Development of the International Discourse on Marx since 1965* (London: Brill, 2016); Ricardo Bellofiore, *Re-reading Marx: New Perspectives after the Critical Edition* (London: Palgrave Macmillan, 2009).

77. See Karl Marx, *Grundrisse: Foundations of the Critique of Political Economy (Rough Draft)*, trans. Martin Nicolaus (London: Penguin Books, 1973), 705.

78. Marx, *Grundrisse*, 705.

79. Marx, *Grundrisse*, 705.

80. Postone would later come out as a conditional basic income supporter in the 1990s. See Moishe Postone, *Time, Labor, and Social Domination: A Reinterpretation of Marx's Critical Theory* (New York: Cambridge University Press, 1995), 21, where he drew on Gorz.

81. Pitts, *Critiquing Capitalism Today*, 144–49.

82. Antonio Negri, *Marx beyond Marx: Lessons on the Grundrisse* (London: Autonomedia, 1991), 211. See also his *Revolution Retrieved: Writings on Marx, Keynes, Capitalist Crisis, and New Social Subjects (1967–83)* (London: Red Notes Italian Archive, 1977).

83. For an overview see Christopher Brooks, "Exile: An Intellectual Portrait of André Gorz" (PhD diss., University of California, Santa Cruz, 2010), passim.

84. Mateo Alaluf, "Qu'est-ce que les grèves de 1960–1961 ont fait à la sociologie?," in *Mémoire de la grande grève de l'hiver 1960–1961 en Belgique*, ed. B. Francq, L. Courtois, and P. Tilly (Brussels: Le cri, 2011), 187–95; F. Perroux and H. Marcuse, *François Perroux interroge Herbert Marcuse … qui répond* (Paris: Aubier, 1969), 1976.

85. See André Gorz, "Le démenti belge," *Les temps modernes* 178 (February 1981), 1055.

86. Cited in Alvin W. Gouldner, "The New Class Project," *Theory and Society* 6, no. 2 (September 1978): 159. See also Mark Poster, *Existential Marxism in Postwar France* (Princeton, NJ: Princeton University Press, 1977), 361–69. Together with Serge Mallet, Alain Touraine, and Pierre Belleville, Gorz was one of the foremost theorists of this "new class" on the left, overlapping with claims about the "professional-managerial classes" in the United States. See Serge Mallet, *Essays*

on the New Working Class (St. Louis, MO: Telos Press, 1975); Barbara Ehrenreich and John Ehrenreich, "The Professional-Managerial Class," *Radical America* 11, no. 2 (March-April 1977): 7–31.

87. André Gorz, *Stratégie ouvrière et néocapitalisme* (Paris: Seuil, 1964).

88. Cited in Lasch, *End of Organized Capitalism*, 210.

89. Lasch, *End of Organized Capitalism*, 210.

90. See Alain Lipietz, "André Gorz and Our Youth," *Vlaams Marxistisch tijdschrift* 46 (2012): 88, for a powerful reflection on this turn in Gorz's thinking.

91. Cited in Steve Meyer," "An Economic 'Frankenstein' ": UAW Workers' Responses to Automation at the Ford Brook Park Plant in the 1950s," *Michigan Historical Review* 28, no. 1 (Spring 2002).

92. Michel Bosquet [André Gorz], *Capitalism in Crisis and Everyday Life* (London: Harvester Press, 1977), 22. See also Michael Scott Christofferson, *French Intellectuals against the Left: The Antitotalitarian Moment of the 1970s* (London: Berghahn Books, 2004), 42–50.

93. André Gorz, *Ecology as Politics* (New York: Blackrose Books, 1980), 77.

94. Cited in Conrad Lodziak and Jeremy Tatman, eds., *André Gorz: A Critical Introduction* (London: Pluto Press, 1997), 66.

95. André Gorz, *Farewell to the Working Class* (London: Pluto Press, 1982), 35.

96. Gorz, *Farewell to the Working Class*, 67.

97. Gorz, *Farewell to the Working Class*, 67.

98. Gorz, *Farewell to the Working Class*, 67.

99. See Michael Scott Christofferson, *Les intellectuels contre la gauche: L'idéologie antitotalitaire en France (1968–1981)* (Paris: Agone, 2014), 12–13; "The Antitotalitarian Moment in French Intellectual Politics, 1975–1984" (PhD diss., Columbia University, 1998), 82–83; Daniel Zamora and Mitchell Dean, *Le dernier homme et la fin de la revolution: Foucault après '68* (Paris: Lux, 2020), 44–45.

100. See Bram van Ojik, *Basisinkomen* (Amsterdam: Politieke Partij Radikalen Studiestiching, 1982), title page. Later examples include Bram van Ojik, "Basisinkomen en arbeidstijdverkorting," *Socialisme en démocratie* 10 (1983): 25–30.

101. Van Ojik, *Basisinkomen*, 15.

102. Van Ojik, *Basisinkomen*, 15.

103. Van Ojik, *Basisinkomen*, 15.

104. Robert Theobald, *Gewaarborgd inkomen in een vrije maatschappij* (Antwerp: Werkgroep 2000, 1967).

105. Cited in F. H. M. Grapperhaus, *Is de negatieve inkomstenbelasting een schrede vooruit op de weg naar de sociale rechtvaardigheid?* (Deventer, 1970), 70.

106. See Jan-Pieter Kuiper, "Arbeid en inkomen: Twee rechten en twee plichten," *Sociaal maandblad arbeid* (1976): 503–12; Jan-Pieter Kuiper, "Inkomen ontkoppelen van arbeid?," *Gids personeelsbeleid* 18 (June 7, 1977): 477. See also

Robert J. van der Veen, *Between Exploitation and Communism: Explorations in the Marxian Theory of Justice and Freedom* (Amsterdam: Wolters-Noordhoff, 1991), 352.

107. See Jan-Pieter Kuiper, "Volwaardige arbeid ook voor minder-validen," *AVO*, December 1976, 9. See also Loek Groot et al., *Basic Income on the Agenda: Policy Objectives and Political Chances* (Amsterdam: Amsterdam University Press, 2011), 219.

108. Roel van Duyn [Duijn], "The Kabouters of Holland," in *The Essential Works of Anarchism*, ed. Marshall D. Shatz (New York: Bantam, 1971).

109. Editors, "Het is weer Amsterdam tegen de provincie," *Trouw*, March 2004.

110. Roel van Duijn, *Provo: De geschiedenis van de provotarische beweging 1965–1967* (Amsterdam: Meulenhoff, 1985), 181.

111. See Roel van Duijn et al., "Wat willen we nu eigenlijk?," *De kabouterkrant* 2 (May 1971): 1.

112. R. Balkker, "Han Schilperoord: Wij willen de handen vuil maken," *Noordnederlandse dagblad*, March 13, 1971. Closely aligned with French situationists, van Duijn later became an eloquent basic income advocate. See R. J. L. Visser, "Discussie over de betogen met reacties van Vogels en van Duijn," in *Natuur en cultuur op gespannen voet: Groen licht voor een nieuw denken?*, ed. Rob Visser (Utrecht: Studium Generale Reeks, 1994), 48.

113. See Roel van Duijn, Michel Foucault, Herbert Marcuse, Gilles Deleuze, and Félix Guattari, *Morgen is het misschien zover: Het nieuwe denken over onze tijd* (Amsterdam: Het Wereldvenster, 1973).

114. Van Duijn, *Provo*, 181.

115. Van Duijn, *Provo*, 181.

116. Van Duijn, *Provo*, 181.

117. Van Duijn, *Provo*, 134.

118. Van Duijn, *Provo*, 134.

119. See Duco van Weerlee, *Wat de provo's willen* (Amsterdam: De Bezige Bij, 1966), 15. For broader overviews of the movement, see Axel Schildt and Detlef Siegfried, *Between Marx and Coca-Cola: Youth Cultures in Changing European Societies, 1960–1980* (New York: Berghahn Books, 2006), 335–38; Richard Kempton, *Provo: Amsterdam's Anarchist Revolt* (London: Autonomedia, 2007), 62–81; F. E. Frenkel, *Provo: Kanttekeningen bij een deelverschijnsel* (Amsterdam: Polak en Van Gennep, 1967).

120. Van Weerlee, *Wat de provo's willen*, 15.

121. Van Weerlee, *Wat de provo's willen*, 16.

122. Van Weerlee, *Wat de provo's willen*, 133. See also Ali Dur and McKenzie Wark, "New New Babylon," *October* 138 (Fall 2011): 37–56; Mark Wigley, *Constant's New Babylon: The Hyper-architecture of Desire* (Rotterdam: 010, 1998); Mark Wigley and Catherine de Zegher, eds., *The Activist Drawing: Retracing Situationist*

Architectures from Constant's New Babylon to Beyond (Cambridge, MA: MIT Press, 2002). Dur and Wark emphasized the influence of Norbert Wiener on Nieuwenhuis plans, and even Henri Lefebvre—classically a critic of cybernetics—evinced enthusiasm.

123. See Constant Nieuwenhuis, *New Babylon* (New York: Notbored, 2009), 3.

124. Nieuwenhuis, *New Babylon*, 134.

125. Cited in Robert J. van der Veen, *Between Exploitation and Communism: Explorations in the Marxian Theory of Justice and Freedom* (Amsterdam: Wolters-Noordhoff, 1991), 352. Also explored in Cor Schavemaker and Harry Willemsen, *Over de arbeid van de mens* (Amsterdam: Samsom, 1984), a book Hans Achterhuis used at the University of Amsterdam during his interactions with the Council.

126. See 19e Kongres van de Partij van de Arbeid, "Resolutie Arbeid," April 23, 1983, 13.

127. Frank Empel and Flip Vuijsje, "Jaap van der Doef en de herverdeling van de arbeid—'Werk moet een recht blijven,'" *De haagse post*, 1980, 2.

128. See Roel van Duijn, *De boodschap van een wijze kabouter: Een beschouwing over het filosofische en politieke werk van Peter Kropotkien in verband met onze huidige keuze tussen katastrofe of kabouterstad* (Amsterdam: Meulenhoff, 1969), 60–61. Van Duijn also postulated that cybernetics had replaced dialectics as the "science of change," using the example of an open grid on which users with bikes could circulate.

129. Van Weerlee, *Wat de provo's willen*, 17.

130. Chris Marker, "Sixties," *Critical Quarterly* 50 (October 2008): 26–32.

131. Chris Marker, *A Grin without a Cat* (film, 1977), at minutes 2–3.

132. See Michel Rocard, "Un puissant parti socialiste: Intervention à la convention nationale du parti socialiste le 25 novembre 1978," in *Parler vrai* (Paris: Seuil, 1979), 176.

133. Michel Bosquet, "Occupons le terrain," *Le nouvel observateur* 166 (August 1976): 23.

134. Pierre Rosanvallon and Patrick Viveret, *Pour une nouvelle culture politique* (Paris: Seuil, 1977).

135. Rosanvallon and Viveret, *Pour une nouvelle culture politique*, passim.

136. Pierre Rosanvallon, "L'état en état d'urgence," *Le nouvel observateur* 670 (September 1977): 49. See in particular Michael Behrent, "Liberalism without Humanism: Michel Foucault and the Free-market Creed, 1976–1979," *Modern Intellectual History* 6, no. 3 (November 2009): 539–68.

137. Pierre Clastres, *La société contre l'état* (Paris: Minuit, 2002), 164–65.

138. Samuel Moyn, "Of Savagery and Civil Society: Pierre Clastres and the Transformation of French Political Thought," *Modern Intellectual History* 1 (2004): 66.

139. Pierre Clastres, *Society against the State* (New York: Zone Books, 2005), 193.

140. Clastres, *Société contre l'état*, 164.

141. Pierre Bourdieu, *On the State: Lectures at the Collège de France, 1989–1992* (London: Wiley, 2018), 8.

142. Michel Messu, "Pauvreté et exclusion en France," in *Face à la pauvreté*, ed. F. Merrien (Paris: Éditions de l'atelier, 1994), 148.

143. Jacques Donzelot, *La police des familles* (Paris: Minuit, 1977).

144. Jeannine Verdès-Leroux, *Le travail social* (Paris: Minuit, 1978).

145. Michel Foucault, "La philosophie analytique de la politique," in *Dits et écrits II*, ed. Daniel Defert and François Ewald (Paris: Gallimard, 1994), 551.

146. Foucault, "Philosophie analytique," 551.

147. Michel Foucault, "Un système fini face à une demande infinie," *Dits et écrits*, 1191.

148. Michael C. Behrent, "Accidents Happen: François Ewald, the 'Antirevolutionary' Foucault, and the Intellectual Politics of the French Welfare State," *Journal of Modern History* 82 (September 2010): 587.

149. François Ewald, *L'état-providence* (Paris: Grasset, 1986), 387.

150. Lionel Stoléru, *Vaincre la pauvreté dans les pays riches* (Paris: Flammarion, 1974), 237.

151. Stoléru, *Vaincre la pauvreté*, 286.

152. Stoléru, *Vaincre la pauvreté*, 287.

153. Stoléru, *Vaincre la pauvreté*, 289.

154. Michel Foucault, *The Birth of Biopolitics: Lectures at the Collège de France, 1978–79* (London: Palgrave, 2008), 115.

155. See also Michael Behrent, "Can the Critique of Capitalism Be Anti-humanist?," *History and Theory* 54 (October 2015): 399.

156. Foucault's postwork sensibility was far from new. In 1978, for instance, in an interview conducted by a young student at the University of Paris, he had insisted on reassessing Paul Lafargue. After discussing themes concerning personal work, the student returned to an earlier statement by Foucault. "You have said," he continued, "that we are forced to work. But do we want to work? Do we choose to work?" "Yes, we desire work," Foucault noted, and "we want to and we love to work, but work does not constitute our essence. To say that we want to work and that we want to ground our essence on our desire to work are two very different things." See Michel Foucault, *Dits et écrits: 1976–1988* (Paris: Gallimard, 1994), 776.

157. Foucault, *Dits et écrits*, 475.

158. Michel Bosquet, "Plaidoyer pour l'entreprise," *Le nouvel observateur* 684 (December 1977): 19–24.

159. Bosquet, "Occupons le terrain," 23.

160. Bosquet, "Occupons le terrain," 23.

161. Bosquet, "Occupons le terrain," 23.

162. Bosquet, "Occupons le terrain," 23.

163. See Gianinazzi, *André Gorz: Une vie* (Paris: La Découverte, 2016), 64. See also Michel Bosquet, "La nébuleuse écologique," *Le nouvel observateur*, August 22, 1977.

164. André Gorz, *Métamorphoses du travail* (Paris: Éditions Galilée, 1988), 79.

165. Paul Kalma, *Het socialisme op sterk water: Veertien stellingen* (Deventer: Van Loghum Slaterus, 1988).

166. See Sicco Mansholt, "Invoering van een basisinkomen een noodzakelijkheid," in *Werkgroep PvdA voor Basisinkomen* (1986), 1. Archives of Collectif Charles Fourier, Université Catholique Louvain-la-Neuve.

167. Mansholt, "Invoering van een basisinkomen een noodzakelijkheid," 1.

168. Mansholt, "Invoering van een basisinkomen een noodzakelijkheid," 1.

169. Mansholt, "Invoering van een basisinkomen een noodzakelijkheid," 1.

170. Wetenschappelijke Raad voor Regeringsadvies, *Waarborgen voor zekerheid: Een nieuw stelsel van sociale zekerheid in hoofdlijnen* (The Hague: Staatsuitgeverij, 1985).

171. Wetenschappelijke Raad voor Regeringsadvies, *Vernieuwingen in het arbeidsbestel* (The Hague: WRR, 1981).

172. Wetenschappelijke Raad voor Regeringsadvies, *Vernieuwingen in het arbeidsbestel*, 181.

173. For overviews, see Archief Stichting Weerwerk (Nijmegen), International Instituut voor Sociale Geschiedenis, Amsterdam.

174. Jan-Willem Bingel, "De Staatsgreep: Het is Niet Of-Of Ofzo," *Luie Donder* 2, no. 2 (1985): 2–3.

175. Folder "Basisinkomen harde grondslag voor sociale zekerheid," Archief Stichting Weerwerk (Nijmegen), International Instituut voor Sociale Geschiedenis, Amsterdam.

176. "Voor Niks Gaat de Zon op," *Nieuwsbrief Weerwerk* 4 (1988): n.p.

177. Philippe Van Parijs, "Pays-bas: Le débat sur l'allocation universelle, ou L'audelà du revenu minimum garanti," *Revue belge de sécurité sociale* 30 (1988): 675–84. The text was later reprinted in *Notes de la Fondation Saint Simon* (September 1, 1988): 15–23. Redirected in correspondence with author, August 30, 2018.

178. Van Parijs, "Pays-bas," 684.

179. Van Parijs, "Pays-bas," 684.

180. Van Parijs, "Pays-bas," 684.

181. However, it was only a few months later, during a stay at the University of Manchester, that Van Parijs learned through economist Richard Blundell about the history of the concept and the vast literature dedicated to the topic, ranging from Friedman to Tinbergen to Kuiper.

182. Philippe Van Parijs, "Les libertariens: Nouvelle droite ou nouvelle gauche?," *La revue nouvelle* 3 (March 1984): 257–65.

183. Philippe Van Parijs, *Real Freedom for All* (Oxford: Clarendon Press, 1995), vii–viii.

184. See G. A. Cohen, "Introduction to the 2000 Edition," in *Karl Marx's Theory of History: A Defence* (Princeton, NJ: Princeton University Press, 2001), xix.

185. Van Parijs, *Real Freedom for All*, vii.

186. Van Parijs, *Real Freedom for All*, vii.

187. Van Parijs, personal correspondence, August 30, 2018.

188. Cited in Daniel Zamora Vargas, "How Poverty Became a Violation of Human Rights: The Production of a New Political Subject, France and Belgium, 1964–88," *History of Political Economy* 52, no. 3 (2020): 507.

189. Philippe Defeyt and Pierre Reman, "Les interlocuteurs sociaux face à la réforme de la sécurité sociale," *Courrier hebdomadaire du CRISP* 38–39, no. 1103–4 (1985): 19.

190. Gilbert Tixier, "L'impôt sur le revenu négatif," *Revue de science financière* 1 (January-March 1969): 112. The proposal later figured in several party platforms such as the liberal PVV (Party for Freedom). See PVV, "De verzorgingstaat aan hervorming toe," July 16, 1982; Els Witte and Jan Craeybeckx, *La belgique politique de 1830 à nos jours* (Brussels: Éditions Labor, 1985), 540–41; Philippe Defeyt, "Les partis politiques face à la réforme de la sécurité sociale," *Courrier hebdomadaire* 1041–42 (1984): 5; CVP, "Bestaanszekerheid voor iedereen," in *Actes du congrès (31 mai au 1er juin)* (January 1981), 56.

191. M. Versichelen, "La misère dans l'état d'abondance: Une étude concrète de 300 miséreux dans notre pays," *Revue belge se sécurité sociale* 9 (September 1970): 11.

192. See Daniel Zamora Vargas, *De l'égalité à la pauvreté: Une socio-histoire de l'assistance en Belgique (1895–2015)* (Brussels: Éditions de l'Université libre de Bruxelles, 2017); Mateo Alaluf, *L'allocation universelle: Un nouveau label de précarité* (Brussels: Couleur livres, 2014).

193. Zamora Vargas, *De l'égalité à la pauvreté*, 211.

194. Écolo, *90 propositions des écologistes—Une autre manière de faire de la politique* (Brussels: Écolo, 1981), 37.

195. Agalev, *Op Mensenmaat: Een groene kijk op de economie* (Brussels: Agalev, 1984).

196. The original can be found in *Le Travail dans l'Avenir* (Brussels: Fondation Roi Baudouin, 1984), 9–16.

197. *Travail dans l'Avenir*, 10.

198. *Travail dans l'avenir*, 10. There has been considerable discussion on the exact status of this foundational text, later recast by its authors as a document meant more to stir up debate than to put forward concrete policy advice. Even when conceived as a "utopia" or as a tool to stir public debate, the text, and the form of utopia it promotes, is of importance.

199. Herman Deleeck, "Noble principe, efficacité douteuse," *La revue nouvelle* 4 (April 1985): 430.

200. Hedwige Peemans-Poullet, "Enfer pavé de mauvaises intentions," *La revue nouvelle* 4 (April 1985): 435.

201. Peemans-Poullet, "Enfer pavé de mauvaises intentions," 435.

202. Peemans-Poullet, "Enfer pavé de mauvaises intentions," 447.

203. Peemans-Poullet, "Enfer pavé de mauvaises intentions," 448–49.

204. Van Parijs, "Libertariens," 257–65.

205. Philippe Van Parijs, "Relever le défi," *La revue nouvelle* 1 (January 1986): 332.
206. Van Parijs, "Libertariens," 265.

207. See Avner Offer and Gabriel Söderberg, *The Nobel Factor: The Prize in Economics, Social Democracy, and the Market Turn* (Princeton, NJ: Princeton University Press, 2019), 180. See also Jenny Andersson, "Neoliberalism against Social Democracy," *Tocqueville Review* 41 (December 2020): 87–107, for an examination of market debates in 1970s Sweden.

208. Offer and Söderberg, *Nobel Factor*, 180–81.

209. Offer and Söderberg, *Nobel Factor*, 180.

210. For references, see Philippe Van Parijs, *Marxism Recycled* (Cambridge: Cambridge University Press, 1993), 168; Van Parijs, "Basic Income Capitalism," *Ethics* 102, no. 3 (April 1992): 465–84, first presented as a paper at a 1991 conference.

211. See Daniel Zamora and Philippe Van Parijs, "The Origins of Basic Income: A Conversation," in *Universal Basic Income in Historical Perspective*, ed. Daniel Zamora, Peter Sloman, and Pedro Ramos Pinto (London: Routledge, 2021).

212. Zamora and Van Parijs, "Origins of Basic Income."

213. Van Parijs here defines a "nonwelfarist" vision of flourishing derived from Ronald Dworkin, in Van Parijs, *Real Freedom for All*, 249. For the original argument, see Ronald Dworkin, "What Is Equality? Part I: Equality of Welfare," *Philosophy and Public Affairs* 10 (1981): 185–246.

214. For overviews of this vision, see Isaiah Berlin, "Two Concepts of Liberty," in *The Liberty Reader*, ed. John Miller (London: Paradigm, 2006), 33–57; John Gray, *Post-liberalism: Studies in Political Thought* (London: Routledge, 2000), 123–55; Quentin Skinner, "The Idea of Negative Liberty," in *Philosophy in History*, ed. R. Rorty, J. B. Schneewind, and Quentin Skinner (Cambridge: Cambridge University Press, 1984).

215. See G. A. Cohen, "The Structure of Proletarian Unfreedom," *Philosophy and Public Affairs* 12, no. 1 (Winter 1983): 3–33. For a critical overview of Cohen's negativist case for Marxism, see John Gray, "On Negative and Positive Liberty," in *Liberalisms: Essays in Political Philosophy* (London: Routledge, 2003), 45–64. See also G. A. Cohen, "Freedom and Money," in *On the Currency of Egalitarian Justice, and Other Essays in Political Philosophy*, ed. Michael Otsuka (London: Oxford University Press, 2011).

216. Van Parijs, *Real Freedom for All*, 18.

217. Van Parijs and Zamora, "Interview."

218. Van Parijs and Zamora, "Interview," 82.

219. John Roemer, "A General Equilibrium Approach to Marxian Economics," *Econometrica* 48, no. 2 (March 1980): 505–30. See also John Roemer and Jon Elster, eds., *Interpersonal Comparisons of Well-Being* (London: Cambridge University Press, 1993), for an attempt to reboot a theory of interpersonal utility comparisons after the Paretian revolution, here enacted through the notion of "envy-free" equality.

220. Philippe Van Parijs, "A Revolution in Class Theory," in *Modern Theories of Exploitation* (Beverly Hills, CA: Sage, 1987), 111–31.

221. Van Parijs and Zamora, "Interview," 231.

222. Van Parijs and Zamora, "Interview," 231.

223. Gorz, *Farewell to the Working Class*, 3.

224. Gorz, *Farewell to the Working Class*, 3.

225. Van Parijs and Zamora, "Interview," 293.

226. See Philippe Van Parijs, "Marx: Een groene jongen?," *Vlaams Marxistisch Tijdschrift* 81 (1985): 28.

227. Van Parijs, "Marx," 33.

228. See Hans Achterhuis, "Arbeid, een eigenaardig fenomeen," *S&D* 9 (2010): 34–40, for a retrospective.

229. See Van Parijs and Vanderborght, *Basic Income*, 278.

230. See Philippe Van Parijs, "Basic Income: A Terminological Note," in *Proceedings of the First International Conference on Basic Income*, Université Catholique de Louvain-la-Neuve, 1986, Archives Collectif Charles Fourier, Université Louvain-la-Neuve, 3.

231. Cited in Peter Sloman, "Basic Income as Technocratic Liberalism: Framing a Policy Idea in Twentieth-Century Britain," in *Universal Basic Income in Historical Perspective*, ed. Peter Sloman, Daniel Zamora Vargas, and Pedro Ramos Pinto (London: Palgrave, 2021), 33.

232. Sloman, "Basic Income," 33.

233. Van Parijs, "Basic Income," 5.

234. Van Parijs, "Basic Income," 5.

235. Van Parijs, "Basic Income," 4–6.

236. Van Parijs, "Basic Income," 4.

237. Van Parijs, "Basic Income," 4.

238. See Philippe Van Parijs, *Arguing for Basic Income: Ethical Foundations for a Radical Reform* (London: Verso Books, 1992), for an overview. For a biographical perspective, see Gianinazzi, *André Gorz*, 215.

239. Gianinazzi, *André Gorz*, 215.

240. Gianinazzi, *André Gorz*, 215.

241. Walter Van Trier, "From 'Second Cheque Strategy' to 'Basic Income'- Why Did André Gorz Change His Mind?," in *Universal Basic Income in Historical Perspective*, ed. Daniel Zamora, Pedro Pinto, and Peter Sloman (London: Routledge, 2021), 81.

242. See Yannick Vanderborght and Philippe Van Parijs, *Basic Income* (Cambridge, MA: Harvard University Press, 2017), 342. The original was published in André Gorz, "L'allocation universelle: Version de droite et version de gauche," *La revue nouvelle*, 1985, 419–28. See also Guy Standing, *Beyond the New Paternalism* (London: Verso, 2002), 285. As Standing notes, Gorz later changed his view when swerving to a postoperaist position.

243. Cited in Gianinazzi, *André Gorz*, 144.

244. Gianinazzi, *André Gorz*, 144.

245. Gianinazzi, *André Gorz*, 144.

246. Gianinazzi, *André Gorz*, 145.

247. See Alain Caillé, Christian Lazzeri, and Dominique Méda, "Table ronde autour de l'allocation universelle," *Cités* 2 (2000): 121; Yoland Bresson, *Le partage du temps et des revenus* (Paris: Economica, 1994).

248. Gianinazzi, *André Gorz*, 160.

249. André Gorz, *Métamorphoses du travail: Quête du sens; Critique de la raison économique* (Paris: Galilée, 1988), 257–65.

250. Gianinazzi, *André Gorz*, 160–80. The *Revue du MAUSS* hosted several discussion forums on the topic throughout the 1980s and 1990s, including conversations with Van Parijs. See André Caillé, "Du revenu social: Au-delà de l'aide, la citoyenneté?," *Bulletin du MAUSS* 23 (1994); "Vers un revenu minimum inconditionnel?," *Revue du MAUSS semestrielle* 7 (1987); *Temps choisi et revenu de citoyenneté: Au-delà du salariat universel* (Paris: MAUSS, 1994). See also David Graeber, "Give It Away," *Free Theory* (2003), for an anglophone perspective on MAUSS activity.

251. Clyde Barrow, "The Dismal Science of Post-Marxist Political Theory: Is There a Future in Postindustrial Socialism?," *Teoria polityk* 2, no. 18 (2018): 217–18.

252. See André Gorz, *Capitalism, Socialism, Ecology* (London: Verso Books, 1994), vii.

253. Gorz, *Capitalism, Socialism, Ecology*, vii.

254. Gorz, *Capitalism, Socialism, Ecology*, vii–viii.

255. Philippe Van Parijs, personal correspondence, August 26, 2018.

256. Van Parijs, "Interview," 286.

257. See Pierre Rosanvallon, *The New Social Question: Rethinking the Welfare State* (Princeton, NJ: Princeton University Press, 2000), 64–65. Rosanvallon's work originally appeared in 1992 and featured a discussion of Van Parijs's plans as well. Rosanvallon himself shared the desire to modernize social security in the 1980s and 1990s. For overviews of Rosanvallon's contribution, see Marc-Antoine Sabaté, "Le revenu de base: Renversement ou renouveau du droit social? Éléments pour une philosophie politique et sociale de l'inconditionnalité" (PhD diss., Université libre de Bruxelles, 2020), 147–48.

258. Pierre Rosanvallon, *New Social Question*, 65.

259. See Wilfried de Vlieghere, "Herverdeling van werk of basisinkomen?," *EcoGroen* 8 (October 1993): 25.

260. See James Heartfield, *Need and Desire in the Post-Material Economy* (London: Sheffield Hallam University Press, 1998), 76.

261. Heartfield, *Need and Desire*, 76.

262. Heartfield, *Need and Desire*, 76.

263. Heartfield, *Need and Desire*, 76.

264. Heartfield, *Need and Desire*, 76–77.

265. See George Caffentzis, "The End of Work or the Renaissance of Slavery?," in *In Letters of Blood and Fire: Work, Machines and the Crisis of Capitalism* (New York: PM Press, 2013), 81.

266. Sloman, "Basic Income," 36.

267. Samuel Moyn, *Not Enough: Human Rights in an Unequal World* (Cambridge, MA: Harvard University Press, 2018).

268. Standing, *Beyond the New Paternalism*, 81.

269. Van Essen, *Kind van de verzoringsstaat*, 55.

270. Hans Achterhuis, "Neem de tijd—Gevangen in de tredmolen als hamsters," *Trouw*, May 19, 2012.

Chapter Five

1. Tito Mboweni, "Foreword by the Minister of Labour," in Guy Standing, John Sender, and John Weeks, *Restructuring the Labour Market: The South African Challenge* (Geneva: ILO, 1996), iii.

2. African National Congress, *Freedom Charter*, 1955.

3. Vella Pillay at a 1989 conference in Switzerland organized by economist Pieter Le Roux of the University of the Western Cape. For the first time ANC economists met face to face with National Party leaders. Pillay quoted in Grace Davie, *Poverty Knowledge in South Africa: A Social History of Human Science, 1855–2005* (Cambridge: Cambridge University Press, 2015), 236.

4. Nelson Mandela, "Preface," in *The Reconstruction and Development Programme (RDP)* (Houghton, South Africa: Nelson Mandela Foundation, 1994).

5. Stephanie Brockerhoff, "A Review of the Development of Social Security Policy in South Africa" (working paper 6, Studies in Poverty and Inequality Institute, Johannesburg, 2013), 23.

6. Guy Standing, John Sender, and John Weeks, *Restructuring the Labour Market: The South African Challenge* (Geneva: ILO, 1996), 482.

7. Standing, Sender, and Weeks, *Restructuring the Labour Market*, 482.

8. James Ferguson, *Give a Man a Fish: Reflections on the New Politics of Distribution* (Durham, NC: Duke University Press, 2015), 136.

9. Ferguson, *Give a Man a Fish*.

10. Personal interview with Guy Standing, May 11, 2021.

11. Davie, *Poverty Knowledge in South Africa*, 258.

12. "Growth, Employment and Redistribution (GEAR): A Macroeconomic Strategy," Department of Finance, Republic of South Africa, 1996, 1.

13. Thabo Mbeki speaking at the June 1996 launching of the GEAR program. Quoted in William Gumede, *Thabo Mbeki and the Battle for the Soul of the ANC* (Cape Town: Zebra Press, 2005), 89.

14. Davie, *Poverty Knowledge in South Africa*, 235.

15. Davie, *Poverty Knowledge in South Africa*, 243.

16. John S. Saul, *A Flawed Freedom: Rethinking Southern African Liberation* (London: Pluto Press, 2014), 94.

17. Nelson Mandela, Address before a Joint Meeting of the United States Congress, 103rd Cong., 2nd Sess., October 6, 1994.

18. Mandela quoted in Hein Marais, *South Africa, Limits to Change: The Political Economy of Transition* (London: Zed Books, 1998), 95.

19. Mandela quoted in Andrew Nash, "Mandela's Democracy," *Monthly Review* 50, no. 11 (April 1999).

20. J. M. Coetzee, "On Nelson Mandela (1918–2013)," *New York Review of Books*, January 9, 2014.

21. Hein Marais, *Economy of Transition* (Cape Town: University of Cape Town Press, 1995), 156.

22. See in particular Saul, *Flawed Freedom*, 9; Franco Barchiesi, "South African Debates on the Basic Income Grant: Wage Labour and the Post-Apartheid Social Policy," *Journal of Southern African Studies* 33, no. 3 (2007): 567; Ingrid Woolard and Murray Leibbrandt, "The Evolution and Impact of Unconditional Cash Transfers in South Africa," in *Annual World Bank Conference on Development Economics 2011: Development Challenges in a Postcrisis World*, ed. Justin Yifu Lin and Claudia Paz Sepulveda (Washington, DC: World Bank, 2013), 368.

23. Brockerhoff, "Review of the Development of Social Security Policy in South Africa," 24.

24. Patrick Bond, *Elite Transition: From Apartheid to Neoliberalism in South Africa* (London: Pluto Press, 2000), 77.

25. For more on the rise of BIG in South Africa see Barchiesi, "South African Debates," and Kumiko Makino, "Social Security Policy Reform in Post-Apartheid South Africa: A Focus on the Basic Income Grant," Report 11 (Berlin: Center for Civil Society Research, 2004), 9.

26. See Andrew Whiteford and Dirk Ernst van Seventer, "South Africa's Changing Income Distribution in the 1990s," *Journal of Studies in Economists and Econometrics* 24, no. 3 (2000): 7–30; Mats Lundahl and Lennart Petersson, "Post-Apartheid South Africa: An Economic Success Story?" (working paper 56, World Institute for Development Economics Research, Helsinki, 2009).

27. Jeremy Seekings and Nicoli Nattrass, *Policy, Politics and Poverty in South Africa* (New York: Palgrave Macmillan, 2015), 151.

28. Republic of South Africa, *Transforming the Present—Protecting the Future*, report of the Committee of Inquiry into a Comprehensive System of Social Security for South Africa (Pretoria: Government Printer, 2002), 61, 25.

29. Davie, *Poverty Knowledge in South Africa*, 272; James Ferguson, "Formalities of Poverty: Thinking about Social Assistance in Neo-liberal South Africa," *African Studies Review* 50, no. 2 (September 2007): 71–86.

30. On the failure of the Taylor Committee to effectively push BIG forward, see Guy Standing and Michael Samson, *A Basic Income Grant for South Africa* (Lansdowne: University of Cape Town Press, 2003): 62–65.

31. Makino, "Social Security Policy Reform, 9.

32. Seekings and Nattrass, *Policy, Politics and Poverty in South Africa*, 154.

33. Seekings and Nattrass, *Policy, Politics and Poverty in South Africa*, 136.

34. Jonny Steinberg quoted in Ferguson, *Give a Man a Fish*, 19.

35. Ferguson, *Give a Man a Fish*, 5.

36. Ferguson, *Give a Man a Fish*, 12.

37. Standing and Samson, *Basic Income Grant for South Africa*, 3.

38. Ferguson, *Give a Man a Fish*.

39. Guy Standing, "How Cash Transfers Promote the Case for Basic Income," *Basic Income Studies* 3, no. 1 (April 2008): 26.

40. Marita Garcia and Charity M. T. Moore, *The Cash Dividend: The Rise of Cash Transfer Programs in Sub-Saharan Africa* (Washington, DC: World Bank, 2012), 12.

41. Herbert Jauch, "The Rise and Fall of the Basic Income Grant Campaign: Lessons from Namibia," *Global Labour Journal* 6, no. 3 (2015): 341.

42. The BIG coalition consists of four large umbrella bodies in Namibia: the Council of Churches (CCN), the Namibian Union of Namibian Workers (NUNW), the Namibian NGO Forum (NANGOF), and the Namibian Network of AIDS Service Organisations (NANASO).

43. Johanna Perkiö, "Universal Basic Income—A New Tool for Development Policy?," *International Solidarity Work*, 2014, 7.

44. Garcia and Moore, *Cash Dividend*, 288.

45. See, for example, Maura Francese and Delphine Prady, "Universal Basic Income: Debate and Impact Assessment Publication," working paper WP/18/273 (Washington, DC: International Monetary Fund, 2018); International Labour Office, *Social Security for All: Building Social Protection Floors and Comprehensive Social Security Systems; The Strategy of the International Labour Organization*, 2012; Ugo Gentilini, Margaret Grosh, Jamele Rigolini, and Ruslan Yemtsov, eds., *Exploring Universal Basic Income: A Guide to Navigating Concepts, Evidence, and Practices* (Washington, DC: World Bank, 2020).

46. Ha-Joon Chang, "Hamlet without the Prince of Denmark: How Development Has Disappeared from Today's 'Development' Discourse," in *Towards New Developmentalism: Market as Means Rather Than Master*, ed. Shahrukh Khan and Jens Christiansen (Abingdon, UK: Routledge, 2010).

47. Guy Standing, "From Labour to Work: The Global Challenge," *World of Work* 31 (September/October 1999): 18.

48. Joseph Hanlon, Armando Barrientos, and David Hulme, *Just Give Money to the Poor: The Development Revolution from the Global South* (Sterling, VA: Kumarian Press, 2010), 162.

49. Martha Finnemore, "Redefining Development at the World Bank," in *International Development and the Social Sciences*, ed. Frederick Cooper and Randall Packard (Berkeley: University of California Press, 1997), 207.

50. Frances Stewart, "Changing Approaches to Development since 1950: Drawing on Polanyi," *History of Political Economy* 50 (2018): 25.

51. Julius K. Nyerere, "The Plea of the Poor: New Economic Order Needed for the World Community," *New Directions* 4, no. 4 (1977): 5–6.

52. Frederick Cooper, *Africa since 1940: The Past of the Present* (Cambridge: Cambridge University Press, 2002).

53. Gunnar Myrdal, *Asian Drama: An Inquiry into the Poverty of Nations* (1977; repr. New York: Penguin, 1977), 108.

54. Samuel Moyn, *Not Enough: Human Rights in an Unequal World* (Cambridge, MA: Harvard University Press, 2018), 103.

55. J. A. Hobson, *Imperialism: A Study* (New York: James Pott, 1902).

56. Jawaharlal Nehru, *The Discovery of India* (Oxford: Oxford University Press, 1946), 406.

57. Mahalanobis quoted in Ashok Rudra, *Prasanta Chandra Mahalanobis: A Biography* (London: Oxford University Press, 1997), 228.

58. Paul Rosenstein-Rodan, "Problems of Industrialisation of Eastern and Southeastern Europe," *Economic Journal* 53, no. 210/11 (1943): 202–11.

59. See David C. Engerman, Nils Gilman, Mark H. Haefele, and Michael E. Latham, *Staging Growth: Modernization, Development, and the Global Cold War* (Amherst: University of Massachusetts Press, 2003); Nils Gilman, *Mandarins of the Future: Modernization Theory in Cold War America* (Baltimore: Johns Hopkins University Press, 2003).

60. On the history of the notion and of Latin American "structuralists," see Margarita Fajardo, *The World That Latin America Created: The United Nations Economic Commission for Latin America in the Development Era* (Cambridge, MA: Harvard University Press, 2022).

61. Andrés Rivarola Puntigliano and Örjan Appelqvist, "Prebisch and Myrdal: Development Economics in the Core and on the Periphery," *Journal of Global History* 6 (2011): 49.

62. Edgar J Dosman, *The Life and Times of Raúl Prebisch, 1901–1986* (Montreal: McGill-Queen's University Press, 2008), Kindle edition.

63. Raúl Prebisch, *The Economic Development of Latin America and Its Principal Problems* (New York: United Nations Department of Economic Affairs, Economic Commission for Latin America, 1950), 1.

64. Prebisch, *Economic Development of Latin America*, 1.

65. Prebisch, *Economic Development of Latin America*, 9.

66. Prebisch, *Economic Development of Latin America*, 10.

67. Prebisch, *Economic Development of Latin America*, 2.

68. Prebisch, *Economic Development of Latin America*, 6.

69. Nils Gilman, "The New International Economic Order: A Reintroduction," *Humanity* 6, no. 1 (Spring 2015): 6.

70. Thomas J. Kelly, *The Effects of Economic Adjustment on Poverty in Mexico* (1999; repr., Abington-on-Thames, UK: Routledge Revivals, 2018), Kindle edition, 19.

71. Rudra, *Prasanta Chandra Mahalonabis*, 228.

72. Resolution on Fundamental Rights and Economic Programme as passed at the Karachi Congress, 1931, and as subsequently varied by the All India Congress Committee at its meeting in Bombay in August 1931, in K. T. Shah, *National Planning Committee Proceedings* (Bombay: National Planning Committee, 1939), 2–3.

73. John K. Galbraith, *A Life in Our Times: Memoirs* (Boston: Houghton Mifflin, 1981), 324.

74. Galbraith, *Life in Our Times*, 408.

75. Resolutions passed at the Conference of Ministers of Industries held in Delhi on October 2–3, 1938, chaired by Sjt. Subash Chandra Bose, in Shah, *National Planning Committee*, 9.

76. Nehru, *Discovery of India*, 398.

77. Nehru, *Discovery of India*, 406.

78. Nehru, *Discovery of India*, 406.

79. Poornima Paidipaty, "Testing Measures: Decolonization and Economic Power in 1960s India," *History of Political Economy* 52, no. 3 (June 2020): 483.

80. Rudra, *Prasanta Chandra Mahalonabis*, 225.

81. Paidipaty, "Testing Measures," 484.

82. Vivek Chibber, *Locked in Place: State-Building and Late Industrialization in India* (Princeton, NJ: Princeton University Press, 2003), 36.

83. See Aaron Benanav, "A Global History of Unemployment: Surplus Populations in the World Economy, 1949–2010" (PhD diss., University of California, 2014), 193.

84. Poornima Paidipaty and Pedro Ramos Pinto, "Revisiting the 'Great Levelling': The Limits of Piketty's Capital and Ideology for Understanding the Rise of Late 20th Century Inequality," *British Journal of Sociology* 72, no. 1 (January 2021): 52–68.

85. See in particular Benanav, "Global History of Unemployment," 191–93.

86. Tirthankar Roy, *The Economic History of India, 1857–2010* (Oxford: Oxford University Press, 2020), 329.

87. Adom Getachew, *Worldmaking after Empire: The Rise and Fall of Self-Determination* (Princeton, NJ: Princeton University Press, 2019), 158.

88. Getachew, *Worldmaking after Empire*, 158.

89. United Nations Conference on Trade and Development, Final Act and Report, Adopted at Geneva, June 16, 1964, E/CONF.46/141, vol. 1 (New York: United Nations, 1964), 3.

90. United Nations Archives, UNCTAD fonds, Arr. 40/1862, box 436, file: Manufactures, TD 428, International Division of Labour, March 12, 1971, Letter from

H. Stordel, Manufactures Division, to Tinbergen, quoted in Johanna Bockman, "Socialist Globalization against Capitalist Neocolonialism: The Economic Ideas behind the New International Economic Order," *Humanity* 6, no. 1 (Spring 2015), 114.

91. Bockman, "Socialist Globalization against Capitalist Neocolonialism," 114.

92. Nyerere, "Plea of the Poor," 5–6.

93. Nyerere, "Plea of the Poor," 5–6.

94. Joanne Meyerowitz, *A War on Global Poverty: The Lost Promise of Redistribution and the Rise of Microcredit* (Princeton, NJ: Princeton University Press, 2021), 57.

95. Gilman, "New International Economic Order," 4.

96. Andrew Martin Fischer, *Poverty as Ideology*, e-book, passim.

97. Meyerowitz, *War on Global Poverty*, 66.

98. Michael Harrington, *The Vast Majority: A Journey to the World's Poor* (New York: Simon and Schuster, 1977), 53.

99. Harrington, *Vast Majority*, 220.

100. Harrington, *Vast Majority*, 91.

101. Pedro Ramos Pinto, "Inequality by Numbers: The Making of a Global Political Issue?," in *Histories of Global Inequality: New Perspectives*, ed. C. O. Christiansen and S. L. B. Jensen (London: Palgrave, 2019).

102. The 1974 *Redistribution with Growth* was the first Bank publication to monetize absolute poverty as living below two arbitrary poverty lines of US$50 or US$75 per year. Only later they would come up with the famous dollar a day line.

103. Daniel Speich, "The Use of Global Abstractions: National Income Accounting in the Period of Imperial Decline," *Journal of Global History* 6 (2011): 10.

104. Speich, "Use of Global Abstractions," 28.

105. Rob Konkel, "The Monetization of Global Poverty: The Concept of Poverty in World Bank History, 1944–90," *Journal of Global History* 9, no. 2 (July 2014): 294.

106. Robert L. Ayres, *Banking on the Poor: The World Bank and World Poverty* (Cambridge, MA: MIT Press, 1983), 89.

107. Konkel, "Monetization of Global Poverty," 208.

108. Harrington, *Vast Majority*, 210.

109. Finnemore, "Redefining Development at the World Bank," 207.

110. McNamara, quoted in Patrick Allan Sharma, *Robert McNamara's Other War: The World Bank and International Development* (Philadelphia: University of Pennsylvania Press, 2017), 3.

111. Sharma, *Robert McNamara's Other War*, 28.

112. Konkel, "Monetization of Global Poverty," 277.

113. Sharma, *Robert McNamara's Other War*, 4.

114. Harrington, *Vast Majority*, 238–39.

115. Konkel, "Monetization of Global Poverty," 291.

116. Finnemore, "Redefining Development at the World Bank," 205.

117. Sharma, *Robert McNamara's Other War*, 58; Mahbub ul-Haq, "In Retrospect," in Mahbub ul Haq, *The Poverty Curtain: Choices for the Third World* (New York: Columbia University Press, 1976), 14. For older views see Mahbub ul-Haq, *The Strategy of Economic Planning* (New York: Oxford University Press, 1963).

118. Mahbub ul-Haq, *The Poverty Curtain: Choices for the Third World* (New York: Columbia University Press, 1976), 14.

119. Haq, *Poverty Curtain*, 16.

120. Haq, *Poverty Curtain*, 17.

121. Haq, *Poverty Curtain*, 17.

122. Mahbub ul Haq, "Crisis in Development Strategies," *World Development* 1, no. 7 (July 1973): 29.

123. Haq, "Crisis in Development Strategies," 30.

124. See in particular Paidipaty, "Testing Measures," 473–97.

125. Paidipaty, "Testing Measures," 487.

126. Paidipaty, "Testing Measures," 492.

127. Haq, "Crisis in Development Strategies," 30.

128. Haq, "Crisis in Development Strategies," 60–69, 70.

129. Moyn, *Not Enough*, 121.

130. Erik S. Reinert, Jayati Ghosh, and Rainer Kattel, *Handbook of Alternative Theories of Economic Development* (Northampton, MA: Edward Elgar, 2016), xxvi.

131. Meyerowitz, *War on Global Poverty*, 76.

132. Ajit Singh, "The 'Basic Needs' Approach to Development vs. the New International Economic Order: The Significance of Third World Industrialization," *World Development* 7, no. 6 (June 1979): 586, 587.

133. Singh, "'Basic Needs' Approach," 587.

134. Singh, "'Basic Needs' Approach," 586.

135. Singh, "'Basic Needs' Approach," 586–87.

136. Singh, "'Basic Needs' Approach," 601.

137. Ayres, *Banking on the Poor*, 80.

138. Konkel, "Monetization of Global Poverty," 291.

139. *Accelerated Development in Sub-Saharan Africa: An Agenda for Action* (Washington, DC: World Bank, 1981), 5.

140. Sharma, *Robert McNamara's Other War*, 113.

141. Getachew, *Worldmaking after Empire*, 139.

142. Excerpt from Fischer, *Poverty as Ideology*.

143. Konkel, "Monetization of Global Poverty," 298.

144. Reinert, Ghosh, and Kattel, *Handbook of Alternative Theories of Economic Development*, xxviii.

145. Reinert, Ghosh, and Kattel, *Handbook of Alternative Theories of Economic Development*, xxviii.

146. "I owe you, I don't deny it; but money to pay back, I don't have."

147. William R. Cline, "Mexico's Crisis: The World's Peril," *Foreign Policy* 49 (Winter 1982–83): 107–18.

148. Eric Toussain, "The Mexican Debt Crisis and the World Bank," *CADTM*, August 4, 2020; https://www.cadtm.org/The-Mexican-debt-crisis-and-the-World-Bank.

149. Kelly, *Effects of Economic Adjustment on Poverty in Mexico*, 19; Arturo Guíllen, "Mexico, an Example of the Anti-development Policies of the Washington Consensus," *Estudos avocados* 26, no. 75 (2012): 58.

150. World Bank data.

151. Guíllen, "Mexico," 60.

152. Martin Ravallion, "Targeted Transfers in Poor Countries: Revisiting the Trade-Offs and Policy Options," World Bank Social Protection Discussion Paper Series, May 2003, 1.

153. Santiago Levy, *Progress against Poverty: Sustaining Mexico's Progresa-Oportunidades Program* (Washington, DC: Brookings Institution, 2006), 1.

154. Tirthankar Roy, *The Economic History of India, 1857–2010* (Oxford: Oxford University Press, 2000), 329–31; Jean Drèze and Amartya Sen, *An Uncertain Glory: India and Its Contradictions* (London: Penguin, 2014), 22–29.

155. Drèze and Sen, *Uncertain Glory*, 40.

156. Sarath Davala, Renana Jhabvala, Soumya Kapoor Mehta, and Guy Standing, *Basic Income: A Transformative Policy for India* (London: Bloomsbury, 2015).

157. For more details about these two programs see Drèze and Sen, *Uncertain Glory*, 199–212; Sakshan Khosla, *India's Universal Basic Income: Bedeviled by the Details* (Washington, DC: Carnegie Publications, 2018), 13–31.

158. For details of the political discussions see Vanya Mehta, "The Great Indian Basic Income Debate," *Open Democracy*, November 14, 2019.

159. Michael Safi, "India: Congress Party Pledges Universal Basic Income for the Poor," *Guardian*, March 25, 2019; "PM Modi May Counter Rahul Gandhi's Income Scheme with Universal Basic Income in Budget," *Hindustan Times*, January 30, 2019.

160. Armando Barrientos and David Hulme, "Social Protection for the Poor and Poorest in Developing Countries: Reflections on a Quiet Revolution," working paper 30 (Manchester: Brooks World Poverty Institute, 2008).

161. Frances Stewart, "Changing Approaches to Development since 1950: Drawing on Polanyi," *History of Political Economy* 50 (2018): 17–38.

162. Oliver W. Kim, "The Real Development Was the Friends We Made along the Way," April 7, 2021; https://oliverwkim.com/Hirschman-Strategy/.

163. Japhy Wilson, *Jeffrey Sachs: The Strange Case of Dr. Shock and Mr. Aid* (London: Verso, 2014), Kindle edition, 60.

164. Sachs, quoted in Wilson, *Jeffrey Sachs*, 62.

165. Wilson, *Jeffrey Sachs*, 10.

166. Chang, "Hamlet without the Prince of Denmark."

167. Nina Munk, *The Idealist: Jeffrey Sachs and the Quest to End Poverty* (Toronto: Doubleday, 2013), 214.

168. Easterly, quoted in Munk, *Idealist*, 214.

169. See in particular Jeffrey Sachs, "Lessons from the Millennium Villages Project: A Personal Perspective," *Lancet* 6, no. 5 (2018); Shira Mitchell et al., "The Millennium Villages Project: A Retrospective, Observational, Endline Evaluation," *Lancet Global Health* 6 (2018): 500–513.

170. William Easterly, "IMF and World Bank Structural Adjustment Programs and Poverty," in *Managing Currency Crises in Emerging Markets*, ed. Michael P. Dooley and Jeffrey A. Frankel (Chicago: University of Chicago Press, 2001); William Easterly, ed., *Reinventing Foreign Aid* (Cambridge MA: MIT Press, 2008); Jessica Cohen and William Easterly, eds., *What Works in Development? Thinking Big and Thinking Small* (Washington, DC: Brookings Institution, 2009).

171. William Easterly, *The White Man's Burden: Why the West's Efforts to Aid the Rest Have Done So Much Ill and So Little Good* (New York: Penguin, 2006), 73.

172. Easterly, *White Man's Burden*, 73.

173. William Easterly, *The Tyranny of Experts: Economists, Dictators, and the Forgotten Rights of the Poor* (New York: Basic Books, 2013).

174. Thomas Frank, *One Market under God: Extreme Capitalism, Market Populism, and the End of Economic Democracy* (New York: Random House, 2010).

175. Hanlon, Barrientos, and Hulme, *Just Give Money to the Poor*, 9–10.

176. Hanlon, Barrientos, and Hulme, *Just Give Money to the Poor*, 11.

177. Hanlon, Barrientos, and Hulme, *Just Give Money to the Poor*, 9.

178. Hanlon, Barrientos, and Hulme, *Just Give Money to the Poor*, 9.

179. Frances Stewart, "Changing Approaches to Development since 1950: Drawing on Polanyi," *History of Political Economy* 50 (2018): 18.

180. Richard Ballard, "Geographies of Development II: Cash Transfers and the Reinvention of Development for the Poor," *Progress in Human Geography* 37, no. 6 (2013): 815.

181. Konkel, "Monetization of Global Poverty," 299.

182. Frances Stewart, "Changing Approaches to Development since 1950: Drawing on Polanyi," *History of Political Economy* 50 (2018): 31.

183. Stewart, "Changing Approaches to Development," 3.

184. International Labour Organization, R202—Social Protection Floors Recommendation, 2012 (no. 202).

185. F. Bastagli, J. Hagen-Zanker, L. Harman, V. Barca, G. Sturge, T. Schmidt, and L. Pellerano, "Cash Transfers: What Does the Evidence Say? A Rigorous Review of Programme Impact and of the Role of Design and Implementation Features," *ODI* (London), July 2016.

186. Oral statement by Mr. Philip Alston, Special Rapporteur on Extreme Poverty and Human Rights at the 35th Session of the Human Rights Council.

187. Philip Alston, "Promotion and Protection of All Human Rights, Civil, Political, Economic, Social and Cultural Rights, Including the Right to Development," Human Rights Council, General Assembly, March 22, 2017, A/HRC/35/26, 18.

188. António Guterres, "Tackling the Inequality Pandemic: A New Social Contract for a New Era, Secretary-General's Nelson Mandela Lecture, July 18, 2020.

189. Ferguson, *Give a Man a Fish*, xi.

190. Chris Hughes, *Fair Shot: Rethinking Inequality and How We Earn* (New York: St. Martin's, 2018), 55. See also Felix Salmon, "Chris Hughes Made Millions at Facebook: Now He Has a Plan to End Poverty," *New York Times*, February 25, 2018; https://www.nytimes.com/2018/02/25/books/review/chris-hughes-fair-shot.html.

191. Hughes, *Fair Shot*, 59.

192. Hughes, *Fair Shot*, 59.

193. Hughes, *Fair Shot*, 59.

194. Hughes, *Fair Shot*, 50.

195. Hughes, *Fair Shot*, 51.

196. Hughes, *Fair Shot*, 52.

197. See in particular Dana Goldstein, "Can 4 Economists Build the Most Economically Efficient Charity Ever?," *Atlantic*, December 21, 2012.

198. GiveDirectly, IPA, Innovations for Poverty Action. Goldilocks Toolkit.

199. For some preliminary results see Dennis Egger et al., "General Equilibrium Effects of Cash Transfers: Experimental Evidence from Kenya," NBER, Working Paper 26600, November 21, 2019.

200. Fischer, *Poverty as Ideology*.

201. Fischer, *Poverty as Ideology*.

202. See Dylan Matthews, "Chris Hughes Wants Another Chance," *Vox*, January 22, 2020.

203. "Fair Shot: Rethinking Inequality and How We Earn," Chris Hughes, Talks at Google, May 2018; https://www.youtube.com/watch?v=p_ELw6-yzvY.

204. Chris Hughes on Founding Facebook and Fighting Inequality, Talks at Goldman Sachs; https://www.youtube.com/watch?v=Qr-w4xlA2b4.

Epilogue

1. https://www.givedirectly.org/covid-19/us/.

2. Adam Smith, "Twitter CEO Jack Dorsey donates $3M to UBI Experiment," *Independent*, July 19, 2020; https://www.independent.co.uk/life-style/gadgets-and-tech/news/twitter-ceo-jack-dorsey-donation-ubi-mgi-experiment-a9611961.html.

3. Guy Standing, "Coronavirus Has Shown Us Why We Urgently Need to Make a Basic Income a Reality," *World Economic Forum Blog*, April 13, 2020; https://www.weforum.org/agenda/2020/04/coronavirus-made-basic-income-vital/.

4. Standing, "Coronavirus."

5. Annie Lowrey, *Give People Money: The Simple Idea to Solve Inequality and Revolutionize Our Lives* (New York: Random House, 2018), 18; Z. Hajnal, "Moral

Economy," in *Words, Objects and Events in Economics: The Making of Economic Theory* (London: Springer Nature, 2020), 81.

6. Steven L. Piott, *Giving Voters a Voice: The Origins of the Initiative and Referendum in America* (New York: Columbia University Press, 2003), 13–15; Thomas Goebel, *A Government by the People: Direct Democracy in America, 1890–1940* (Chapel Hill: University of North Carolina Press, 2003), 70–75. This variant of "populism" needs to be distinguished from its nineteenth-century incarnations, which were far less insistent in their preference for direct democracy and in fact preferred interest formation in cooperative bodies and parliaments above plebiscite politics; see Anton Jäger, "State and Corporation in Populist Political Philosophy, 1877–1902," *Historical Journal* 64 (2021): 1035–59; Leon Fink, "Labor, Liberty, and the Law: Trade Unionism and the Problem of the American Constitutional Order," *Journal of American History* 74 (1987): 913.

7. Melinda Cooper, "Infinite Regress: Virginia School Neoliberalism and the Tax Revolt," *Capitalism: A Journal of History and Economics* 2, no. 1 (Winter 2021): 41–87; Kevin Starr, *Golden Dreams: California in an Age of Abundance, 1950–1963* (New York: Oxford University Press, 2011).

8. Fred Turner, *From Counterculture to Cyberculture: Stewart Brand, the Whole Earth Network, and the Rise of Digital Utopianism* (Chicago: University of Chicago Press, 2010).

9. Guida West, *The National Welfare Rights Movement: The Social Protest of Poor Women* (New York: Praeger, 1981).

10. Andrew Blauvelt, Greg Castillo, and Esther Choi, *Hippie Modernism: The Struggle for Utopia* (San Francisco, CA: Clarke Walker Art Center, 2015); Amia Srinivasan, "Stop the Robot Apocalypse," *London Review of Books* 37, no. 8 (September 2015): 12–14.

11. Peter Schwarz and Kevin Kelly, "The Relentless Contrarian: At 86, Peter Drucker Remains the Most Astute Observer of Modern Corporate Society; Maybe Society, Period," *Wired*, January 1996; Kevin Kelly, "Wealth Is Overrated," *Wired*, March 1998, 44. Drucker himself predicted a guaranteed income in *The New Society*.

12. Charles Murray, *In Our Hands: A Plan to Replace the Welfare State* (London: Rowman and Littlefield, 2016).

13. Murray, *In Our Hands*, 5.

14. Charles Murray, *Coming Apart: The State of White America, 1960–2010* (New York: Crown Books, 2012); Charles Murray, *Losing Ground: American Social Policy, 1950–1980* (New York: Basic Books, 2015). See also Dean E. Robinson, "'The Black Family' and US Social Policy: Moynihan's Unintended Legacy?," *Revue française d'études américaines* 3, no. 97 (2003): 118–228.

15. Michael Tanner, "The Pros and Cons of a Guaranteed National Income," *Cato Institute — Policy Analysis* 773 (May 2015): 1–36; Richard K. Caputo and Larry Liu, *Political Activism and Basic Income Guarantee: International Experiences and*

Perspectives Past, Present, and Near Future (New York: Springer, 2020); Miranda Perry Fleischer and Daniel Hemel, "The Architecture of a Basic Income," *University of Chicago Law Review* 87, no. 3 (May 2020): 625–710.

16. Alex J. Wood, *Despotism on Demand: How Power Operates in the Flexible Workplace* (Ithaca, NY: Cornell University Press, 2019); Ursula Huws, *Labour in Contemporary Capitalism: What Next?* (New York: Springer, 2019).

17. For the "protocollary" nature of this new digital sphere, see Alexander Galloway, *Protocol: How Control Exists after Decentralization* (Cambridge, MA: MIT Press, 2006); Geert Lovink, *Social Media Abyss: Critical Internet Cultures and the Force of Negation* (London: Wiley, 2017). For a recent overview, see Alex Williams, "Control Societies and Platform Logic," *New Formations* 84/85 (2015): 209–27.

18. Chris Hughes, *Fair Shot: Rethinking Inequality and How We Earn* (New York: St. Martin's, 2018), 58.

19. Frances Coppola, *The Case for People's Quantitative Easing* (London: John Wiley, 2019); Tooze, "Gatekeeper," 18.

20. Coppola, *Quantitative Easing.*

21. Coppola, *Quantitative Easing.*

22. See Dale Russakoff, *The Prize: Who's in Charge of America's Schools?* (New York: Houghton Mifflin Harcourt, 2015).

23. See Sam Altman, "Basic Income"; https://ycombinator.wpengine.com/basic-income/.

24. See Nitasha Tiku, "Y Combinator Learns Basic Income Is Not So Basic After All," *Wired*, September 27, 2018.

25. See the detail of the proposal here: Basic Income Project Proposal, Open-Research, Overview for Comments and Feedback, January 2020.

26. For an overview of the preliminary results see Stacia West, Amy Castro Baker, Sukhi Samra, and Erin Coltrera, "Preliminary Analysis: SEED's First Year," *SEED*, 2021.

27. https://www.economicsecurityproject.org/guaranteedincome/.

28. https://www.economicsecurityproject.org/guaranteedincome/.

29. For a survey of the ongoing pilots all around the United States, see Mayors for a Guaranteed Income, "Year in Review, 2020–2021, 2021"; https://www.mayorsforagi.org/resources.

30. Eileen Guo, "Universal Basic Income Is Here—It Just Looks Different from What You Expected," *MIT Technology Review*, May 7, 2021.

31. The complete list of grantees is available on Dorsey's website: https://start small.llc/#list.

32. For broader histories of this specifically American associational trajectory and the rise of PR politics, see Theda Skocpol, "Advocates without Members: The Recent Transformation of American Civic Life," in *Civic Engagement in American Democracy*, ed. Theda Skocpol and Morris P. Fiorina (Washington, DC: Brookings

Institution Press, 1999), passim; Theda Skocpol, *Diminished Democracy: From Membership to Management in American Civic Life* (Norman: University of Oklahoma Press, 2013); Brian Balogh, *The Associational State: American Governance in the Twentieth Century* (Philadelphia: University of Pennsylvania Press, 2015); Karen Ferguson, *Top Down: The Ford Foundation, Black Power, and the Reinvention of Racial Liberalism* (Philadelphia: University of Pennsylvania Press, 2013). For deindustrialization, see Judith Stein, *Pivotal Decade: How the United States Traded Factories for Finance in the Seventies* (New Haven, CT: Yale University Press, 2010); Judith Stein, *Running Steel, Running America: Race, Economic Policy, and the Decline of Liberalism* (Chapel Hill: University of North Carolina Press, 2000); Robert Gordon, *The Rise and Fall of American Growth: The U.S. Standard of Living since the Civil War* (Princeton, NJ: Princeton University Press, 2016), 600–630.

33. Zygmunt Bauman, *Liquid Modernity* (New York: John Wiley, 2013); Zygmunt Bauman and Thomas Leoncini, *Born Liquid* (New York: John Wiley, 2018).

34. Alex Heath, "Why Mark Zuckerberg Is Advocating Universal Basic Income in the US," *World Economic Forum* (July 10, 2017); https://www.weforum.org/agenda/2017/07/why-mark-zuckerberg-is-advocating-universal-basic-income-in-the-us.

35. Heath, "Why Mark Zuckerberg Is Advocating."

36. Robert J. van der Veen and Philippe Van Parijs, "A Capitalist Road to Communism," *Theory and Society* 15, no. 5 (September 1986): 635–55.

37. Peter Mair, *Ruling the Void: The Hollowing of Western Democracy* (London: Verso Books, 2013); Wolfgang Streeck, "The Politics of Exit," *New Left Review* 88 (July-August 2014): 121–29; Peter Mair, "Ruling the Void: The Hollowing of Western Democracy," *New Left Review* 42 (November-December 2006): 25–51.

38. Peter Mair, "Partyless Democracy: Solving the Paradox of New Labour," *New Left Review* 2 (March-April 2000): 21–35. See also John B. Judis, *The Populist Explosion* (New York: Columbia Global Reports, 2018); Benjamin Moffitt, *The Global Rise of Populism: Performance, Political Style, and Representation* (Stanford, CA: Stanford University Press, 2017); Peter Csigo, *The Neopopular Bubble: Speculating on "the People" in Late Modern Democracy* (Budapest: Central European University Press, 2017).

39. Pierre Rosanvallon, *Le siècle du populisme: Histoire, théorie, critique* (Paris: Seuil, 2020), passim; Pierre Rosanvallon, *Le parlement des invisibles* (Paris: Seuil, 2014).

40. Christopher Bickerton and Carlo Invernizzi Acetti, "Populism and Technocracy," in *Oxford Handbook of Populism*, ed. Cristobal Rovira Kaltwasser et al. (New York: Oxford University Press, 2017), 326.

41. Guy Standing, *The Precariat: The New Dangerous Class* (London: Bloomsbury, 2016).

42. Hillary Clinton, *What Happened* (New York: Simon and Schuster, 2017), 239. For inspiration, see Peter Barnes, *With Liberty and Dividends for All: How to*

Save Our Middle Class When Jobs Don't Pay Enough (New York: Berrett-Koehler, 2014); Klaus Schwab, *Stakeholder Capitalism: A Global Economy That Works for Progress, People and Planet* (London: John Wiley, 2021).

43. Clinton, *What Happened*, 119.

44. Paolo Gerbaudo, *The Digital Party: Political Organisation and Online Democracy* (London: Pluto Press, 2019).

45. For overviews see Michael E. Gardiner, "Automatic for the People? Cybernetics and Left-Accelerationism," *Constellations*, March 2020, 1–15; Aaron Benanav, *Automation and the Future of Work* (London: Verso Books, 2020), 102–4; Andrew Yang, *The War on Normal People: The Truth about America's Disappearing Jobs and Why Universal Basic Income Is Our Future* (New York: Hachette, 2018); Erik Brynjolfsson and Andrew McAfee, *The Second Machine Age: Work, Progress, and Prosperity in a Time of Brilliant Technologies* (London: W. W. Norton, 2014); Yann Moulier-Boutang, "Le revenu garanti ou salariat affaibli: Condition structurelle d'un régime vivable du capitalisme cognitif," *Multitudes* 4, no. 27 (2006): 97–106; Kathi Weeks, *The Problem with Work: Feminism, Marxism, Antiwork Politics, and Postwork Imaginaries* (Durham, NC: Duke University Press, 2011), 143–50.

46. Brent Ranalli, *Common Wealth Dividends: History and Theory* (Cham: Palgrave Switzerland, 2021), 32–38.

47. Paul Fain, "Huge Budget Cut for the University of Alaska," *Inside Higher Ed* (June 29, 2019); https://www.insidehighered.com/quicktakes/2019/06/29/huge -budget-cut-university-alaska. For a broader overview, see Karl Widerquist and Michael Howard, *Alaska's Permanent Fund Dividend: Examining Its Suitability as a Model* (New York: Springer, 2014).

48. Richard Parker, *John Kenneth Galbraith: His Life, His Politics, His Economics* (Chicago: University of Chicago Press, 2005), 93–94.

49. John Kenneth Galbraith, *The Affluent Society* (New York: Houghton Mifflin, 1958), 251.

50. Galbraith, *Affluent Society*, 251.

51. Peter Sloman, *The Liberal Party and the Economy, 1929–1964* (London: Oxford University Press, 2015); "Redistribution in an Age of Neoliberalism: Market Economics, 'Poverty Knowledge,' and the Growth of Working-Age Benefits in Britain, c. 1979–2010," *Political Studies*, 2018, 1–20; Tony Cutler, John Williams, and Karel Williams, *Keynes, Beveridge and Beyond* (London: Routledge, 2013), 1–5.

52. Maurice Dobb, "Review: The Economics of Socialism," *Science and Society* 4, no. 4 (1940): 448.

53. Dobb, "Review: The Economics of Socialism," 448.

54. John O'Neill, "Who Won the Socialist Calculation Debate," *History of Political Thought* 17, no. 3 (Autumn 1996): 431–42; John O'Neill, "Knowledge, Planning, and Markets: A Missing Chapter in the Socialist Calculation Debates," *Economics and Philosophy* 22, no. 1 (2006): 55–78; John O'Neill, "In Partial Praise of

a Positivist," *Radical Philosophy* 74 (November-December 1995): 29–38; Michael Turk, *Otto Neurath and the History of Economics* (London: Routledge, 2018).

55. Antonio Negri built on Deleuze's and Guattari's philosophy predicting the advent of a new mode of "molecular politics" in the 1970s, when the more large-scale "'molar' politics" of parties, unions, and councils seemed increasingly obsolete. (Guattari himself came out as a basic income enthusiast in a 1989 book.) See also Guy Standing, *Beyond the New Paternalism* (London: Verso, 2002), 7.

56. Félix Guattari, "The Three Ecologies," *New Formations* 8 (Summer 1989): 131–47.

57. Susanne Wengle and Michael Rasell, "The Monetisation of l'Goty: Changing Patterns of Welfare Politics and Provision in Russia," *Europe-Asia Studies* 60, no. 5 (July 2008): 739–56.

58. Mark Mazower, *Dark Continent: Europe's Twentieth Century* (London: Vintage Books, 2000), 340. See also Eric Hobsbawm, *Age of Extremes: The Short Twentieth Century, 1914–1991* (New York: Michael Joseph, 1994), 282–83. Hobsbawm himself spoke of "a facetious regeneration of *Gemeinschaft* in an increasingly remote *Gesellschaft*"; Eric J. Hobsbawm, *Globalisation, Democracy and Terrorism* (London: Abacus, 2008), 83.

59. Mazower, *Dark Continent*, 340.

60. Mazower, *Dark Continent*, 341.

61. Mazower, *Dark Continent*, 341.

62. Mazower, *Dark Continent*, 341.

63. N. P. Barry, *Welfare* (Milton Keynes, UK: Open University Press, 1990). See also John Holmwood, "Three Pillars of Welfare State Theory: T. H. Marshall, Karl Polanyi and Alva Myrdal in Defence of the National Welfare State," *European Journal of Social Theory* 3 (February 2000): 29.

64. Ulrich Beck, "Goodbye to All That Wage Slavery," *New Statesman*, March 5, 1999.

65. "Meaningful Work Survey," *Olivet Nazarene University* (September 2019), 5–6. For broader cultural histories of the work ethic, see Daniel Rodgers, *The Work Ethic in Industrial America, 1850–1920* (Chicago: University of Chicago Press, 1979); Daniel Markovits, *The Meritocracy Trap* (London: Penguin, 2020).

66. Figures cited in Kim Moody, "Workers of the World: Growth, Change, and Rebellion," *New Politics* 18, no. 2 (Winter 2021), http://links.org.au/workers-of-the-world-growth-change-and-rebellion. See also Aaron Benanav, "A Global History of Unemployment: Surplus Populations in the World Economy, 1949–2010" (PhD diss., University of California, Los Angeles, 2014), passim; Aaron Benanav and John Clegg, "Crisis and Immiseration: Critical Theory Today," in *Sage Handbook of Critical Theory* (New York: Sage, 2019), 1629–48; Mike Davis, *Planet of Slums* (London: Verso Books, 2000); Branko Milanović, *Capitalism, Alone: The Future of the System That Rules the World* (Cambridge, MA: Harvard University Press, 2019); Marcel Van der Linden, "San Precario: A New Inspiration for Labor Historians,"

Labor Studies in Working-Class History of the Americas 11, no. 1 (March 2014): 9–21.

67. The Invisible Committee, *The Coming Insurrection* (New York: Semiotexte, 2019), 15.

68. For the contrast, see Erik Olin Wright, "Why Something Like Socialism Is Necessary for the Transition to Something Like Communism," *Theory and Society* 15, no. 5 (September 1986): 657–72; Robert J. van der Veen and Philippe Van Parijs, "Universal Grants versus Socialism: Reply to Six Critics," *Theory and Society* 15, no. 5 (September 1986): 723–57; Bruce Ackerman et al., *Redesigning Distribution: Basic Income and Stakeholder Grants as Cornerstones of a More Egalitarian Capitalism* (London: Verso, 2006); Erik Olin Wright, *Envisioning Real Utopias* (London: Verso Books, 2010).

69. André Gorz, *Capitalism, Socialism, Ecology* (London: Verso Books, 1994), viii.

70. Siegfried Kracauer, *Jacques Offenbach and the Paris of His Time* (London: Zone Books, 2002), 24.

71. Avner Offer, "The Market Turn: From Social Democracy to Market Liberalism," *Economic History Review* 70, no. 4 (November 2017): 1051–71; Avner Offer and Gabriel Söderberg, *The Nobel Factor: The Prize in Economics, Social Democracy, and the Market Turn* (Princeton, NJ: Princeton University Press, 2019); Ben Jackson, "Putting Neoliberalism in Its Place," *Modern Intellectual History* (2021), published online, passim; Daniel Zamora Vargas, "Introduction: How Neoliberalism Reinvented Democracy," *Tocqueville Review* 41, no. 2 (December 2020): 7–17.

72. Mair, "Ruling the Void," 27.

73. Paul Pierson, *Dismantling the Welfare State? Reagan, Thatcher and the Politics of Retrenchment* (New York: Cambridge University Press, 1995), 181.

74. Pierson, *Dismantling the Welfare State?*, 181.

75. Amy C. Offner, *Sorting Out the Mixed Economy: The Rise and Fall of Welfare and Developmental States in the Americas* (Princeton, NJ: Princeton University Press, 2019), 289.

76. Schiller, "Regulation and the Collapse of the New Deal Order," 185.

77. Schiller, "Regulation and the Collapse of the New Deal Order," 185.

78. Marcel Gauchet, *La réligion dans la démocratie: Parcours de la laïcité* (Paris: Gallimard, 1998), 117.

79. Gauchet, *Réligion*, 117.

80. Marcel Gauchet, Éric Canon, and François Azouvi, *Comprende le malheur français* (Paris: Stock, 2016), 277. See also Michael Behrent, "Age of Emancipation," *Dissent*, Winter 2018, 125–31. See Annelien De Dijn, *Freedom: An Unruly History* (Cambridge, MA: Harvard University Press, 2020), passim, for a parallel overview of the same "individualization" of freedom.

81. Benjamin Y. Fong, "From a Community of Citizens to a Network of Users," *European Journal of Psychoanalysis*, April 2020, 1–10; Marcel Gauchet and Alain

Badiou, *Que faire? Dialogue sur le communisme, le capitalisme, et l'avenir de la démocratie* (Paris: Philomag, 2014), 138.

82. Eric Hobsbawm, "Democracy Can Be Bad for You," *New Statesman*, March 5, 2001, 27.

83. Gauchet, *Réligion*, 120.

84. Gauchet, *Réligion*, 118.

85. István Hont, *Politics in Commercial Society: Jean-Jacques Rousseau and Adam Smith* (Cambridge, MA: Harvard University Press, 2015); Albert Hirschman, *The Passions and the Interests* (Princeton, NJ: Princeton University Press, 1998); Paul Cheney, "István Hont, the Cosmopolitan Theory of Commercial Globalization, and Twenty-First-Century Capitalism," *Modern Intellectual History*, March 2021, 1–29.

86. Gauchet, *Réligion*, 118. Questions about monetary welfare date back at least to the Speenhamland debate; see Karl Polanyi, *The Great Transformation: The Political and Economic Origins of Our Time* (Boston, MA: Beacon Press, 2001), 81; Frederick Harry Pitts, Lorena Lombardozzi, and Neil Warner, "Speenhamland, Automation and the Basic Income: A Lesson from History?," *Renewal* 25 (December 2017): 145–55; Eric Hobsbawm, *Industry and Empire: From 1750 to the Present Day* (New York: New Press, 1999), 82–85; Eric Hobsbawm and George Rudé, *Captain Swing* (London: Phoenix Press, 1969); Fred Block, "In the Shadow of Speenhamland: Social Policy and the Old Poor Law," *Politics and Society* 31, no. 2 (June 2003): 283–323.

87. Gauchet and Badiou, *Que faire?*, 89. "Dès lors que l'indépendance des acteurs individuels est consacrée de la sorte, la coordination de l'ensemble prend nécessairement la forme d'un marché, c'est-à-dire d'un arbitrage plus ou moins automatique entre les initiatives, les offres et les demandes des différents acteurs impliqués. En elles-mêmes, ces idées n'ont rien de nouveau. La nouveauté réside dans l'étendue de leurs applications. Elles se mettent à modeler de part en part la vie sociale effective" (our translation).

88. Ignacio Ramonet, trans. Ed Emery, "A World Transformed," *Le monde diplomatique*, October 1997. Ramonet's concept is taken up again in Wolfgang Streeck, *Critical Encounters: Capitalism, Democracy, Ideas* (London: Verso Books, 2020). See also Castoriadis's notion of a "second disenchantment"; Cornelius Castoriadis, "Entretien," in *La compagnie des contemporains*, ed. Roger Pol-Droit (Paris: Odile Jacob, 2002), 44; Marcel Gauchet, *L'avènement de la démocratie 4: Le nouveau monde* (Paris: Gallimard, 2017).

89. Jean Baudrillard, *The Transparency of Evil: Essays on Extreme Phenomena* (London: Verso Books, 1993), 33, 35.

Archives Consulted

Internationaal Instituut voor Sociale Geschiedenis/International Institute for Social History, Amsterdam

Jan-Pieter Kuiper Archieven

Basisinkomen Archieven

Archief SDAP

Weerwerk Archieven

Archief Vlaams Marxistisch Tijdschrift, Dacob Archief, Brussels

Werkgroep Arbeid en Milieu Papers, Amsab Instituut voor Sociale Geschiedenis, Ghent

BIEN and Philippe van Parijs Papers, Université Catholique de Louvain, Louvain-la-neuve

James and Grace Lee Boggs Papers, Walter P. Reuther Library, Detroit

Wilbur Ferry Papers, Center for the Study of Democratic Institutions Collection, Vanderbilt University, Nashville, TN

Robert Lampman Papers, Institute for Research on Poverty, University of Wisconsin–Madison

Milton Friedman Papers, Hoover Institute, Stanford University, Palo Alto, CA

George Stigler Papers, University of Chicago, Chicago

Robert Lampman Papers, University of Wisconsin–Madison

Center for the Study of Democratic Institutions Archives, University of California, Santa Barbara, Santa Barbara

Yale Brozen Papers, Hoover Institute, Stanford University, Palo Alto, CA

Abba P. Lerner Papers, Library of Congress, Washington, DC

Index

www.ingramcontent.com/pod-product-compliance
Ingram Content Group UK Ltd.
Pitfield, Milton Keynes, MK11 3LW, UK
UKHW042319050225
454727UK00001B/1